MW01078914

THINKING

LIKE A

POLITICAL

SCIENTIST

Chicago Guides
to *Writing,* Editing,
and Publishing

THINKING LIKE A

POLITICAL SCIENTIST

A PRACTICAL GUIDE

TO RESEARCH METHODS

CHRISTOPHER HOWARD

The University of Chicago Press

Chicago and London

The University of Chicago Press, Chicago 60637
The University of Chicago Press, Ltd., London
© 2017 by The University of Chicago
Published 2017

Printed in the United States of America

26 25 24 23 22 21 20 19 18 17   1 2 3 4 5

ISBN-13: 978-0-226-32740-2 (cloth)
ISBN-13: 978-0-226-32754-9 (paper)
ISBN-13: 978-0-226-32768-6 (e-book)
DOI: 10.7208/chicago/9780226327686.001.0001

Library of Congress Cataloging-in-Publication Data

Names: Howard, Christopher, 1961– author.
Title: Thinking like a political scientist : a practical guide to research methods /
Christopher Howard.
Other titles: Chicago guides to writing, editing, and publishing.
Description: Chicago ; London : The University of Chicago Press, 2017. | Series: Chicago
guides to writing, editing, and publishing | Includes bibliographical references and index.
Identifiers: LCCN 2016015890 | ISBN 9780226327402 (cloth : alk. paper) | ISBN 9780226327549
(pbk. : alk. paper) | ISBN 9780226327686 (e-book)
Subjects: LCSH: Political science—Methodology. | Political science—Research. |
Research—Methodology.
Classification: LCC JA71.H69 2017 | DDC 320.072—dc23 LC record available at
https://lccn.loc.gov/2016015890

♾ This paper meets the requirements of ANSI/NISO Z39.48-1992 (Permanence of Paper).

CONTENTS

PREFACE FOR STUDENTS

If you're like most of the students I have taught, then you're not exactly look-ing forward to reading any book about research methods. You'd rather be reading about politics. I definitely understand your hesitation. In college I never took a general research methods course because, well, none was re-quired. Only later did I realize what I had missed. I worked hard in college, putting in long hours, but I didn't always work smart. While brute trial and error is one way to learn, it's usually not the most efficient. What I really needed was some practical guidance about how to identify a good research question and how to answer it systematically and persuasively. In part to keep other students from repeating my mistakes, I have been teaching a basic methods course for over a decade. This course is where students really learn how to think like political scientists.

Teaching Research Methods has been one of the more rewarding parts of my professional career. (And that's not because the rest of my career has been pitiful.) Students' written evaluations at the end of the semester typi-cally start out by expressing their opinion of the subject matter: "incredibly boring" and "horrid," among others. However, many quickly add that mine was one of the most useful and practical courses they have ever taken. Some say it already helped them write a better paper in another class they were tak-ing that semester. Others can now see possibilities for a future independent study project or honors thesis. Once in a while, students tell me in person how they came to genuinely like the course. In short, after a basic introduc-tion to the nuts and bolts of research, many recognize that their minds now can do things they couldn't do before.

No student has ever said that my methods class convinced them to pur-sue a PhD and become a professional political scientist, which is fine by me. That's not one of the main ways I measure success. I am more interested in helping students develop skills that will lead to success in college and wher-ever they go after graduation. After all, it's not just people who've earned a PhD who need to work with abstract concepts, evaluate the adequacy of ex-planations, and piece together evidence from documents. We all do.

My ultimate goal in writing this book is to help more people reap these kinds of benefits. You might finish this guide and want to deepen your rep-ertoire of skills, perhaps by taking a course about statistics, experiments, case studies, field research, or mass surveys. That would be great. For now, though, I hope that you will acquire certain skills used by experienced political analysts and enjoy the process of learning those skills. Yes, enjoy. Admittedly, making research methods fun is no small task. No guide or textbook that I have read even tries. Maybe my occasional off-beat example or colorful analogy will trigger a little smile. If nothing else, some humor will make the whole process less . . . horrid. At a deeper level, I hope that you gain real satisfaction from learning how to conduct research like a professional analyst and how to read published work intelligently. That sort of satisfaction lasts a long time. To inject some joy into research methods, I have deliberately written an unusual book. This one combines everyday intuition, formal concepts, a wide variety of examples (some academic, some not), practical exercises, plain English, and a little playfulness. With a nod to Stephen Colbert, perhaps the goal I have in mind is *Research Meth-audacity*.

PREFACE FOR TEACHERS

Every year, thousands of college students sign up for a research methods course taught by someone in their Political Science/Politics/Government Department. Not because they want to—because they have to. A methods course is often required to major in political science, much like immunizations are required to enter kindergarten. Most college students look forward to their methods course about as much as having a needle stuck in their arm. That's a shame, because Research Methods could be one of the most eye-opening and useful courses that students ever take.

Having taught Research Methods for many years, I can definitely sympathize with students who don't look forward to this course. In my experience, they have at least three reasons to be wary. Part of the appeal of political science is the opportunity to take courses such as International Security, Ethnic Conflict, Modern Political Campaigns, and Environmental Policy—courses that investigate real-world issues, some of them literally life-and-death. Many students enjoy learning about terrorism, democratization, US presidential elections, and the like, and so do I. But Research Methods is all about the process of thinking systematically, which is not nearly as sexy. I have considered changing the course title to "Harry Potter and the Sinister Methods" or to "Better Thinking = Better Job," but I'm pretty sure that my department chair and the college's curriculum committee would object.

A second problem is that Research Methods is routinely taught as this weird hybrid between a methods course and a statistics course. Think about it: while your typical Economics, Mathematics, Psychology, and Sociology Departments offer a semester-long introduction to statistics, we in the Political Science Department think it's possible to teach the basics in, oh, three to six weeks. Which could mean that (1) our students are much smarter than everyone else's, (2) we're fooling ourselves, or (3) we're fooling ourselves. It gets worse. All those weeks that we kinda, sorta teach statistics come at the expense of topics that truly belong in a methods course but are either dropped or treated superficially. Students could finish the course thinking that statistical analysis is the only respectable way to study politics, which is not true. College students are taught how to work with numbers much more than with written documents, even though both provide essential evidence for political arguments. Technically, then, the standard course should probably be called Research Method, not Methods.

Don't get me wrong, I'm a big fan of numbers. I have used tables and regression models in my own research, and I regularly encourage college students and my own children to take a statistics course. For better or worse, statistics has become the de facto foreign language requirement in the social sciences. Nevertheless, if a basic methods course is supposed to prepare students to read a wide range of scholarly work and to conduct their own research, then it should not lean so heavily on statistical techniques and numbers. Students also need to know how to analyze single cases in depth, carefully compare two or three cases, and work with written documents—and most textbooks do a poor job of teaching those skills.

In my ideal world, undergraduates who major in political science would take at least two methods courses—a general introduction, followed by a more in-depth course devoted to some widely used technique for studying politics such as statistics, experiments, case studies, survey research, or field research. That way, students would be broadly familiar with different research tools and truly skilled at one of them. Their chances for success, in college and beyond, would improve. But I know that the odds of my ideal world becoming reality anytime soon are slim. Departments all over the country would have to modify their requirements; some existing courses might not be taught as often or at all. In the meantime, this book offers a fresh approach to that intro course while serving as a useful companion to a more traditional methods course. For departments that don't offer or require a methods course, this book can provide students with a useful introduction to the process of thinking like a political scientist.

A third reason why students dread taking Research Methods is the textbook. I have assigned different ones over the years, and by the end of the semester students judge the textbook to be somewhere between a necessary evil and soul-crushing. With good reason. Many of these textbooks are too long and literally overflowing with information. The writing can be highly technical, and the joy of studying politics is easily lost. If you have ever read the owner's manual for an automobile, not the skinny "basics" version but the full 475-page monster, then you get the idea. It wouldn't be surprising to find, somewhere in a standard methods textbook, a passage like "This concludes our discussion of sample-population congruence. In the next section we will learn about optimal transmission-gear ratios." By contrast, introductory textbooks in American politics, comparative politics, and international relations—filled with real people and important disputes over power, freedom, and equality—feel like beach reading.

If the main problems with the methods textbook were just flat prose and abstract concepts, a good teacher could overcome them. But the problems go deeper. In the typical textbook, hundreds of important and not-so-important concepts vie for the reader's attention. It's often hard to tell the big ideas from the small ones. Feeling overwhelmed, many students, even the truly dedicated ones, can become frustrated. Some might stop reading altogether. Others will spend the whole semester staring at the proverbial trees without seeing the forest. Moreover, students might spend so much time trying to absorb new information that they don't have enough time to practice their new skills, and practice is essential.* The irony here is that many textbooks preach the virtues of "parsimony" or "analytic leverage"—of identifying a few key factors that might account for a large portion of some pattern in politics—without realizing that parsimony can be a virtue in a textbook as well. A student who learns a dozen general lessons well is probably better off than one who tries to memorize four hundred definitions.

There has to be a better way to teach students how to think systematically about politics. There just has to be a better way. That is the basic premise of this book.

* To become a great chef, you can't just read cookbooks. You have to practice cutting, roasting, sautéing, and baking—over and over. Great athletes don't just watch videotapes; they practice for thousands of hours. Becoming proficient at political research also requires a lot of practice creating good hypotheses, choosing the right research design, picking cases, and other skills.

INTRODUCTION

Let's start at the beginning. What, exactly, should happen in an introductory methods course? What are students supposed to learn? One common way of answering this question is to think in terms of producers and consumers. After taking an initial methods course, students will be better able to produce research on their own and to consume what others have written. This metaphor seems half-right to me. Teachers do want students to produce at a higher level: to write better papers in their politics courses; to work effectively on professors' research projects, if they have a chance; and to conduct many different kinds of research after college, whether in jobs, graduate school, or their personal lives. But "consume"? Usually when we consume something, it goes away and no one else can benefit from it; think food or gasoline. Knowledge isn't really consumed in the same way. When you finish reading a particular book or article about politics, other people can still do the same. Knowledge is more of a public good than a private good. A related problem with this metaphor is that ordinarily, whatever we consume but can't use is transformed into some waste product that often pollutes the environment. While political research may be ignored by "consumers," it doesn't fill the skies with sulfur dioxide or litter the highways with trash. (As an occasional "producer," I certainly hope not.)

Here's a better analogy. A good introduction to research methods should enable students to become the equivalent of careful home inspectors when they read political analysis, and competent home builders when they undertake their own research. The ultimate objectives are more about building and inspecting than producing and consuming.

For those of you unfamiliar with home inspectors, I will briefly describe what these remarkable people do. Home inspectors are hired by individuals who are serious about buying a house, but haven't yet signed a contract. While a house may appear to be in good shape, who knows what problems lurk below the surface? The average person can't tell. In the span of a few hours, a good home inspector can check the roof, walls, and foundation for cracks and evidence of moisture or termite damage; make sure that all windows and doors open and close properly; and test the home's plumbing, heating/cooling, and electrical systems, down to the last wall socket. This is really impressive, considering that the inspector had never set foot inside the house before the day of the inspection. Typically, home inspectors carry around a detailed checklist to make sure they cover every important part of the house. It does not matter much what architectural style the house had been built to reflect, or how large it is, or how old. The main items on the checklist are still the same. Potential home buyers pay good money for this service, because buying a house with hidden defects could be a very costly mistake. They expect an honest and thorough evaluation; they want to hear the good and the bad. Although the home inspector doesn't need to be an experienced builder, she or he must know what goes into a well-built house.

Reading a journal article or academic book is much like conducting a home inspection. Readers should always enter into the process with a critical eye. Just because research has been published doesn't mean that the results should be completely trusted. Even the best work has limitations. When reading political analysis, it helps to have a mental checklist for identifying which parts of an argument are in good shape, which need repair, and which are just plain missing. For example, much as a home inspector might check the foundation of a home, we should note whether a scholarly book or article clearly builds on previous research. Poorly crafted hypotheses, like a leaky roof, might lead to the equivalent of water damage. An outdated furnace might be akin to an outdated list of sources in that neither one is likely to hold up for very long. Such a checklist will be useful whether students are reading about the proliferation of nuclear weapons, party politics in Japan, or the US Supreme Court. It will be useful whether the analysis is performed by academics, policy makers, pundits, or advocates. A good grasp of research methods will help you develop that checklist.[1]

What is missing from a home inspector's report is almost as important as what's included. A well-crafted report doesn't dwell on factual minutiae. "Grout in upstairs bathtub appears to have been purchased from Home Depot." Not important. "Found old paper bag in crawl space under house." Unless there's a severed head or poisonous snake in that bag, who cares? Nor does the inspector's report dwell on features that are obvious to all. "In my professional judgment, the carpet in the living room is tan." Unfortunately, too many readers try to remember these kinds of details instead of focusing on the more important structural features of a scholarly article or book. This guide will help break that habit and create more sophisticated readers.[2]

When teachers tell their students to conduct research and write papers, they are training students to build arguments. A good argument is like a well-built house. Homes don't need an original design to be valuable; many neighborhoods are filled with homes that are based on a few basic floor plans. A good home should be built to last, with certain essentials like indoor plumbing, electricity, doors, and windows. Similarly, most undergraduate papers don't have to offer a truly original argument.[3] In fact, originality may be a bit overrated.

> Original ideas, those hinges on which an era turns, are rare. It is unlikely that you will write *The Origins of Species*. Or that you will be Emerson. But originality and profundity are not identical. Profound ideas bear repeating, or rediscovery, and many original ideas do not.[4]

Students are often asked to analyze familiar but important problems such as the impact of divided government in the United States, or reasons why democracies have been difficult to establish in the Middle East. Nevertheless, teachers expect the argument, even if familiar, to be well constructed. This means more than its having an introduction, a body, and a conclusion. For example, the argument should not be a tautology, and therefore true by definition (e.g., "Democracies have more competitive elections than dictatorships"). Arguments about some factor A causing some outcome B should have more proof than arguments simply claiming that A and B regularly occur at the same time. By the same token, we expect a home builder to use quality materials, just as teachers, employers, and judges expect arguments to be supported with substantial evidence from high-quality sources.

While it is possible for a home inspector to become a home builder, the two jobs are different. The standards for obtaining a license are usually more demanding for builders than inspectors, a sign that builders need more expertise. Similarly, students should expect that becoming a skilled researcher and writer will take longer than becoming a skilled reader. Whereas a good home inspection can be completed in an afternoon, a house takes months to build. Students may be able to read an article or chapter in a few hours, but they would be hard-pressed to crank out a decent research paper in the same amount of time. And the work of a home builder is by definition more visible to the rest of the world. Students must be prepared to share the results of their research with the attitude of "Here's what I built, and I stand behind my work."*

Building and inspecting are fundamentally harder tasks than looking. Literally anyone can look at a house or a political argument. Looking requires little time or effort. When college students write, "This paper looks at partisan polarization in Congress" or "In this paper, I will look at foreign

---

*In case building and inspecting homes don't grab your interest, think in terms of being trained as a chef and a food critic. Either way, the key point here is acquiring certain skills that will help you to create and to appreciate what others have created.

aid," their teachers can see trouble coming. These students probably have a general topic but lack a specific argument. To be a good inspector or builder requires time, skill, and a critical mind. You must adopt certain standards of quality and judge the work, whether it's your own or someone else's, against those standards. Trained political scientists do more than just look.

After you study politics for a while, people may assume that you know a lot of Important Facts. Maybe you can name the current Speaker of the US House of Representatives and the year India became an independent state. You can probably spell out NAFTA and NATO, IMF and WHO. But so can a philosophy major, a chemistry major, your cousin who's in the fifth grade, and that guy who drives the UPS truck in your neighborhood—so can almost anyone who has access to the Internet and can use a search engine like Google. Sure, a trained political scientist can name these facts two or three minutes sooner than anyone else, but in the grand scheme of things, that's not much of an advantage. In the age of *Wikipedia* and other virtual warehouses of information, the value of majoring in political science increasingly depends on general skills acquired rather than specific facts memorized. (Actually, this statement holds true for any college major.) While factual knowledge about politics will always be important, you could soon be replaced by a couple of cell phone apps if that's all you possess.

Of course, writing well and speaking effectively in public are essential skills that all students should develop. Any number of college courses can help cultivate those abilities, and students should take as many of those courses as they can. On the other hand, the special skills a political science major should have are different: knowing, for instance, how to work intelligently with "big" concepts such as democracy, terrorism, political tolerance, and civic engagement; how to distinguish causation from correlation; and how to pick good cases for testing a hypothesis. Ideally, those skills will later be reinforced and refined in upper-level courses. And they're hard to acquire with just a cell phone.

In effect, this book identifies several of the essential skills needed to become a capable inspector and builder of empirical arguments about politics. My experience teaching research methods indicates that students are better off learning a handful of skills, and learning them well, rather than being overwhelmed by a multitude of concepts and formulas. Consequently, this book is relatively short by design (and less expensive than its rivals). Years of experience also tell me that students need to practice these skills to become proficient. It's no coincidence that the old Chinese proverb "I hear and I forget; I see and I remember; I do and I understand" is invoked so often on the syllabi of methods courses.

The organization of this guide is unusual, maybe even unique. It begins with the premise that students should learn how to ask good questions about politics and how to generate good answers. Teaching these two skills makes up the two main parts of this book. Political scientists ask many different questions, but at the end of the day they usually boil down to some variation of "What happened?" "Why?" and "Who cares?" This is true whether the subject is social movements, the impact of money on elections, conflict in Sudan, you name it.* Most published work in political science tries to answer two of these questions, and often all three. Each question raises a particular set of issues and requires a distinct set of skills. That terrain will be covered in part I of this guide.

The Who Cares / So What question concerns the larger significance of a research project. Typically, authors raise this question at the very beginning of their paper, journal article, or book, which is one reason I discuss it first (in chapter 1). If the initial answers are not compelling, or at least intriguing, then readers might find something else to do. When answering this question, authors must think about the intended audience for their work. It could be a small group of specialists, a larger number of social scientists, policy makers, or some segment of the general public. The broader the audience, the bigger the inferences authors will make about their research. "This isn't just a story about the Chewa and Tumbuka peoples of Africa," an author might claim. "In fact, it might provide valuable insights into how cultural differences can lead to political conflict all over the world."[5] That type of appeal will grab my attention, even though I'm not a specialist in African politics. Chapter 1 describes a few common strategies that authors use to persuade their audience to care about their arguments. Of course, anyone can make bold claims about the implications of their work. As careful readers, we should examine such claims closely, even skeptically.

It's one thing to state that you're tackling an important problem and quite

---

* Political theorists, on the other hand, tend to ask more normative questions. What makes a government legitimate? How should values of liberty and equality be balanced? Under what circumstances are countries morally justified in going to war? The political scientists I have in mind are interested more in empirical questions—in studying what is rather than what should be. They are the ones teaching courses in comparative politics, American politics, international relations, and public policy. Nevertheless, empirical political science is often animated by normative concerns, as we shall see in the next chapter.

another to show that you have something new or important to contribute. Both are essential in answering the Who Cares / So What question. In academic writing, a literature review helps readers to understand how previous scholars have studied a given problem and what they have found. A good literature review serves as a kind of springboard for the rest of the article or book. It usually identifies the descriptive or causal hypotheses worth investigating. It indicates how the author plans to contribute to our collective understanding of democratization, retirement policy, human rights, or whatever topic is being studied. Even authors writing for a more general audience point out, early on, whom they are agreeing with or arguing against. Most undergraduates, however, have little to no experience in conducting a literature review, and they don't fully appreciate its importance when reading the work of published authors. Chapter 1 will help to develop those skills.

Chapter 2 is titled "What Happened?" and that turns out to be a deceptively simple question. True, some events or trends are fairly easy to describe. Social insurance programs first appeared in Europe in the late nineteenth and early twentieth centuries. Iraqi troops invaded Kuwait in 1990. In cases like these, the more interesting and complicated question is, why? Suppose we want to know why some Asian countries are more democratic than others. Before we can consider the possible causes, however, we need to define *democracy* and figure out how to measure it in different countries. Problem: there is no universally accepted definition of *democracy*, and some of the data we might need to measure democracy are not available for every Asian country. We would therefore need to choose a general definition and specific measures, and then defend our choices. Similar difficulties would arise if the topic was terrorism, and we were trying to explain why the number of terrorist attacks has varied over time. Terrorism means different things to different governments. Chances are good that not all countries count terrorist attacks the same way, making it harder for us to observe general trends. Even seemingly simple concepts like voter turnout can be hard to describe accurately. In short, figuring out what happened in politics requires us to think carefully about concepts and measures.

Determining what happened could require describing a possible relationship between variables, which is also discussed in chapter 2. Initially, we might want to determine whether the values of two variables change in any regular pattern. We are testing descriptive hypotheses, with no claims (yet) about any causal relationship. Perhaps we want to find out whether affluence and democracy are related across countries. Or whether gender and attitudes toward the death penalty are related among adults.

More often than we care to admit, scholars have tried to explain some pattern in politics without establishing that such a pattern truly exists. When that pattern turns out to be wrong, a lot of time and effort go down the scholarly drain. Sometimes the problems with the pattern are conceptual, sometimes they are rooted in measurement error, and sometimes they reflect a failure to consider alternatives. To illustrate the latter, suppose we found that women are more likely than men to oppose the death penalty. Before declaring that gender and the death penalty are correlated, we would be smart to check if both were connected to some third factor, such as political ideology or party identification (and probably other factors as well). Put more generally, we ask, "Are *A* and *B* related, controlling for *C*?" Asking questions in this manner will enable us to generate more accurate descriptions of what happened.

Causal knowledge is highly prized by political scientists, and the Why question probably receives more attention than any other. For many, the ultimate goal of political science is to explain general patterns of behavior. Why do democracies rarely go to war with other democracies? Why do some people participate in politics more than others? Why has polarization increased in the US Congress? These are big, important questions, and not surprisingly, people will routinely disagree about the answers. After being exposed to these different debates, we could conclude that "hey, there appear to be many different explanations, and they all seem pretty plausible to me." While this sort of attitude could indicate open-mindedness, too often it reveals a lack of critical judgment. Chapter 3 will introduce readers to the design of causal questions—featuring independent, dependent, and intervening variables—as well as the process of answering these questions.

In some respects, scholars answer Why questions much as they answer What Happened questions: by determining whether two variables are correlated, and whether that relationship holds even after controlling for other relevant variables. Both steps are important. In addition, those who wish to demonstrate a causal connection need to establish the right sequence of events. If they think that *A* led to *B*, they need to show that *A* happened before *B*.[6] Moreover, scholars need to show how *A* led to *B*, which means identifying one or more causal mechanisms. This is one of the big differences between correlation and causation—locating a path between cause and effect. Take the well-known example of democracy and war. Maybe democracies rarely go to war with each other because of their shared commitments to diplomacy and human rights. Alternatively, this pattern could occur because democracies have regular elections, which give ordinary citizens a way to punish their leaders if and when wars go badly. The first path is rooted in values, the second more in institutions. We can imagine other causal mechanisms as well. The main point I want to stress for now is that good answers to <u>why</u> in politics usually require good answers to <u>how</u>. Chapter 3 takes up these issues in more depth.

Choosing a good question and knowing what constitutes a good answer are essential parts of the research process. "Well begun is half done," in the words of Aristotle. The other half, however, is also crucial. The other half requires some strategy for answering the question, which is the subject of part II of this guide.

The first step in generating good answers is choosing an appropriate research design (discussed in chapter 4). Such a design functions like the blueprints used by home builders. Typically, there's a big gap between the types of research design that undergraduates can execute on their own and the types they will encounter in the professional literature. Trained political scientists increasingly use experimental designs, for instance, to test their hypotheses. Although experiments have been more prominent in the study of American politics, specialists in comparative politics and international relations are catching up. Many of those designs are frankly too complicated, expensive, or time-consuming for undergraduates to use in their own research. Nevertheless, as inspectors-in-training, students should know the main elements of experimental designs, along with their classic advantages and disadvantages.

Likewise, many undergraduates lack the statistical know-how to compare many cases using SPSS, Stata, or some other software package (at least, not beyond calculating simple percentages and generating bar charts). Creating contingency tables and multiple regression models requires at least a semester of statistics, and the more sophisticated work that appears in print is often based on several semesters' worth of statistical training. Still, we need to start somewhere. Statistical designs are ubiquitous in political science, and students need to learn some of the main variants along with their characteristic strengths and weaknesses. Experimental and statistical research designs will both be discussed in chapter 4.

The one design that students probably have the most experience using is ironically the one that traditional textbooks devote the least attention to—case studies. Rarely if ever will undergraduates be expected to conduct an experiment, and few are the times when statistical prowess will be required of them. Instead, teachers assign case studies. In their introduction to American politics course, for example, students might have written a paper analyzing how Barack Obama won the presidential election in 2008, or explaining why a specific interest group is widely considered to be influential. Students in a basic comparative politics course might have been told to investigate party politics in a particular country and write up their findings.

Many scholars employ this design in their own work. Although case studies are in some respects easier to conduct than experiments or statistical analyses, they're also easy to screw up. I have seen plenty of college students use case studies to accomplish what they are ill-suited to do. It's a bit like watching someone try to install a roof with a paintbrush. Case studies will be the third research design covered in chapter 4.

Regardless of which general design is selected, scholars must then choose specific cases to analyze. A case could be an individual, an election, a nation, a bill, a war; there are many other possibilities as well. The number of cases in a given study could range from one to many thousands. Individual cases could be selected at random or quite deliberately by the investigator. With so many decisions, the odds of making a mistake increase, which is one reason why case selection must be performed carefully (explained in chapter 5). Perhaps the main insight to pass along at this point is that cases are usually selected in such a way as to make useful inferences possible. Suppose we plan to survey 1000 people in order to learn something about racial attitudes in the United States, whose total population exceeds 300 million. How can we pick the right people? Or suppose we want to understand the prospects for democratization among developing countries. What general lessons, if any, can we draw from comparing countries like Mexico and Tunisia? One of the more common criticisms leveled at published work is that the cases chosen don't enable anyone to generalize very far, or with much confidence.

Once we have settled on a research design and chosen our cases, we need to collect and analyze evidence—empirical evidence, the kind that can be observed in the real world. Without such evidence, we quickly enter the realm of personal belief, parable, collective myth, or conspiracy theory.[7] To continue with the housing metaphor, evidence constitutes the building materials—the bricks, wood, vinyl, nails—of an argument. Without enough evidence in the right places, an argument will sag or fall apart.

By and large, political scientists work with two kinds of evidence, words and numbers. (Those who study political communication might also use visual images as evidence.) The two are by no means mutually exclusive: most scholars use words and numbers as evidence in their research, and many find ways to convert words into numbers or numbers into words. Not surprisingly, those who use statistical analysis to make comparisons across many cases rely heavily on numbers such as voter turnout rates, per capita income, and years of education. Those who perform in-depth case studies are more likely to cite government documents, newspaper articles, biographies, speeches, and personal interviews as evidence.

Standard textbooks spend lots of time teaching students how to analyze numbers and relatively little on how to work with documents. This guide gives equal time to each type of evidence, because both are important, and equal time here means one chapter each (chapters 6 and 7). These chapters will offer some suggestions for finding good sources of written and numerical information. The primary emphasis, however, will be on how to analyze that information. With documents, we need to be sensitive to problems such as bias and selectivity. The remarkable increase in websites, blogs, think tanks, and self-publishing has made it possible for many, many individuals and organizations to share their thoughts with the rest of the world. In their haste to publish, some of these sources could be inaccurate. The authors could be writing more as advocates than analysts, and we would be smart to double-check their claims. Even more authoritative sources can be biased in ways that raise concern. When working with numbers, we must learn which statistical tests are appropriate for which kinds of data. We need to appreciate the difference between the statistical significance of a relationship and its substantive importance. And we need to understand that statistical techniques are usually better suited to test some elements of a causal relationship than others. In short, the "facts" rarely speak for themselves, whether they are based on words or on numbers.

Each chapter in this book has two main sections. The first and longest section introduces key terms such as *literature review*, *hypothesis*, *internal validity*, *external validity*, *research design*, *triangulation*, *statistical significance*, and many others. This material is similar to what you would find in a traditional textbook, although the presentation of that material is often quite different. The real emphasis, though, is on general strategies and practical advice—what to do and what not to do, and why. Throughout the book, I illustrate these lessons with examples drawn from comparative politics, American politics, international relations, and public policy.

The second section of each chapter gives readers a chance to apply these concepts and skills. My suggestion is to start practicing the role of "inspector" by reading good examples of published research. The specific topics may be unfamiliar, which is a good test of what you are learning. Despite knowing little about Italian regional governments or international disputes over fishing rights, can you determine whether the author's argument is structurally sound? If you or your teacher has different examples in mind, fine; the main point is to move from memorizing facts to evaluating the general structure of the argument. To help readers become better "builders," I conclude each chapter with a few exercises. Just as inspecting and building homes require a mixture of book learning and hands-on practice to master them, so do inspecting and building arguments about politics.

PART ONE

ASKING GOOD QUESTIONS

1

WHO CARES?

Imagine that someone starts talking to you, at length, about bananas. About how they cost more at Kroger than at Walmart; then again, the ones at Walmart sometimes have more brown spots on the outside, and sometimes those spots mean a bruise but, you know, not always. About how bananas are a great source of potassium, but lima beans and acorn squash are even better sources. This person asks you, "Isn't it odd that grocery stores will let their customers shuck fresh corn yet won't let them peel bananas (or grapefruit, for that matter) before they check out? Did you know that monkeys peel bananas from the bottom, while humans do it from the top?" If this person happens to be anyone that you truly care about, then you may nod your head and try to look interested. With just about anyone else, your eyes will start to glaze over, and the voice inside your head will be screaming, "WHY are you WASTING my TIME?! Why should I CARE?"

When we talk or write, it's easy to assume that our audience will be fascinated by what we say. That assumption is perfectly reasonable for those of us who are under the age of eight, or who are dealing with people who love us unconditionally. Otherwise, it makes more sense to assume that our audience is really busy and doesn't share our particular passion. To truly connect with people, we need to persuade them to stop, listen, and engage.

Granted, the example of bananas is vivid but trivial. Suppose instead that you are writing a college paper about democratization in Eastern Europe or land reform in Brazil. Or suppose that you work at a "real" job analyzing environmental regulations, military budgets, court cases, medical costs, or consumer behavior. No matter what the issue, almost everyone you hope to communicate with is feeling inundated, maybe even overwhelmed, with information. In any given day at the office, people (and that includes college instructors) deal with dozens and dozens of e-mails, phone calls, memos, reports, meetings, and conversations with coworkers. While some of these messages are expected, many are not. A significant number of these exchanges are distracting or pointless. In addition, apart from work, the average American received an estimated 74 gigabytes of data from television, radio, cell phones, personal computers, and the like in 2015—every single day. That's the equivalent of nine DVDs of words, sounds, and images, every single day. The amount of data aimed at us is staggering, literally staggering, and it keeps growing.[1]

To keep our heads from exploding, we've developed a number of coping strategies. Much of this information is simply ignored. Other times, we quickly skim a document, or read the first lines carefully and then skim. One recent study found that most people stop reading the average web article when they are halfway through—and halfway means only a few paragraphs.[2] Many items are mentally filed under "If I Have Time Later . . . ," but that time rarely comes. Not when there are deadlines to meet, groceries to buy, clothes to wash, and ballgames to attend. Clearly, anyone trying to send a message, and have it heard, will find the odds stacked against them.

Many students, however, don't realize this. For years they have inhabited this strange world where their written work has been guaranteed one reader—their teacher. After all, it was the teacher who had created the assignment in the first place, and that teacher is paid to read and comment on whatever the student writes. Students write for their teacher. That mindset works fine if you plan to take orders from one person for the rest of your life. It doesn't work well anywhere else. Ideally, students will start to view research and writing less as an exercise in power (or, more accurately, powerlessness) and more as an opportunity for persuasion.

Professional scholars realize how difficult it is to capture a reader's attention. They understand that motivating their readers is important, which is why they usually answer the Who Cares / So What question early in their article, chapter, or book. Before they describe what happened and explain why, social scientists have to generate interest in their work. Otherwise, people will stop reading and find something better to do. Later, in the conclusion, these authors usually highlight the larger significance of their research findings. Generally speaking, answers to the Who Cares question appear at the beginning and the end of a project, while answers to <u>what happened</u> and <u>why</u> occupy the middle.

As careful readers, students need to recognize how authors frame the Who Cares question. Scholars employ a variety of techniques to establish the larger significance of their research, and I will discuss several of them in this chapter. Choosing among these techniques depends in part on the intended audience, which can range from a small group of academic specialists to the general public. Knowing these strategies will also help students when they conduct their own research. In particular, it will help them make that crucial leap from finding a topic that interests them to identifying a specific research question that will interest many others.

CHAPTER ONE

My brother is a high school English teacher, and a few years ago he introduced me to a terrific book about writing called *They Say, I Say*.[3] One of the authors' core insights is that all writers, no matter what their topic, are part of some larger conversation that extends across time. Writing is both a solitary activity and a collective enterprise. Except for personal diaries, we write to communicate with other people.

For many scholars, these conversations take place primarily with other academics. This is especially true of writing that takes the form of articles appearing in scholarly journals or books published by university presses. No one expects the average person to read the latest issue of the *American Political Science Review* or *International Organization*. Most of the books published by Oxford University Press and the University Press of Kansas never reach the shelves of our local bookstore. Yet professional scholars know that these kinds of journals and books are where they can go to join a good conversation. As a practical matter, many scholars also realize that contributing to these conversations is necessary if they want to earn tenure and promotion (and maybe even honor and respect) within their profession.

These scholarly conversations can be quite disjointed and hard to follow. They involve people who might never meet face to face. Participants often want to shift the conversation in new directions. And these conversations could persist, off and on, for years or even decades. It is therefore essential that scholars clearly indicate which conversation they are trying to join. They typically do this early in their written work, and they do it fairly quickly, because they realize that few readers will want to spend much time rehashing old arguments. This part of the project is called the **literature review** (better known as the **lit review**), which has nothing to do with reading Charles Dickens or Toni Morrison but everything to do with joining and contributing to a scholarly conversation. In the lit review, scholars summarize what is already known about some event or pattern in the political world. Most lit reviews also indicate what we don't know, and thus how additional research could enrich our collective understanding of that event or pattern. To return to the house metaphor introduced earlier, a lit review provides the foundation on which the rest of the scholarly edifice is built.[4]

How scholars design their literature review tells us a lot about the intended audience for their work (Who) and the potential significance of their research (Cares). Readers should pay close attention to which literatures are being invoked. Someone analyzing the outcome of the 2008 US presidential election, for example, could start by engaging with past studies of the presidential campaigns in that year. After digging through articles and books, he or she might identify a group of analysts who believe that Barack Obama won because his campaign did a better job of mobilizing new voters, and another group believing that John McCain lost because he blundered in choosing Sarah Palin as his running mate. A broader literature review might encompass multiple US elections before 2008, with a focus on the role of economic conditions. These elections could be presidential, congressional, or both. Maybe the 2008 election needs to be examined against a larger pattern in which incumbent parties do poorly when the economy falters.

In principle, there's no reason why the 2008 election has to be analyzed strictly from the perspective of American politics. Perhaps the larger question is how members of marginalized groups manage to overcome historical obstacles and win national elections. Obama was, after all, the first African American to win the US presidency. From this angle, previous studies of female prime ministers (e.g., in Israel, England, India, Mozambique) could be relevant. The target audience would now include scholars of comparative politics, not just American politics. There are undoubtedly many other ways to use the 2008 election to further a scholarly conversation. Same case, different literatures. Nevertheless, it is hard to imagine any single book or article embracing all these literatures; a certain degree of analytic focus is important and usually expected.[5]

Unless our collective knowledge of a topic is quite limited, it will be practically impossible for scholars to cite, much less summarize, every previous study in their lit review. (Nor should they try before verifying that their health insurer offers a full range of mental health benefits.) Scholars will need to generalize, they will need to condense, and they will need to discuss a number of studies while leaving some out. Most lit reviews are therefore organized around schools of thought rather than individual authors or studies. The two most common designs for a literature review represent some variant of the Conventional Wisdom and the Ongoing Debate.

With some questions, most political scientists agree on what happened or why. Among specialists in international relations, for instance, the conventional wisdom is that democracies rarely go to war with each other, hence the "democratic peace." Although democracies certainly go to war with non-democracies (think World War II), and they regularly spy on other democracies, full-fledged war between democracies is rare.[6] In comparative politics, the conventional wisdom is that electoral systems based on proportional representation give third parties more voice in government than do systems based on single-member districts. Both of these generalizations describe important patterns in politics. A review of either literature could cite multiple published studies and historical examples.

Conventional Wisdoms describing what happened in politics are probably more common than Conventional Wisdoms explaining why, but the latter do exist. Most specialists in American politics would agree on some of the reasons why public trust in government declined after the 1960s. According to the American National Election Studies, three-quarters of Americans in 1964 felt they could trust the national government most of the time or almost always. By 1980, that figure had dropped to one-quarter.[7] Why did that happen? The conventional wisdom is that the Vietnam War and the Watergate scandal diminished trust in government. As a second example, experts generally agree that party identification plays a larger role than specific issues (e.g., abortion) or candidate traits (e.g., intelligence, honesty) in determining how people vote in US national elections. For most Americans, knowing that Obama was a Democrat and McCain a Republican provided important information in deciding whom to vote for in 2008.

On most questions, though, political scientists actively disagree. Sometimes these Ongoing Debates divide scholars into two main camps—not necessarily equal camps, but each side big enough to sustain a meaningful debate. Any question involving the impact of something—such as UN peacekeeping missions, school reforms, gender quotas in national legislatures, economic sanctions against "rogue" nations—can pit those who claim the effort was effective versus those who say it was ineffective. To determine impact, we must figure out what happened. Theoretical debates, centered on the Why question, are very common in political science. A literature review about inequality might feature two camps: those who argue that the roots are primarily economic, and those who say the roots are political. Similarly, studies of international migration might pit those who stress "push" factors versus those emphasizing "pull" factors as the main causes. In these examples, a literature review would summarize the basic logic and some of the key evidence for each side.[8]

Such debates can easily expand to include more than two sides. A debate over the effectiveness of some agency or program might boil down to those who believe it is usually, sometimes, or seldom effective. A debate over the causes of inequality might feature economic, political, and cultural arguments. Introductory textbooks in international relations often frame the main theoretical debates as a contest among realism, liberalism, and constructivism. Three sides is by no means the upper limit. Over the years, scholars have offered many different reasons why the American welfare state seems to lag behind its European counterparts, including highly fragmented institutions; core values of individualism and limited government; the absence of strong left-wing political parties and labor unions; the power of business interests; and the historical importance of racial divisions.

One function of the literature review, then, is to signal which conversation the author hopes to join. Authors say, in effect, "I'm talking specifically to these political scientists who generally agree about *X*." Or, "I'd like to weigh in on this argument between these two groups of scholars over *Y*."* But that's not enough. Authors also need to set up the Conventional Wisdom or the Ongoing Debate in such a way that they can contribute something new. This step is crucial. A professional literature review does more than simply show that the author has read the classic studies in her field. It does more than provide accurate summaries of those studies. A strong lit review helps readers recognize potential gaps and misunderstandings in our collective knowledge of some part of the political world. It makes readers feel that they want to learn more. Who + Cares. The rest of the paper, article, chapter, or book will start to fill in these gaps or correct these misunderstandings.

In more formal terms, a good lit review generates one or more hypotheses that the author plans to investigate more fully. A **hypothesis** is an educated guess, in this instance an educated guess about some feature of the political world, whether that's a single event such as the 2008 US election or a general pattern such as the democratic peace. A hypothesis is "educated" in the sense that it's informed by prior research or experience. It is a "guess" in the sense that it could turn out to be true or false, depending on the evidence. For instance, given what scholars have learned about US elections in the twentieth century, we would expect economic factors to have played a role in the 2008 election—but we won't know for sure until we research this case more thoroughly.[†]

---

* For the general reader, it can be helpful to introduce the authors cited in the literature review. For example, when Richard Valelly was summarizing past work about black enfranchisement, he started one sentence with, "As Katherine Tate, a leading scholar of African American political behavior, observes . . ." He then described the scholar Michael Dawson as "co-investigator of the 1993–94 National Black Politics Study" (*The Two Reconstructions: The Struggle for Black Enfranchisement* [Chicago: University of Chicago Press, 2004], p. 14). No long biography needed, just a quick phrase to indicate why these particular authors deserve our attention.

[†] By contrast, my hypothesis that fans of the New York Yankees like to kick puppies is based on neither research nor experience, but on my prejudice as a Boston Red Sox fan. That's not exactly an educated view (though I could still be right). And my hypothesis

Anyone trying to contribute to a conversation has a few options, and the same is true for political scientists. Broadly speaking, research tries to extend, refine, or challenge what we (think we) know about the political world.[9] This is admittedly a simple list of options, and the choices aren't mutually exclusive, but as an initial framework it will do the job. Imagine, for example, that you were conducting research in the year 2000 on the so-called resource curse in comparative politics. After reading numerous studies, you would probably notice a piece of conventional wisdom: countries that rely heavily on oil for revenue often suffer from poor economic growth. They also tend not to be strong, healthy democracies. An abundance of oil turns out to be a curse. So far, this is a descriptive hypothesis; it indicates a relationship without explaining how or why oil impedes development.[10]

The question you now face as a researcher is how to advance our collective understanding of this pattern. As you read the relevant literature, you might wonder just how far the conventional wisdom can apply. Oil isn't the only natural resource that matters. Some countries rely heavily on precious minerals or natural gas. Does this curse extend beyond oil to these other resources? Good question. That kind of insight might lend itself to a statistical analysis of many mineral-rich countries, which would be a genuine addition to the literature.[11] Or, you might notice that proponents of the resource curse all tend to cite the same examples—Libya, Nigeria, Saudi Arabia. After summarizing key findings from these countries, you might ask, "Does this pattern extend to other oil-rich countries such as Indonesia and Venezuela?" In that event, a detailed case study might be appropriate.[12] Alternatively, a lit review on this topic might demonstrate that most of the evidence comes from the last fifty years. Does the resource curse extend even farther back in time? Any one of these extensions, across space or over time, could provide a test for the resource curse hypothesis. None of them would be possible, however, without a careful reading of past studies.

Designing the lit review to extend an argument offers a few advantages in terms of gaining an audience. First, it is usually nonthreatening. An extension will probably not antagonize anyone who has already published in this area, which could be important, given that most scholarly work must undergo peer review before it can be published. (Sure, peer reviewers should be big enough to accept criticism of their work, but there are petty people in every walk of life, and academia is no exception.) Even if the extension turns out to deviate from the conventional wisdom—for example, a case study

---

that Barack Obama won the 2008 US presidential election would not really qualify as a guess.

of Canada will probably not illustrate the resource curse—the scholar can identify the outer boundaries of that wisdom without rejecting it. Second, designing the lit review for a possible extension will appeal to scholars who want to generalize as broadly as possible about politics.

On the other hand, a proposed extension could be so modest that it fails to generate much interest. Allow me to continue with the resource curse example. If the lit review points out that past studies of the resource curse have focused heavily on oil but overlooked cobalt, well, I have a hunch that few readers are dying to learn more about this one mineral (call that my cobalt interest hypothesis). Moreover, the prospect of simply extending any argument might not generate as wide an audience as a frontal assault on a well-known description or explanation. Some people genuinely enjoy watching a good fight. At a deeper level, certain members of the audience might believe that the fastest way to make intellectual progress is to attack the conventional wisdom, not extend it.

A literature review designed to refine a Conventional Wisdom or an Ongoing Debate looks a bit different. With an extension, the basic argument in the literature is clear; we just don't know yet for how many cases or for what span of time it holds true. When the argument is fuzzy or incomplete, though, we may need to refine it. Let's revisit the question of trust in government. The conventional wisdom is that trust declined sharply in the United States during the 1960s and 1970s, in no small part because of Vietnam and Watergate. Key evidence in practically all these studies comes from opinion polls. After reviewing the past research, however, you notice that scholars have combined survey questions about trust in institutions such as Congress with questions about individual politicians such as Richard Nixon. Conceptually, the two might be distinct. In fact, you know that Americans generally think more positively about their own representatives in Congress than they do about Congress as a whole. Your lit review might therefore make the case that we need to refine our understanding of trust in government by analyzing government institutions and specific public officials separately. In effect, you would argue that the variable "trust in government" has been measured too crudely in the literature. We need to look more closely at what happened.

Causal hypotheses often need to be refined.[13] The steps connecting cause and effect (e.g., the intervening variables) might be missing. Even if one causal pathway has been established, a second pathway involving some of the same variables might exist. Returning to the example of trust in government, we might review the literature and still not find a clear explanation of exactly how the Vietnam War diminished the public's trust. Was it because the media fed the public a steady diet of negative stories about the war? Or was it some combination of negative media coverage plus official statements that the US war effort was going well? Was it because so many Americans died in Vietnam or were closely related to someone who was killed? We can imagine other links as well. A literature review could thus indicate one or more gaps in the causal story, paving the way for new empirical research that would help fill in those gaps.

Another common way to refine a causal hypothesis is by adding independent variables. The existing argument isn't so much wrong as incomplete; more causes may be involved. A literature review about trust in government might quickly summarize previous research concerning Watergate and Vietnam and then suggest that economic factors such as unemployment and inflation might be important as well. Why would we think that? Well, maybe these factors have been shown to affect trust in other countries, or maybe they have been shown to influence voting behavior in US elections. (Hint: it pays to read widely and capitalize on insights from related literatures.) Either way, we could make an educated guess from these other literatures that in the United States, economics might also influence trust. The rest of the project could then investigate whether, to what extent, and how economic factors affected trust. This kind of revision is common among political scientists who want their explanations to be as complete as possible, even if their accounts become a little messy and complicated. Those who favor lean, parsimonious explanations will be less inclined to take this path.

Alternatively, scholars can try to revise an Ongoing Debate by saying, "Hey, you're both right." This type of literature review would summarize the well-established reasons why A might lead to X, and why B might lead to X, and then argue that both could be true. We need to add two separate causes, A and B, into our explanation for X. A lit review focused on the 2008 presidential race might suggest that both Obama's get-out-the-vote drive and McCain's poor choice of a running mate were decisive. The rest of the argument would have to offer concrete evidence to support or reject this hypothesis. Another twist on this approach would be to argue that the interaction of A and B ($A \times B$, not $A + B$) might be important. Biddle, Friedman, and Shapiro do just that when reviewing previous explanations for levels of violence in Iraq. Whereas some scholars believe that the dramatic decrease in violence after 2007 was due largely to the surge in US troops, others claim that it was triggered by local Sunni tribes rebelling against al-Qaeda. On the surface, those seem like two very different explanations, one rooted in external force and the other in domestic politics. And they have very different implications for foreign policy. Yet the authors suggest early on in their article that the interaction between these two developments may have been crucial.[14]

The high-risk, high-reward strategy is to enter a scholarly conversation and openly challenge what one or more key participants have been saying. Forget extending or refining what we know; we should reject, or at least seriously question, what other scholars have claimed to be true.[15] Consider the important book by Pauline Jones Luong and Erika Weinthal, *Oil Is Not a Curse*. Chapter 1 contains their literature review, and from the very start (literally, page 1) they cite previous scholars who refer to the resource curse as a law or fact. Nevertheless, these same scholars disagree about why oil has such negative effects. Thus, readers are quickly introduced to a Conventional Wisdom about what happened and an Ongoing Debate about why. Luong and Weinthal then suggest (not prove, but suggest) that this entire line of inquiry is misguided. By itself, oil might not be a curse; the real problem could be who owns the oil. This problem has not been apparent to other scholars because virtually all their cases have been countries where the government owns or controls the oil. Scholars should therefore compare countries where the oil is privately owned versus publicly owned, which in Luong and Weinthal's book essentially pits Russia and Kazakhstan versus Turkmenistan and Uzbekistan. Chapters 2 through 9 provide detailed evidence from these countries, with sustained attention to the role of ownership and control. Those chapters test the hypotheses introduced in the first chapter. As you can tell from the book's title, the authors conclude that the resource curse has been exaggerated.[16]

Challenges don't have to be this sweeping. Sometimes scholars join an Ongoing Debate to find out which side is closer to the truth. Writing this sort of lit review can be tricky. Because some of these debates have been going on for years and the arguments are well known, adding a simple "Yeah, like he said" on behalf of one side won't count as much of a contribution. Instead, scholars might use the lit review to offer a new reason why explanation A is better than explanation B, or perhaps to identify a new set of cases where we can compare the validity of A and B. Early in his famous study of Italy, Robert Putnam introduces economics and culture as two leading explanations for why some governments perform better than others. (This is a long-running debate in comparative politics.) He then proposes to use the introduction of regional governments in Italy during the 1970s as a novel test of both explanations.[17]

Some challenges go beyond reinforcing one side of a debate, yet stop short of rejecting all sides. Take, for instance, a published study of European attitudes toward immigrants. In their literature review, John Sides and Jack Citrin identify interests and identities as the two leading explanations for such attitudes. People might express negative views toward immigrants

22   CHAPTER ONE

if they felt their jobs and wages were threatened, or if their sense of national character was under attack. The first explanation stresses material reasons, while the second is more symbolic. The authors then introduce a third possible explanation, information, which they say has been overlooked by other scholars. The role of information could reinforce either of the prevailing explanations. If people lack accurate information about immigration, then they could be more likely to feel that their pocketbooks or their culture is being threatened. Those were the authors' educated guesses, not statements of fact. The bulk of the article uses evidence from the European Social Survey to test the role of information and interests versus information and identities.[18]

In short, there is no one right way to address the Who Cares question. Other than the need to deal with this question from the very beginning, researchers have a number of options. Their intended audience could be fairly limited or quite broad—the difference between talking just to specialists in Italian politics or to many comparativists, in Putnam's case, or between communicating with experts who study World War II versus those interested more generally in the democratic peace. We can also find some middle ground, such as if Putnam had aimed his book at specialists in European politics.

By the same token, scholars have options in how they characterize prior research and try to say something new. After studying past work, we might perceive a Conventional Wisdom, an Ongoing Debate, or both; the resource curse literature is a case in point. I mentioned before that the welfare state literature is a many-sided debate, and it could be too unwieldy or confusing to deal with all these explanations simultaneously. We might decide to work with only two or three of them in a given project, or we might combine explanations in interesting ways (e.g., top-down versus bottom-up theories of change). Scholarly debates can be characterized in multiple ways, which means the lit review offers a chance to demonstrate real insight and creativity.

If we are reasonably satisfied with the soundness of an argument, we can try to extend it in new directions and see if it applies to more cases (i.e., more countries, elections, agencies, etc.) or to different periods of time. Whether the argument does or does not hold when stretched is not that important; either way, we have a better understanding of its scope. On the other hand, if we have serious doubts about previous scholarship, then we can try to revise or challenge it. The basic point, and it's essential, is to figure out a way to move the conversation forward, even if only a little bit.

So far, we have discussed ways of joining a conversation led by political scientists. Sometimes, however, we want to communicate with academics from other disciplines. Historically, political scientists have reached out to experts in psychology, economics, sociology, history, law, and, more recently, biology. The basic choices involved with entering these conversations are still the same. Someone working at the intersection of political science and psychology, for instance—maybe conducting a study of racial attitudes in South Africa—could potentially tap into literatures about South African politics, African politics, racially divided societies, transitional justice, racial prejudice, prejudice in general, threat perception, and probably several others. Because trying to speak to all these audiences at once would be foolhardy, the researcher would have to choose carefully among them. Once that choice has been made, the next step would be to determine the extent of agreement or disagreement among scholars in that area, and then how best to enhance our collective understanding.[19]

Perhaps the main difference between research produced from a political-science standpoint and research of an interdisciplinary nature involves the outlet in which the latter is published. Numerous journals hope to promote conversations between political scientists and other disciplines. Examples include *Political Psychology*, the *Journal of Law, Economics, and Organization*, and the *Journal of Policy History*. Some book publishers do the same. See, for instance, the Political Economy series from Cornell University Press.

From time to time, political scientists try to join conversations that extend beyond academia. They believe that their research could interest policy makers and members of the general public. Some political scientists even feel a genuine obligation to venture outside the ivory tower (a feeling I share). Writing for periodicals like *Foreign Affairs*, *Democracy: A Journal of Ideas*, the *Atlantic*, and *Boston Review* would fit in this category. Virtual publications like the *Monkey Cage* could qualify as well.

Although the average reader of these publications and the *American Political Science Review* is probably two different people, the process of joining these conversations is fairly similar. Authors usually begin by identifying a Conventional Wisdom or an Ongoing Debate. They might not cite prior research in as much detail as in a scholarly article or book—publications with a broader audience often discourage footnotes, endnotes, or formal bibliographies—but they do signal whom they plan to argue with or against.

In a recent issue of *Foreign Affairs*, political scientists Henry Farrell and Martha Finnemore begin their article, "The End of Hypocrisy," by noting the widespread belief among US government officials that leaks of classified documents pose a great threat to the nation. Farrell and Finnemore then suggest that policy makers misunderstand the true danger. "The deeper threat that leakers such as [Bradley] Manning and [Edward] Snowden pose is more subtle than a direct assault on U.S. national security; they undermine Washington's ability to act hypocritically and get away with it."[20] That hypothesis ought to raise a few eyebrows. To back up their core claim, the authors quickly discuss the concept of "soft power," which is well known among international relations scholars and was introduced years ago by Joseph Nye, a professor at Harvard University. Nowhere, however, do Farrell and Finnemore provide explicit references to speeches, congressional testimony, or reports that would document this widespread but mistaken fear about leaking. Nor do they mention Nye or cite any of his books. Adding that sort of scholarly scaffolding is simply not the practice at *Foreign Affairs*. Nevertheless, the authors make it clear from the start which conversation they are joining and what they hope to add to that conversation.

RAISING THE STAKES

Good scholarship promises to increase our collective understanding of the world around us, which political scientists view as a worthy objective. Yet that alone may not be enough to grab the audience's attention. As mentioned above in connection with cobalt and the resource curse, a proposed expansion could be so minor that it triggers a collective yawn. Even a bold assault on some piece of conventional wisdom might suffer the same fate if it involved the role of the lieutenant governor in Kentucky politics during the nineteenth century, or the lobbying clout of sheep farmers in New Zealand. The fact is, we don't fully understand many, many features of the political world. But that doesn't mean that all are equally worthy of study. Authors need to figure out what makes a political puzzle so important that readers will devote some of their scarce time and attention to understanding it better.

One way authors accomplish this is by arguing that their particular project will shed light on a fundamental problem in politics. The trick is to imply, in the humblest manner possible, that their research represents a major intellectual breakthrough. In the introduction to this guide, I mentioned an article by Daniel Posner about two African tribes, the Chewas and the Timbukas, who live in Zambia and Malawi. To me, a specialist in American politics, this topic sounds pretty obscure. Not much different from studying old lieutenant governors from Kentucky. And yet somehow it was published in the premier journal of my profession, the *American Political Science Review*, which has an article acceptance rate of less than 10 percent. How did this author manage to pull that off (he asked, with some envy)? One reason is evident from the start, in the abstract that appears right after the article's title. First sentence: "This paper explores the conditions under which cultural cleavages become politically salient." A truly significant topic. In the second paragraph of the article, Posner lists several places in the world—ranging from New York City and Northern Ireland to Rwanda, Sri Lanka, and Sudan—where cultural differences have and have not been politically salient. The message is clear to anyone who reads just the first page of this article: the potential significance of this research goes way beyond two African countries.[21]

In some ways, this is the "go big or go home" strategy that football coaches and presidential wannabes are fond of invoking. True, this kind of research tends to get published in the most prestigious venues and win the major professional awards. Nevertheless, "going big" often entails a sizable leap from the evidence in hand to the larger pattern of interest, and that leap makes the author vulnerable. Do we really believe that whatever happened in Malawi and Zambia can help us understand politics in New York City and Northern Ireland, as Posner suggests? On the first page of *Making Democracy Work: Civic Traditions in Modern Italy* (one of the most heralded books in political science during my lifetime), Robert Putnam states that problems of poor government performance extend "from Moscow to East St. Louis, from Mexico City to Cairo"—a pretty sweeping claim. Do we really believe that whatever happened to regional governments in Italy can teach us something about institution-building in Egypt and the former Soviet Union? Stated more generally, what prevents political scientists from making wild-ass claims just to attract a bigger audience? Frankly, this is where the peer-review process is supposed to help, weeding out potential books and articles that promise way more than they can deliver. Still, even research that successfully passes through peer review can be guilty of exaggerating its larger significance. After we review the case-selection process in more depth in chapter 5, you may feel better equipped to judge for yourself whether a given piece of research might actually have broader implications. In the meantime, it will help to be aware of how authors are trying to attract an audience, and to resist accepting those claims at face value.

A second tactic, also common, is to portray the research as a solution (probably a partial solution) to some tangible problem affecting many people. The problem could be large and immediate, such as the hardships created by a major recession. It could be modest in size but growing, such as an aging population. Think of this as the *Law & Order*, "ripped from the headlines" approach to attracting an audience. The author says to the reader, in effect, "I know what may be troubling you, and I think my research can help remedy your problem."

This tactic is adopted frequently by political scientists who publish in journals aimed at a broader audience. This is not surprising, given that these journals exist largely to diagnose and remedy public problems. When writing recently about food safety in *Democracy: A Journal of Ideas*, Adam Sheingate opened with a vignette about a mother of three from Colorado who ended up in a coma due to listeria poisoning. By the third paragraph, he was informing readers that 48 million Americans each year suffer from some food-borne illness. It doesn't take a math whiz to figure out that many of us or people we know could fall victim. Numbers and stories like these will grab our attention. They might even make us want to learn more about two government bureaucracies, the Food and Drug Administration and the US Department of Agriculture, which are central to the rest of Sheingate's article.[22]

When the primary audience consists of policy makers rather than the general public, authors may appeal to their self-interest by helping them solve problems they encounter in their professional lives. In "The End of Hypocrisy," Farrell and Finnemore were joining an active and highly contentious debate over US foreign policy. Their audience included experts in national security from the executive and legislative branches of government, the legal profession, think tanks, and mass media. All of them were trying to figure out how much damage recent security leaks had caused; what punishment, if any, should be handed out to the responsible parties; and what could be done to prevent leaks in the future. Farrell and Finnemore wanted to channel that debate in a new direction, toward what they viewed as a more accurate description of the problem and thus more useful solutions.

Many political scientists use this same tactic in their more scholarly writings. For Putnam, the problems facing places like Mexico City, Moscow, and Cairo include clean air and safe streets. Government performance has a very palpable impact on citizens' lives. If scholars can figure out why some governments perform better than others, then we might be able to improve the standard of living for millions of people. In the first few pages of his book, Putnam thus appealed to a wide range of academics, policy makers, and citizens to learn more about regional governments in Italy. Likewise, when Biddle, Friedman, and Shapiro wrote about the surge in Iraq, they were tackling a problem that concerns military strategists in many countries, as well as scholars specializing in security studies. Alexander Lee analyzed the backgrounds of over seven hundred activists from the Bengal province of India during the early twentieth century, which might seem to be an esoteric topic. His article opens, however, with a contemporary debate among policy makers and scholars over the best way to combat the sources of terrorism. Among those who believe that poverty is a root cause, Lee mentions George W. Bush and Al Gore. Other analysts question this view, pointing out that many terrorists are relatively well-off in their home countries. Hence, we have a live debate about terrorism, a problem that affects people all over the world and that involves destruction and death. In this context, Lee used evidence from India to help us figure out why some individuals become terrorists, while many others do not. With stakes that high, many readers might find it worthwhile to learn more about Indian politics from one hundred years ago.[23]

Finally, authors often address the Who Cares question by appealing to widely held values. This tactic may seem out of place, since I declared in the introduction to this guide that it would focus on empirical and not normative questions. The clear division of labor seems to be that empirical work is done by political scientists, and normative work by political theorists or political advocates. In practice, however, this line is fuzzy. Political scientists engaged in empirical work often invoke normative claims to justify why their work is important. Someone who argued that Mexico ought to have at least two viable political parties, and then gave reasons why, would be making a normative argument about how Mexican politics should work. This kind of argument would be well suited to an op-ed or a position paper. On the other hand, someone who claimed that competitive parties should be considered a hallmark of democratic governments (normative), and then explained how Mexico managed to operate for decades under one-party rule (empirical), would be engaged in the kind of research familiar to many political scientists. The initial normative claim would be made early and relatively quickly; most of the book or article would be devoted to answering the empirical questions of what happened and why.

The basic message is, "If you care about [insert prized value here], then you should be interested in my research." The list of prized values that could be invoked is a long one: majority rule, minority rights, freedom of expression, equality of opportunity, security, accountability, rule of law, efficiency, compassion, and many more. Again, in the name of focus and clarity, authors would probably invoke only one or two values in order to spark interest in their work; throwing out a whole bunch of values and hoping that one of them will resonate with readers feels a bit, well, desperate. Such values are typically mentioned in the introductory section of a research project and in the conclusion. After summing up the main empirical findings in the conclusion, an author may draw out implications for the same values that animated the study in the first place. Perhaps, in the case of party politics in Mexico, one lesson could involve the obstacles to establishing a healthy, vibrant democracy. The latter is very much a value-laden concept. Returning to the example of the democratic peace, an author might open and conclude an empirical project by linking the peace to human suffering or international stability. People often care passionately about values such as these, and scholars are smart to consider ways of engaging the readers' heads and hearts.

Political scientists routinely invoke these kinds of values. In the examples offered earlier in this chapter, most of the authors mentioned at least one normative dimension to their research. Some raise it early in their article or book. When Gary Orren wrote about declining trust in government, he started out by claiming that "today's discontent is neither transient nor shallow and . . . it holds profound (and negative) consequences for governance. . . . Public dissatisfaction also harms democracy."[24] Other scholars bring in values toward the end of their study as they consider the larger significance of their findings. Sides and Citrin conclude their analysis of immigration attitudes with these thoughts about tolerance and inclusion:

> Indeed, the problem of redefining nationhood to accommodate cultural differences seems significant in Europe, in part because so many of the immigrants to Europe are Muslims with cultural traditions about family life that diverge sharply from the current European mainstream. One is left to wonder whether outside the intelligentsia the abstract values of Rawlsian liberalism and cosmopolitan humanitarianism are a strong enough impetus to incorporate immigrants into the political and welfare institutions that remain grounded in the eroding but not yet vestigial nation-state. Among ordinary people, a thicker cultural brew may be needed to sustain social solidarity and welcome newcomers into a democratic welfare state.[25]

And nothing prevents scholars from starting and ending their empirical analysis with normative concerns.

Keep in mind that these different ways of "raising the stakes" and grabbing a reader's attention aren't mutually exclusive. Political scientists can and do use more than one of these in a given project. And sometimes they use none of them. That kind of research is almost by definition aimed solely at other political scientists.

GETTING STARTED

Simply in terms of pages, most published research in political science is devoted to figuring out What Happened and Why. None of that information will be terribly compelling, however, without a good answer to the Who Cares question. My hope is that this chapter will help readers recognize different ways of answering this question when they read academic books and articles. This is part of your training as high-powered home inspectors in the realm of politics. It also should be useful when conducting your own research and building your own arguments.

Undergraduates often have a decent idea of how to frame their research question in ways that could attract policy makers and ordinary citizens. They stay informed about current events; indeed, the original inspiration for their research paper may have come from a recent news story or op-ed. Students have an intuitive and sometimes even a well-developed understanding of values such as equality and freedom. Making a connection between their specific research puzzle and some larger question of general concern isn't terribly difficult. Suppose a student wanted to investigate the prolonged civil war in Sri Lanka. Unfortunately, this is not exactly a part of the world most people care or think much about. However, if general readers knew that tens of thousands of people had been killed, or had a sense that a greater understanding of Sri Lanka might help world leaders better deal with current conflicts in Syria or Sudan, then they might read with interest. Finding these expository "hooks" requires some thought, but not a lot.

Joining a scholarly conversation is different. For seasoned professionals, this isn't a big deal. They have been immersed in the scholarly literature for years. They have attended many academic conferences, workshops, and presentations. They know what kinds of conversations are taking place, and that awareness makes it easier for them to identify pieces of Conventional Wisdom and Ongoing Debates. For them, researching and writing the literature review is not a tall hurdle. For everyone else—and that includes trained political scientists who want to move out of their comfort zone and tackle new kinds of problems—crafting the lit review can be a daunting task. Put bluntly, there's so much f!*%# stuff to read! How can anyone possibly catch up on a high-powered conversation that has been going on for years?

Fortunately, we now have several ways to get up to speed on a large number of literatures in political science. This is the point where one's interest in a general topic ("Mr. Howard, I want to write a paper about terrorism," or "I think I want to do something with the Senate filibuster") becomes connected to specific puzzles that interest academic experts. Or, this is the point where interest in a specific question (e.g., "I am simply dying to explain why the European Union admitted Bulgaria and Romania in 2007") becomes linked to a larger literature (e.g., expansion of the EU). Either way, this is how an individual writer starts finding a potential audience. Strong hint: a crude Google search won't prove very helpful here. Type in the word *terrorism* and you could easily get 25 million hits. Very fast, but pretty useless. Let me suggest some more targeted approaches.

Annual Review volumes. Most disciplines in the sciences and social sciences have a special edited volume that captures the latest scholarship. The Annual Reviews organization covers everything from condensed matter physics to public health. The *Annual Review of Political Science* has been published every year since 1998, and it can be very helpful. Its chapters cut across the major subfields within political science, making each volume rather eclectic. To illustrate, the 2014 edition includes chapters concerning violence against civilians, state and local government finance, public attitudes toward immigration, and the political economy of development in China and Vietnam.[26] Searching online for a specific topic would therefore make more sense than going to the library and checking the table of contents for every single year. Type in the term *terrorism* in the Annual Reviews database and you will soon find the chapters "Terrorist Decision-Making" (2003), "Domestic Terrorism" (2009), and "Terrorism and Democracy" (2013) in the *Annual Review of Political Science*. There is also one chapter in the 2005 volume that is focused specifically on the September 11 attacks.[27] Reading all these chapters might give more direction to a research project, pointing out certain Conventional Wisdoms and unresolved debates. In addition, the bibliographies in each chapter would provide valuable clues about what to read next.

Handbooks. A number of academic publishers have started to issue large edited volumes covering a host of topics in political science. Like the Annual Reviews, the contributing authors to these handbooks are all experts in their respective fields. Each handbook is designed to summarize the state of the art and to suggest paths for future inquiry. In other words, every single one is chock-full of literature reviews. If you consult the *Oxford Handbook of Comparative Politics* (2007), you'll find chapters devoted to national identity, civil wars, party systems, federalism, and many more topics.[28] The *Cambridge Handbook of Experimental Political Science* (2011) includes chapters about various types of experimental designs and about the use of experiments to analyze different aspects of political life (e.g., voter mobilization, trust, racial attitudes). The *Routledge Handbook of Global Environmental Governance* (2014) includes chapters about international environmental law, environmental security, and hazardous wastes. Each handbook is therefore more organized, thematically, than the *Annual Review of Political Science*. (No single handbook, however, is published annually.) These volumes often contain thirty to forty chapters, so they're a veritable gold mine of information. A student who wanted to learn more about the Senate filibuster, for instance, would be smart to consult the *Oxford Handbook of the American Congress* (2011). Although no chapter contains *filibuster* in the title, a quick scan of the index for this term would lead to a chapter titled "The Supermajority Senate." That sounds promising.

Other edited volumes. The Annual Reviews and handbooks share a basic model: round up a bunch of smart people and task each one with distilling his or her corner of political science into a fifteen- to thirty-page chapter. That model can work elsewhere, too. In the early stages of the research process, we want to find edited volumes designed to synthesize what we know about some political phenomena and to open up new avenues for research. Many edited volumes won't accomplish these objectives; the individual chapters are only loosely related to one another, and the editor(s) fail to provide a strong introductory or concluding chapter.[29] But some volumes will. For instance, many scholars have turned to *The Tools of Government*, edited by Lester Salamon, to help them understand the "new governance" in which public policies are implemented by networks of public and private organizations. Anyone starting a research project in this area might begin by reading Salamon's introductory chapter and perhaps skimming the final five or six chapters, which analyze cross-cutting themes emerging from the case studies in chapters 2 through 15. That volume is now over a decade old, which could make it a bit dated. Nevertheless, it might serve as a decent starting point for a new project. Subsequent investigation may reveal that scholars are still wrestling with similar questions, or that some of the contributors to that initial volume have continued to publish in that area.

Review articles/essays. Book reviews are common in a number of political science journals. Review articles or essays are less common but potentially more valuable. In these, the author tries to pull together and critically assess research by several experts, and not just review one book. Some essays are like the one Christopher Blattman wrote for *Perspectives on Politics*. On the surface, he analyzes three new books about child soldiers. In the process, however, he references earlier research on this topic as well as general studies of warfare. The entire essay and its bibliography thus provide a quick introduction to the larger literature regarding child soldiers.[30] My second example comes from the realm of American politics. In recent years, there's been a mini-explosion of studies concerning polarization. With so much activity, it's not always clear who is agreeing or disagreeing with whom. To bring some order to this situation, Marc Hetherington published an extended review essay that divides the literature into general categories (measuring polarization, leading causes, major consequences) and then identifies places of scholarly consensus and dispute. For someone new to these conversations, this essay provides a handy road map.[31]

✦ Books and journal articles. Of course, it's always possible to read a recent book or article of interest and see how that author sizes up the existing literature. My suggestion is to pay particular attention to the lit reviews created by younger scholars, who are often graduate students or assistant professors. This may sound like strange advice coming from a seasoned (i.e., middle-aged) professional, so let me explain. Literature reviews by younger scholars often emerge from their dissertations, and graduate students devote considerable time and energy trying to master the literature in their field. They may have read an enormous amount, from the classics to the cutting edge, and thus may be unusually well equipped to make sense of the literature. More senior scholars might offer an equally comprehensive literature review, or they might assume that readers already know the previous research well enough that citing a few books and articles here and there will suffice.

You can also examine the concluding section of articles and books, where scholars often discuss the larger implications of their findings and suggest promising avenues for future research. In effect, strongly written conclusions indicate where the conversation should go next. Here I would pay more attention, all else being equal, to the conclusions of more established scholars. Freshly minted PhDs sometimes have trouble recognizing the broader significance of their work. They have spent so much time identifying new "trees" that they have difficulty seeing the "forest." Two decades ago, I was certainly in that camp. The risk, however, in relying on senior scholars to light the way is that they will be so entrenched in established ways of thinking that they won't be able to direct the conversation in a truly novel direction.

Textbooks. Introductory textbooks do more than convey a boatload of factual knowledge about politics. They also introduce students to important theories and controversies. Basic textbooks in comparative politics, for example, will usually present cultural and institutional approaches to analyzing politics within countries. Some of these texts may mention a specific topic like the resource curse (aka the resource trap, the paradox of plenty), but some may not. Those that do mention it may not provide many suggestions for additional reading. I have an entire shelf filled with introductory textbooks in American politics. When it comes to ideology and values, most of them do a much better job of analyzing the meaning of *liberal* and *conservative*, *Democrat* and *Republican* than they do analyzing, say, public trust in government. Consequently, I rarely if ever advise my students to look only at textbooks when building their literature reviews. These should be combined with some of the other resources listed above.

All these sources should be considered as starting points. Reading a good handbook chapter or review essay is no substitute for reading the books and articles that are cited. The people who write these chapters and essays make many judgments about how best to condense and classify prior research, and sometimes those judgments are questionable. Think of it this way: while you might love to read movie reviews, you still want to see many of these movies yourself.

PRACTICE: INSPECTING

In the introduction to this book, I mentioned the importance of practicing the skills used by political scientists. Telling you what to look for or what to do isn't enough; you need opportunities to apply these lessons. Remember that proverb I quoted earlier: "I see and I remember; I do and I understand." Now that you have read about the different ways that scholars answer the Who Cares question, it is time to study a few examples in more depth. Collectively, these examples illustrate different ways of building a literature review, generating hypotheses, and demonstrating the larger significance of the research. They are deliberately varied in topic and place of publication in order to demonstrate the widespread applicability of these skills. As you read each one, ask yourself:

1. When surveying previous studies, does the author perceive a Conventional Wisdom, or an Ongoing Debate? What, specifically, is/are the main school(s) of thought?

2. What do you notice about the number and variety of previous studies cited? Just one or two, several, or dozens and dozens? Were most written by the same author, or by a variety of authors? Published by academic journals and book publishers, or somewhere else?

3. Can you name one or two specific hypotheses that emerge from the literature review? Try to state each one clearly and concisely.

4. What is supposed to be new here? Does this research seem like a modest extension of an existing argument, a direct challenge to established ways of thinking, or something in between? Explain.

5. Does the author give any reasons why someone besides a political scientist should care about this research? Explain.

EXAMPLES

Tiffany D. Barnes and Stephanie M. Burchard, "'Engendering' Politics: The Impact of Descriptive Representation on Women's Political Engagement in Sub-Saharan Africa," *Comparative Political Studies* 46, no. 7 (July 2013): 767–90; focus on pages 767–72.

Sumit Ganguly, "Nuclear Stability in South Asia," *International Security* 33, no. 2 (Fall 2008): 45–70; focus on pages 45–49 and 65–70.

John G. Geer, "The News Media and the Rise of Negativity in Presidential Campaigns," *PS: Political Science and Politics* 45, no. 3 (July 2012): 422–27.

Charles Lipson, *Reliable Partners: How Democracies Have Made a Separate Peace* (Princeton, NJ: Princeton University Press, 2003). Chapter 1 is available online at http://press.princeton.edu/chapters/s7651.pdf; focus on pages 1–11.

Yotam Margalit, "Explaining Social Policy Preferences: Evidence from the Great Recession," *American Political Science Review* 107, no. 1 (February 2013): 80–103; focus on pages 80–84, 98–99, and the References section.

Lauren McLaren, "Immigration and Trust in Politics in Britain," *British Journal of Political Science* 42, no. 1 (January 2012): 163–85; focus on pages 163–68 and 183–85.

Theda Skocpol, "Why the Tea Party's Hold Persists," *Democracy: A Journal of Ideas* 31 (Winter 2014): 9–14.

PRACTICE: BUILDING

1. Suppose you wanted to research and write about the resource curse. You don't want to know the state of the debate in 2000, which was mentioned earlier in this chapter. You want to know where that literature stands now. With a little research, you find the following sources:

   Stephen Haber and Victor Menaldo, "Natural Resources and Democracy in Latin America: Neither Curse nor Blessing," in *The Oxford Handbook of Latin American Political Economy*, ed. Javier Santiso and Jeff Dayton-Johnson (New York: Oxford University Press, 2012), pp. 493–512;

   Pauline Jones Luong and Erika Weinthal, "Rethinking the Resource Curse: Ownership Structure, Institutional Capacity, and Domestic Constraints," *Annual Review of Political Science* 9 (2006): 241–63;

   Kevin M. Morrison, "Whither the Resource Curse?," *Perspectives on Politics* 11, no. 4 (December 2013): 1117–25.

   After reading these overviews, do you see any pieces of conventional wisdom? What are the major ongoing debates? Did the authors identify any promising directions for future research? What would be the next five to ten books or articles that you would read to deepen your understanding of previous scholarship?

2. Your turn: Pick a topic that interests you deeply, and write a literature review. Identify a piece of conventional wisdom or an ongoing debate, and then describe at least one way that additional research could contribute to this scholarly conversation.

2

WHAT HAPPENED?

During the 1980s and 1990s, many observers of American politics worried that voter turnout was dropping to dangerously low levels. In some national elections, barely half the electorate voted. Considering how central elections are to democratic government, this seemed like a really disturbing trend. Analysts identified a variety of causes and possible remedies, such as changes to voter registration laws and media coverage of campaigns. Only later did it become clear that voter turnout hadn't declined as much as they thought. Their measure of turnout was faulty. Oops.[1]

The terrorist attacks of September 11, 2001, heightened interest in foreign affairs among many scholars, policy makers, and regular citizens. The attacks focused attention on Iraq and Saudi Arabia in particular. Some experts, upon analyzing the state of the world, claimed that Muslim countries as a group suffered from a democracy gap or deficit. Stated more formally, they depicted an inverse relationship between the extent of democracy in a country and the percentage of Muslims in that country's population. More Muslims, less democracy. The larger puzzles they wrestled with were how and why Islam inhibited democracy, and what might be done to overcome those barriers. Implicit in some of these formulations was the question, how can we reduce the Muslim threat to our way of life? Other scholars, however, questioned the accuracy of the initial description. They made a good case that the least democratic countries were Arab, not Muslim. They pointed to largely Muslim countries such as Turkey, Indonesia, and Mali that still managed to hold reasonably competitive elections. Democracy thus seemed more closely related to region than religion.[2]

These two examples illustrate a nagging problem in political science. In our rush to explain events or patterns, we may fail to describe them accurately. Like Don Quixote, we end up tilting at windmills. Instead of fighting imaginary giants, political scientists battle one another in an effort to explain political phenomena whose very existence is questionable. Not good. And when poorly crafted descriptions eventually lead to ineffective or counterproductive remedies, then the initial mistake is compounded.

These examples also illustrate two main types of description in political science. The first involves the measurement of individual concepts, and the second concerns the relationship between concepts. The first leads to a crucial question, is that really the best way to measure . . . ? This question could be asked of voter turnout, corruption, welfare state spending, terrorism, or any other political concept. In fact, as builders and inspectors of political arguments, you should ask this question routinely. The answers to this question will often be vulnerable to challenge, a fact that makes life harder for us as builders but a bit easier for us as inspectors. The second type of description, concerning relationships, leads us to ask what else might be going on. Are concepts A and B truly related, or might some other concept C diminish, maybe even negate, that relationship? Because of the nearly infinite supply of other relevant concepts, this question is tough to answer definitively. Nevertheless, the difficulty of finding perfect answers should not stop us from asking how best to measure concepts and to describe relationships between them.

In the view of many political scientists, good descriptions are important, largely because they provide the raw material for good explanations, and the ultimate goal of political science is causal knowledge. This is what many social scientists, including economists and sociologists, do for a living: they try to explain why the world works in certain ways. They create theories that capture some pattern in which certain causes regularly lead to certain effects. Most political scientists feel that uncovering why something happened is harder than figuring out what happened. From this perspective, what happened is a less interesting, less challenging question than why.

I do not share this view. Oh, rest assured that good explanations occupy a special place in this political scientist's heart. But so do good descriptions. My fondness for the whole descriptive side of political science is partly autobiographical. In my capacity as a trained inspector of political research, I have often found problems in the ways undergraduates define and measure their key concepts. From time to time I have encountered similar problems when reviewing book and article manuscripts written by more advanced scholars. By pointing out these problems and suggesting ways to fix them, I like to think that I have been helpful. To the extent I have made a name for myself as a builder of arguments, it's largely because I challenged the conventional portrait of the American welfare state. The explanatory variables in my research are pretty standard; the more distinctive features concern the size, shape, and historical development of US social policy. If you believe my argument that the United States is not the "welfare state laggard" that many experts in American and comparative politics have claimed it to be, then many of the usual scholarly debates over why seem misplaced.[3]

So much for my fondness. My respect is based on the knowledge, after years of teaching, researching, and writing, that political life can be really hard to describe accurately and clearly.[4] As we will see in the next chapter, political scientists generally agree on certain standards for judging a causal explanation. There are some clear-cut reasons for rejecting an explanation. This is less true for descriptions. Suppose I define a welfare state as what governments do to fight poverty and to insure everyone against risks of income loss due to old age, sickness, disability, or unemployment. Another scholar might define this concept to mean only what government does to fight poverty. The American welfare state that I describe will therefore be much bigger, because mine includes Social Security and Medicare and his does not. Whose description is correct? Tough to say. Although I would defend my definition as being consistent with scholarly tradition, I would be hard-pressed to name an objective standard against which to judge our two definitions. I couldn't even point to a sacred text, locked away at the American Political Science Association headquarters, that gives the definitive meanings of key concepts. Many other concepts besides welfare state are just as contentious.

As historians know well, constructing a narrative of what happened requires a series of judgments. Any given event can be told many different ways. Next time you visit a major bookstore, notice how many books have been written about World War II or the American Civil War. Even for less momentous events, such as a mayoral election, descriptive accounts might feature many parts: individual candidates, political parties, campaign staff, voters, interest groups, election officials, candidate debates, local issues, national concerns, media coverage, maybe even the weather on Election Day. Including all of that is probably too much for any one story to contain (at least, a story that would attract much of an audience). Someone writing this story will need to decide which parts to delete or minimize and which parts to emphasize.

The next section of this chapter takes readers through the process of describing concepts. The basic idea is to move deliberately from abstract ideas to concrete measures. Although we can't literally see power or tolerance, we may be able to identify specific measures of these concepts. The voter turnout example shows what can happen when concepts aren't measured well. Good measures should be reliable and valid, and political scientists have several ways of satisfying these criteria. Once we have a handle on individual concepts, we can describe relationships between them. Describing relationships is one of the more common and essential tasks of the political scientist. Among countries, is there a strong connection between democracy and religion? Or is some other concept, like region, more closely related to democracy? Before we become convinced that a relationship exists, we need to ask whether other factors might be involved.

Throughout this guide, I have put key terms in boldfaced type. This chapter features more of those terms than any other chapter. Political scientists have a distinctive vocabulary, and students should become familiar with these terms as quickly as possible. (My way of teaching these terms is a little different from most political scientists, though.)

MOVING FROM CONCEPTS TO MEASURES

Imagine that you were injured badly and fell into a coma. After you have been taken to a hospital, a family member will probably ask a doctor, "So, how bad is it?" (If no one cares enough to ask this question, then being comatose is only one of your problems.) Being told that you were running a slight fever, with a temperature of 99.5 degrees, would not be enough for most people. They would want to know, "How bad is the coma?" Some doctors might shrug their shoulders and reply, "Eh, I've seen worse." That's not very helpful. Being told that your coma was "pretty typical" or that you were showing "some signs" of improvement would still leave a lot of questions unanswered.

The basic definition of a coma is a prolonged state of unconsciousness. Being classified as comatose could require a yes/no judgment, yet doctors have recognized for a long time that some comas are worse than others. About forty years ago, two neurosurgeons in Scotland developed a more precise measure. Now called the Glasgow Coma Scale, it enables doctors to assign a specific number to each patient. The scale has three main components—motor response (ranging from 1 to 6), verbal response (1–5), and eye response (1–4); each component is scored separately and then added together. Thus, the scale ranges from 3 to 15. Someone who could not move, speak, or open his or her eyes would be given a score of 3. On the other hand, someone who could obey simple commands to move (motor = 6) but seemed confused when talking (verbal = 4) and opened his or her eyes only in response to pain (2) would be a 12. With this scale, doctors all over the world now had a way to describe comas more precisely, and they could carefully track changes in a patient's condition over time.

Of course, being told that your coma is a 9 might not mean much to your friends and family. Doctors often convert these numerical scores into common-language categories—severe, moderate, and mild—when communicating with laypeople. A severe coma usually means any score between a 3 and an 8, while a mild coma ranges from 13 to 15. In this scenario, your coma would be classified as moderate.

What does the Glasgow Coma Scale have to do with political analysis? A lot, actually. Initially, political scientists might ask questions like, "Has China become more democratic in recent decades?" Not asking why, just whether it has. A good answer to this question would describe democracy in China at several points in time. We can't begin to answer the question, however, without some clear definition of *democracy*. In addition, we would need to identify some specific measures of this concept that we could find evidence for over time. A better way to ask this question would be, "Has China become more democratic in recent decades, and here 'democratic' means . . ." Another research question might start out as, "In the United States, are men more likely than women to participate in politics?" This question would be improved by adding, "and here 'political participation' means . . ."[5]

In medicine, some **concepts** like fever are pretty straightforward to define and measure. Many medical concepts are more abstract. Besides coma, examples include disability, high-risk pregnancy, and stages of cancer. These concepts are constructs that contain a mixture of objective elements and subjective judgments. The same situation exists in politics. Some concepts in that field can be defined and measured fairly easily, such as midterm elections. The vast majority of political concepts, however, are quite abstract: terrorism, pluralism, socialism; democracy, autocracy, meritocracy; tolerance, governance, influence; mandate, weak state, personality trait; superpower, ivory tower, air power; political participation, regional cooperation, policy innovation; gridlock, deficit hawk, Doomsday Clock; party competition, issue coalition, loyal opposition; civil war, cold war, trade war, and more (you get the idea). Working with such concepts is seldom easy. We can't see, hear, or touch them directly. Somebody, somewhere, will disagree with how any of them are defined or measured, just as doctors and social workers can argue over what it means to be disabled. Often the best we can do is to be systematic and transparent when working with these concepts.

Step one for researchers, then, is defining the key concepts in their project. This is the point where some undergraduates reach for a dictionary, a habit I usually discourage. We're not joining a conversation with Merriam or Webster. We're talking with political scientists, and maybe with policy makers and the general public, too. A better place to find a good definition would be previous studies involving the same concept.[6] This is another possible function of the literature review—to identify points of agreement and disagreement in the treatment of core concepts. For instance, although scholars of comparative politics may disagree why a resource curse exists, or how many countries it affects, it's quite possible that they agree on the

CHAPTER TWO

meaning of the general concept. During our investigation of what happened, we could follow suit.

In a number of cases, and democracy is certainly one of them, the definition of a concept will be contested. Consequently, when we ask what happened (e.g., whether China has become more democratic), we will need to make some choices. If a certain definition of a concept is employed by most scholars in a given field, then we could use it and simply acknowledge alternative definitions in a note. Sometimes competing definitions overlap, and we could highlight their common elements. Alternatively, we could introduce two or three competing definitions of a concept, measure each one, and then see if the results of our empirical analysis differed much depending on our initial choices. It could be true that men participate in politics more than women whether you limit the concept of political participation to elections, or broaden it to include any effort designed to influence the actions of government. (That in itself would be an interesting finding.) The one choice we should not make in these circumstances is thinking that our definition of a key concept is the only one possible.

Political scientists often distinguish between **conceptual definitions** and **operational definitions**. The former are more general and indicate the main elements or dimensions of the concept; the latter specify exactly how the concept will be measured. A simple conceptual definition of *conservatism* could stress the degree to which individuals prefer limited government. The operational definition could then indicate that such a preference would be determined based on opinions about taxes, gun control, and environmental regulations. *Labor power* might be defined conceptually as the ability of workers to influence the terms of their employment. The operational definition might focus on the extent to which labor unions influence wages, benefits, job security, and workplace safety. "Cyber warfare," according a recent study, "employs computer network attacks as a use of force to disrupt an opponent's physical infrastructure for political gain."[7] The author then specifies that such infrastructure would include electric power grids, air traffic control, water distribution, and financial data. For my purposes, the distinction between conceptual and operational definitions is less important than knowing how to move from the abstract to the concrete, from concept to measure.[8]

The second step involves noting the **unit of analysis**, meaning "the entity to which the concept applies."[9] In the definition of *conservatism* mentioned above, the unit of analysis is clearly the individual. Later on, we would therefore collect evidence at the individual level, such as responses to survey questions about taxes. *Democracy* is usually defined as a characteristic of countries; a related concept, support for democracy, could be a characteristic of individuals. *Accountability* might be defined such that government agencies would be the unit of analysis. Some concepts can apply to more than one unit, making it imperative that researchers specify their unit of analysis. Political tolerance, for instance, could apply to individuals or countries. In the former case, we might use mass surveys and small focus groups for evidence; in the latter, perhaps laws or court rulings. A study that defined a concept for one unit of analysis but presented evidence from another unit could seem confused or unconvincing.

To illustrate, let's return to some of the published studies mentioned in chapter 1. When Luong and Weinthal analyzed the resource curse, their unit of analysis was the country. Previous studies had examined countries such as Libya and Nigeria, and their study focused on parts of the former Soviet Union. In order to challenge the conventional wisdom directly, they kept the same unit of analysis. The authors did not collect information at the individual level, asking if people felt cursed by a tank of gasoline or a pair of diamond earrings. That's not really what the resource curse means. For part of Putnam's book about Italian politics, the unit of analysis was the region. Posner's study of the Chewas and Tumbukas in central Africa featured ethnic groups as the unit.

The article about immigration attitudes, by Sides and Citrin, is more complicated. The title of their article refers to "European opinion," which makes it sound as though Europe, a large geographic region, is their unit of analysis. Some of the article's tables and figures, however, display results by individual country. Which is the true unit: all of Europe, or each of its countries? Technically, neither one; the original unit of analysis in Sides and Citrin's study was the individual. They collected responses from over thirty thousand people who participated in the European Social Survey. They analyzed individual attitudes. The authors then aggregated the results by country, and again for all of Europe. This is a common practice in studies of public opinion. We ask questions of individuals in order to say something about the attitudes of groups, such as men and women or old people and young people. Other kinds of studies aggregate as well. Whereas Putnam gathered most of his evidence from multiple regions in Italy, sometimes he grouped them into North and South.[10]

After defining the concept clearly and specifying the unit of analysis, the next step any researcher must take is identifying one or more **measures** for each concept. A measure is an objective indicator. We can't observe education in any individual, but we can usually measure her years of formal schooling. We can use that measure as a proxy for the concept of education.

Although we can't see or touch political participation, we can measure voter turnout, and we may also be able to discover how many people work in campaigns or engage in some form of public protest. We could then use those measures to describe levels of political participation among different groups of people. When political scientists say they are analyzing the relationship between two or more concepts, they are actually analyzing the relationship between measures of those concepts. This distinction is really important. The leap from concept to measure creates the potential for measurement error, a pervasive problem in the analysis of politics.

Many of the most important concepts that political scientists work with are rich and complex. These concepts will have multiple attributes or dimensions. Building on the well-known work of Robert Dahl, for example, many scholars believe that the concept of democracy has two underlying dimensions—contestation and inclusiveness.[11] At a minimum we would need two measures, one for each dimension, when analyzing democracy in any country. In practice, scholars regularly identify multiple indicators for each of these dimensions. Contestation could refer to both regular elections and the presence of two or more viable political parties. It might also include freedoms of speech and assembly, which would allow opposing voices a chance to be heard. Inclusiveness might refer to widespread adult suffrage as well as eligibility to serve in public office.[12] Conceptually, these two dimensions are distinct. A country that held elections every five years, featured three major political parties, and extended voting rights only to men could score high on contestation but low on inclusiveness. In contrast, we can imagine a country with close to 100 percent turnout in elections that featured just one candidate (hello, North Korea).

Sometimes it helps to create a visual image of what we are doing. Table 2.1 presents two simple diagrams of the measurement process, one for the concept of coma and the other for democracy.[13] The basic idea here is moving from a general concept to specific measures while keeping the unit of analysis in focus. These examples also illustrate the points that two concepts may not have the same number of attributes, and that two attributes may not have the same number of measures. Determining the right number of attributes and measures involves a combination of art and science. Finally, please remember that the diagram for democracy is purely an illustration; many other and perhaps better ways of measuring this concept are possible.

One of my favorite examples of measurement comes from the tiny Himalayan country of Bhutan. For years the government there tried to promote the concept of gross national happiness as a more humane alternative to gross national product. Originally, the government decided that happiness

Table 2.1. Moving from concept to measures

		Example 1	
Concept		Coma	
Attributes/ dimensions	Motor response	Verbal response	Visual response
Measures	Motor scale	Verbal scale	Visual scale
Unit of analysis		Individual	

		Example 2	
Concept		Democracy	
Attributes/ dimensions	Contestation		Inclusiveness
Measures	Regular elections		Adult suffrage
	Party competition		Eligibility for
	Freedom of speech		public office
	Freedom of assembly		
Unit of analysis		Country	

rested on four pillars: the economy, culture, environment, and government. A later formulation identified nine domains of happiness, ranging from psychological well-being and community vitality to time use and living standards. For each pillar or domain, the government listed several indicators, for a grand total of seventy-two. Those indicators were then combined, using a fairly complicated formula, into a single number with the help of trained social scientists and (but of course) a Gross National Happiness Commission.[14]

Measuring happiness in Bhutan may seem a bit extreme, but this basic approach is used in many walks of life. Take a complex concept, describe its main dimensions or attributes, identify at least one measure for each, and then combine all the measures into a summary indicator. College rankings, based on multiple components such as student-teacher ratio, endowment, and selectivity of admissions, are a prime example. Fans of college basketball will recognize the Ratings Percentage Index, which ranks teams depend-

	Nominal	Ordinal	Interval	Ratio
Distinct values	✓	✓	✓	✓
Clear order to those values		✓	✓	✓
Uniform distance between values			✓	✓
Total absence indicated by value of 0				✓

Figure 2.1. Levels of measurement.

ing on their win-loss record and their strength of schedule. You've probably read about crash safety ratings for automobiles, based on tests of front, rear, and side collisions. You should also pay attention to the overall sanitation grades for restaurants, which include measures of worker hygiene, the cleanliness of the kitchen, and the performance of refrigerators and freezers. In short, we already recognize that important concepts have multiple parts, and that each part needs to be included in order to describe these concepts well. We need to apply that same mindset to politics (see box 2.1, "Building an Index," at the end of this chapter).

When moving from general concept to specific measure, be sure to note the **level of measurement** (fig. 2.1). In essence, you want to know how precise the indicators are. Although this may sound like the job of an accountant or auditor, political scientists need to know the level of measurement for a couple of reasons. Basically, it will connect later with the collection and analysis of evidence. Certain statistical tests, for instance, are appropriate for one level of measurement but not another (discussed in chapter 7).

The most basic level of measurement is **nominal**. A nominal measure features mutually exclusive categories, but they aren't ranked in a meaningful order or given a numerical value. Religion is a good example. A study analyzing the relationship between religion and political tolerance among Americans might rely on survey data, and the survey could include a question about the individual's religious affiliation, with the possible answers of Catholic, Protestant, Jewish, Muslim, Other, None.[15] Each person would be asked to self-identify and check off one of those boxes. A similar study investigating political tolerance by region might group responses based on whether individuals lived in the Northeast, Midwest, West, or South. We can't say that one religion or one region is of a higher value than another, only that they are different. The usual measures for race and ethnicity are nominal. The same is true for sex/gender, though recent developments are making this concept more complicated.

An **ordinal** measure is more precise than a nominal one. The possible values are mutually exclusive, and they can be ordered. Typically, the order goes from more to less (or from less to more) of some attribute, and the possible values are expressed with words, not numbers. One of the classic "trust in government" questions gives people the option of replying Just About Always, Most of the Time, or Some of the Time. Another question for this same concept can be answered A Great Deal, A Fair Amount, Not Very Much, or None at All. A measure of education level might include separate values for high school dropout, high school graduate, some college, and college graduate. Following the 9/11 terrorist attacks, the George W. Bush administration developed a color-coded threat scale, with five levels ranging from red (severe) to green (low). Strictly speaking, we don't assume that the values of an ordinal measure are evenly spaced along some imaginary line called trust, education level, security threat, or whatever concept we are handling. We are not sure, for instance, that moving from high school dropout to graduate represents the same increase in education as moving from high school graduate to some college. All we know is that one value is more or less than another.[16]

While religion is nominal, a related concept called religiosity could be considered ordinal. Religiosity, broadly speaking, reflects the intensity of a person's connection to any given religion. It could be measured by how often in a typical year that person attends services at a church, synagogue, mosque, or other place of worship. The possible answers might be Never, A Few Times, Once or Twice a Month, Every Week, or Every Day. Note that if we converted these categories into numbers—0, 3–5, 12–24, 52, 365—they wouldn't be evenly spaced.

The most precise measures are **interval** and **ratio**. Here we can assign different values, order them, and attach a number to each value. The distances between each value are the same. The main difference is that the number 0 has no real meaning in an interval measure. The classic example is air temperature, where 0 degrees Fahrenheit doesn't indicate the complete absence of temperature. Likewise, polling organizations sometimes use what is known as a feeling thermometer in mass surveys. They might ask, on a scale from 0 to 100, how people feel about a particular candidate, policy, or aspect of government. Typically, a score of 50 means neutral, while 0 means very cold and 100 very warm. The 0 does not indicate an absence of feeling; in fact, the feelings are quite strong and negative. Take a look sometime at the thermometer scores for public figures or Congress and you will see that many people are willing to say zero.

In practice, ratio-level measures are more common than interval measures. Anything that can be expressed in dollars or percentages is considered a ratio measure. Zero dollars given to election campaigns means no money. Zero percent civilian casualties during a war means that no civilians died. The zeroes in ratio measures mean something. In most instances, if we can count it, we can assign a ratio-level measure such as months of combat, pages of regulations, votes in Parliament, and number of trade agreements.[17] As the term *ratio* implies, we can compare different values for each measure with precision. Voter turnout of 60 percent in one election is twice as much as the turnout of 30 percent in another election. Someone who donated $1000 to a candidate gave 6.7 times more than someone else who gave $150. In contrast, we are limited to basic comparisons of more or less when we use ordinal measures.

You can probably imagine why many political scientists are keen to work with interval and ratio measures. For one thing, these measures lend themselves easily to statistical analysis, as we will see in chapter 7. One assumption to keep in mind is that all the values are supposed to be spaced apart equally. Moving up or down one unit always implies the same amount of change. When the Freedom House organization ranked countries according to their protection of political rights in 2014, the gap separating the United States (overall score of 1) and Peru (2) was the same as that separating Angola (6) from Belarus (7). On the surface, those seem like four very different polities. Are we sure that such precision is warranted? When we measure education by the number of years of schooling, we assume that going from 8 to 9 means the same thing as going from 11 to 12 (and presumably earning a high school diploma).[18] Hmmmm. Not everyone is comfortable with these types of assumptions, which is why political scientists may prefer to work with ordinal measures in certain circumstances. It might make more sense, for instance, to work with educational categories that distinguished among college graduates, high school graduates, and high school dropouts instead of counting years of schooling. Freedom House even groups countries under three general labels—*free*, *partly free*, and *not free*—for those who feel its numerical scores are too exact. The United States and Peru were both labeled *free*, while Angola and Belarus were *not free*.

There are also instances when precise data are simply unavailable. Take political corruption. For practical and intellectual reasons, we would like to know how often public officials use their office for private gain, and in what ways. Giving substantial amounts of foreign aid to a highly corrupt government would probably be unwise. How could we measure the level of political corruption in a government when much of it may go unreported or uncounted? Strong "watchdog" agencies within government may be absent. Sending a survey to public officials, asking about the extent of their corrupt actions, would seem like a nonstarter. Relying on members of the local media may not help much if they feel that publishing stories about official corruption would put them in danger. One reasonable alternative might be to collect estimates of corruption from political experts of the countries in question and then classify these countries as highly, moderately, mildly, or not corrupt. Sometimes an ordinal measure is the best we can do.*

If every case shares the same observed value for that measure, then we have a **constant**. We might measure the concept of legislative-executive relations nominally with just three values—parliamentary, presidential, or mixed. A study limited to the United States would assign every case to the presidential category, making it a constant. A measure is a **variable** if it takes on two or more different values among the cases under investigation. In a cross-national study involving the United States and Europe, legislative-executive relations would be a variable, because different countries operate under different systems. In theory, then, a given concept could be a constant or a variable, depending on the nature and scope of our research project. In practice, most of the measures that political scientists work with are variables.

All this sounds rather technical, more like accounting than politics. What would happen if we failed to follow these steps when describing political concepts? Chances are good that our research would be unconvincing at best, sloppy or lazy at worst. By framing our research question poorly, we would then run a greater risk of constructing a shoddy answer. Suppose a student of American politics wanted to analyze presidential effectiveness and, without defining the concept clearly or specifying its dimensions, moved straight to a comparison of Bill Clinton's success in reducing the

---

* **Dichotomous** measures (sometimes called dummy variables) can be tricky to classify. At first glance, they appear to be nominal, because they can have only two possible values. "Has this country agreed to limits on their greenhouse gases, as set forth by the Kyoto Protocol? Yes/No." "What region in the United States is this person from? South/Non-South." Some analysts treat such measures as ordinal, arguing that the two values form a continuum, such as from Yes to No. And some treat dichotomous measures as ratio, because all the values are equally distant from each other. They have to be, given the single space between the two values. Dichotomous measures should therefore be handled with care. (Sometimes it seems like you can't live with them or without them.)

national deficit, George W. Bush's failure to find Osama bin Laden, and Barack Obama's executive order to combat wildlife trafficking. Forget apples and oranges—this person is literally comparing turtles and terrorists. The student's project somehow mashes up domestic and foreign affairs, presidential actions that do and do not require cooperation from Congress, and policy outputs (executive orders) and policy outcomes (lower deficits)—all under some vague heading of "stuff presidents do." To make this kind of comparison systematic, and fair, the researcher should begin with a definition of *presidential effectiveness*, followed by some justification for dividing this concept into separate dimensions. He would then present evidence for every case on each dimension. Thus, if handling the economy turns out to be one dimension of presidential effectiveness, and the size of the budget deficit is one measure of that dimension, then the researcher would cite deficit figures for Bush and Obama as well as Clinton.

DETERMINING THE QUALITY OF MEASURES

Building a house badly is easy. Measuring a concept badly is even easier, if only because it takes less time. No one can physically stop me from defining *political tolerance* as "the extent to which an individual supports free speech," and then measuring people's reactions to uncensored episodes of the TV show *South Park*. Nevertheless, the initial definition seems too one-dimensional, and the specific measure sounds like a joke. It would be really helpful if political scientists had some standards (even if the head writers of *South Park* do not).

As mentioned earlier, political scientists are destined to argue over the definitions of many concepts. Their specific measures, however, may be evaluated more readily. To political scientists, a good measure is **reliable** and **valid**. A reliable measure gives us the same reading after repeated use. It is consistent. As an everyday example, a scale that weighs me in at 200 pounds today, 225 pounds tomorrow, and 185 pounds the next day is probably not very reliable. If I identify certain indicators of democracy and apply them to China, then my results should be very similar to those of another researcher who used these same indicators on this same case. The more our judgments differ, the less reliable are my measures. This test is called **inter-rater** or **inter-coder reliability**, and is used quite often in the social sciences. A team of scholars, or their graduate research assistants and maybe even their undergraduate assistants, would be trained in the use of a measure and then given a number of examples to code. Do these development projects in Africa look like they were completely successful, partly successful, not successful, or counterproductive? Or maybe, on a scale of 1 to 7, how would you rank these countries in protecting civil liberties? The more often the coders agreed, the more reliable the measure.

The Glasgow Coma Scale has been challenged on this very ground. Medical professionals have to make a number of judgment calls in evaluating each patient. Someone measuring a patient's verbal ability might have to decide whether the choice of words was inappropriate (verbal score = 3) or confused (4), a distinction I find hard to apply to my own speech. The level of training in the use of this scale differs, with neurologists more trained than intensive-care nurses. For these and other reasons, a number of clinical studies have found the inter-rater reliability of the Glasgow Coma Scale to be lacking and have proposed alternative measures.[19]

Another way of testing reliability is to see if the measure gives the same result at different points in time, known as the **test-retest method**. A survey of attitudes toward the death penalty would be reliable if your answers on Monday were the same as your answers on Thursday. Using this approach assumes, of course, that whatever we are measuring should not be changing over time, and that assumption could be highly questionable. If your coma score was a 9 every day for two weeks, that would appear to be a reliable measure. But if your underlying condition had indeed changed, the score would not be valid, that is, accurate. This type of measurement error could be disastrous if your treatment actually needed to be modified. A study of democracy in China over the last few decades might employ a measure that produced the same result every year, which could seem reliable but might not be valid. The true level of democracy could have gone up or down. In fact, the test of inter-coder reliability might also produce an invalid measure. Everyone involved on the research project might agree on how to measure a concept, yet all do so inaccurately. In short, reliable measures aren't necessarily valid.*

Political scientists thus worry more about the validity of their measures. A measure that's valid is also reliable; it is accurate no matter who is using it or when it's used. Scholars have a few ways of determining whether a measure is valid. The first is called **face validity**, and it requires a simple test: does this look right? I'm serious, this really is the test. In some studies it even boils down to the author asking, "Does this look right to me?" The answer tends to be a simple yes rather than an extended justification. When authors rely on face validity, they are appealing to our common sense or

---

*A scale that gave my weight as 125 pounds every single day for a month would be reliable, but it wouldn't be valid. Not even close.

common knowledge of a particular concept. On the face of it, they claim, this measure looks accurate. Imagine a project in which the author planned to measure political knowledge among Americans by asking them to name as many current members of Congress, up to 535, as they could. We could say, "Wow, that seems pretty stupid," or we could be more polite and raise the possibility of poor face validity.

Content validity is a more rigorous standard. It requires identifying all the major attributes of a concept and providing at least one measure for each attribute. The architects of the Glasgow Coma Scale believed that comas have three main attributes—motor, verbal, and visual—and created a measure for each. Their overall measure has content validity as long as we agree that those are the right dimensions. Assuming that democracy has two essential dimensions, contestation and inclusiveness, we would need at least two measures. Of course, we don't know how accurate any one of those indicators might be. Content validity is more a test of the comprehensiveness of a measure.

A measure could lack validity if its content was too large or too small. A "maximalist" index of democracy, for example, might incorporate too many measures. Along with indicators of contestation and inclusiveness, it might have measures of economic inequality and collective bargaining in each country. Now we seem to be blending a political concept with economic components that may not be relevant given our definition of *democracy*. To make matters worse, the more we stuff our concepts with different measures, the harder it will be for us later to test relationships involving those concepts. Using a maximalist index, we might not be able to examine a relationship between democracy and economic inequality, because the latter would already be embedded in our measure of democracy. In effect, we have created a partial tautology, a relationship that will be true by definition. On the other hand, a "minimalist" approach also would lack content validity, because key attributes or dimensions of a concept were missing. A summary index of democracy based on several indicators of contestation but none for inclusiveness would lack content validity.[20]

Demonstrating **construct validity** takes more work. It requires comparing our measure A of concept A to a good measure B of related concept B. The more closely correlated the two measures are, the more construct validity measure A has. A specific example can help illustrate construct validity. In chapter 3 of *Making Democracy Work*, Putnam developed a measure of institutional performance for Italy's regional governments. He built an index out of many components, which produced a single score for each regional government. To test the construct validity of his index, Putnam compared it to surveys of Italians who were asked how satisfied they were with their regional government. Those surveys were not part of Putnam's index. We might think of these two general concepts as institutional performance and perceived institutional performance. For the most part, those two measures were closely correlated. The regional governments that Putnam measured as high performers were the same ones that had the most satisfied citizens. That was good evidence for the construct validity of Putnam's measure.[21]

In developing a mental checklist, we now have several questions to ask ourselves when reading a piece of political research, and when crafting our own. Several of these questions highlight potential sources of measurement error, a problem that can bedevil practically any type of empirical research. It doesn't matter whether the topic is impediments to democracy in the Arab world, the American welfare state, ethnic conflict in central Africa, the democratic peace, or attitudes toward immigrants in Europe. The questions are the same:

> Have the key concepts been clearly defined? Where did the definitions come from? Can we identify or imagine other plausible definitions of this same concept?
>
> Does the general concept have the correct attributes or dimensions? What is the unit of analysis?
>
> What level(s) of measurement is/are involved? Would it make sense if the level were more precise or less precise? Why or why not?
>
> Do the measures of each concept (including any summary index or scale) seem valid? Explain.

DESCRIBING RELATIONSHIPS

Sometimes I ask my students what family therapists, King Henry VIII, undercover spies, and political scientists have in common. After a puzzled silence: "They're all masters of deception?" Ouch. No student has ever guessed the right answer, or at least the answer I have in mind: all of us are interested in relationships. That answer usually elicits a mix of wry smiles and muffled groans. But my lame attempt at a joke does point out an important truth, which is that political scientists are constantly analyzing relationships. They want to understand how the many and varied parts of the political world are connected.

Occasionally, political scientists engage in research that is exploratory, where they initially have little idea of which relationships to investigate. On those occasions they may act more like cultural anthropologists, immersing themselves in unfamiliar surroundings and waiting for patterns to emerge. More often—and this is true for virtually every project conducted by undergraduates—they already have some idea of which relationships are worth analyzing. In chapter 1, the process of conducting a literature review helped focus our attention on a relatively small number of descriptive or causal hypotheses.

These hypotheses are designed to cover multiple instances of some political phenomenon. They are generalizations that may be more or less true for any particular instance, or case. Thus, when political scientists ask, "What happened?" they start by focusing on patterns. Their answers will contain evidence about specific cases, maybe even just one case (discussed in chapter 5). But that evidence is usually supposed to shed light on some larger pattern.

When trying to describe relationships between concepts (e.g., democracy and natural resources, tolerance and education), political scientists ask themselves two basic questions. Are the measures of each concept correlated? Is the apparent relationship spurious, in other words fake? If we can answer "yes" to the first question and "no" to the second, then we feel confident that a descriptive relationship exists. Answering the first question requires a strategy of verification: we need evidence showing that the concepts are indeed related. Answering the second questions entails a process of falsification, meaning that we are trying to rule out competing accounts. The first question is usually easier to answer than the second. Both are important to address.

Correlation is a statistical term, but the basic idea can be understood intuitively as well. It applies whether we are working with precise numbers or more general categories. At issue is the extent to which the values of our measures covary across some set of cases. This is not a yes/no question; we want to know how much the values covary. Among other things, this means that our hypothesis will need to have a direction. It's not enough to hypothesize that labor repression and economic growth are related among countries, or that the duration of wars is related to geography. Our hypotheses need to be more specific than that.

When there is a **direct relationship** between two measures, higher values of one are associated with higher values of the other. Lower values are likewise associated. Studies routinely find that levels of democracy and economic development are directly related. More affluent countries tend to be more democratic. While there are exceptions—Bahrain and Singapore come to mind—this pattern holds true for most countries. An **inverse relationship** exists when higher values of one measure are typically associated with lower values of the other measure. Among individuals, we might expect to find an inverse relationship between income and support for progressive taxation. If true, the richest group would offer the least support.[22] It is also possible that our initial hypothesis would lead us to expect no relationship, in which case that hypothesis would be called a **null hypothesis**. Previous studies might lead us to believe that no relationship exists between age and support for the death penalty, and we could test that hypothesis with evidence from one or more countries. If that hypothesis were true, then young people and old people should have similar views.*

Direct and *inverse* both refer to linear relationships, and those are the main types that political scientists look for and work with. Relationships can, however, be **nonlinear** or **curvilinear** and still exhibit covariation. The relationship between voting and age in the United States looks a bit like an upside-down bowl: voter turnout is lower when people are in their twenties, rises steadily and peaks in their fifties and sixties, and then declines during their seventies and eighties. This pattern is regular but not linear. Other relationships in politics could be U-shaped. Support for a given political party could be high among high school dropouts and people who attended graduate school, but low among high school and college graduates. Although statisticians have developed ways of testing for nonlinear relationships, running those tests requires a level of training that many undergraduates lack. As an alternative, graphing the data may offer powerful clues about the presence of a curved relationship. Otherwise, we might conclude that no relationship exists when the reality is that no linear relationship exists.

If we are working with many cases (20 to 25 or more), the standard method for determining covariation relies on statistics such as correlation coefficients (see chapter 7). Not surprisingly, in the 2012 US presidential election, the feeling thermometer scores for the Democratic and Republican candidates were strongly and inversely related. The more warmly someone felt about Obama, the less warmly that person felt about Romney. There was, however, essentially no relationship between an individual's political ideology and her feelings toward Congress.[23] With fewer cases, we eyeball the

---

* These relationships are sometimes referred to as positive and negative rather than direct and inverse. Those terms, however, contain a normative element that can be misleading. If I discuss a positive relationship between ethnic diversity and the chances of civil war, some readers might get the impression that I looked favorably upon such a relationship. *Direct* and *inverse* are more neutral adjectives.

data and judge whether the two measures are directly or inversely related most of the time. Covariation doesn't have to be perfect—political scientists deal in regularities, not iron laws of nature—so there can be exceptions. Sometimes those exceptions are large enough, though, to call the whole relationship into question.

In my field of social policy, one piece of conventional wisdom is that the American welfare state has two distinct tiers: an upper tier of social insurance programs that are large, generous, and politically powerful (e.g., Social Security), and a lower tier of public assistance programs that are small, inadequate, and politically vulnerable (e.g., public housing). Look carefully, and the exceptions start to pile up. Two of the five programs in the upper tier, unemployment insurance and workers' compensation, don't fit this pattern very well. Nor do two of the largest programs in the lower tier, Medicaid and the Earned Income Tax Credit. Moreover, many social programs run through the tax code don't fit easily in either tier. We probably need some better way of describing the structure of the American welfare state.[24]

One of the easiest ways to rule out a relationship is when one of the measures exhibits little variation, and may even be a constant. Students of international relations may want to know what kinds of countries signed on to the Kyoto Protocol, a treaty concerning the emission of greenhouse gases. Maybe signing was related directly to a country's income, or to the size of its manufacturing sector, or to the power of its left-wing political parties. It will be hard to test any of these relationships, however, because practically every country on Earth—rich and poor, left-wing and right-wing—has signed on to this treaty. It might be wiser to study what kinds of countries agreed to binding targets for their emissions, a much smaller number. By the same token, someone analyzing traffic fatalities in Nevada, Nebraska, and North Dakota might not find much of a relationship with speed limits in those states, because the legal maximum in all three is seventy-five miles per hour.

Checking for covariation isn't that complicated. The bigger problem is **spuriousness**. *Spurious* isn't a word used to describe cowboys; it means "false" or "fake." Even though two measures might seem directly or inversely related, their relationship might be an illusion created by some third factor we haven't considered. A classic example is the direct relationship between sales of ice cream and deaths by drowning. This may sound like the beginning of a lawsuit against Ben & Jerry's, but all the relationship really reflects is summer, whose higher temperatures are associated with more ice cream and more swimming. The possibility of a spurious relationship in politics

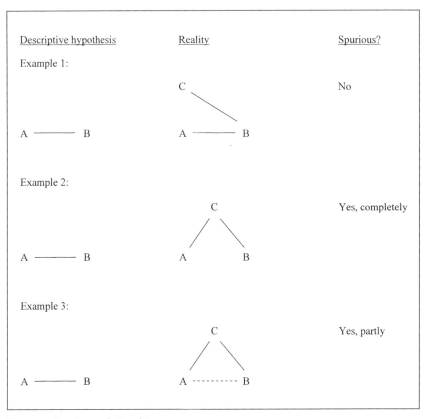

Figure 2.2. Spurious relationships.

was raised at the start of this chapter: are democracy and Islam related, or is region related to democracy and to Islam? Political scientists aren't as worried that some other factor might be related, in addition to those under scrutiny. Our hypotheses are always simplifications of reality. The real concern is that one of those other factors might more or less wipe out the relationship we thought we observed. Figure 2.2 illustrates the difference between those types of problems. The first example, involving a relationship between generic factors A and B, is not spurious. The second example is completely spurious, and the third is partly spurious.

To appreciate just how badly we want to avoid spurious relationships, imagine an episode of the *Dr. Phil* talk show. Dr. Phil McGraw, for those of you unfamiliar with TV psychologists, specializes in messy divorces, unruly teenagers, emotional abuse, and the like. In this scenario, a couple in their

CHAPTER TWO

forties walks onstage and sits across from Dr. Phil. We are told their names are Leslie and Tim. Their four kids, ages eight to sixteen, follow, and sit down on a nearby couch. Leslie then tells her kids that she has some difficult news for them, and maybe Dr. Phil can help them understand. (He nods.) She starts by telling each child, by name, that she really, really loves them. Then the show gets interesting. "Kids, I want to tell you today that Tim and I are not married and never have been." The children look confused. "In fact, Tim isn't even your biological father." Loud gasps from the audience. Tim looks down at the floor. Dr. Phil tilts his head to one side. "Your father is actually Reverend Jim, who works at that little church we go to sometimes, next to the Pizza Hut." Dr. Phil leans in, wide-eyed. A couple of the children seem close to tears. "And kids, Reverend Jim also happens to be Tim's father." At that point all hell breaks loose, and Dr. Phil tries to keep the two oldest kids from physically attacking their so-called parents.

This whole scenario is desperately sad, but what makes it spurious? The children were convinced they had a certain relationship with their parents. But in fact, a third person they barely thought about had a powerful relationship with their parents and with them. Leslie and Tim still acted as parents in many ways, so their relationship with their children was not entirely spurious (akin to example 3 in figure 2.2). Even so, the Reverend Jim angle does alter their relationship in fundamental ways. Emotionally, the kids are probably scarred for life. Dr. Phil's ratings, on the other hand, just got a huge boost.

None of us want to discover that our relationship is spurious, and that includes political scientists. Knowing to watch out for spuriousness will be a big step for many undergraduates. The tendency, however, is to show that two measures covary, and then stop. Students often settle for a plausible answer without subjecting it to much scrutiny. They need to take the next step, which is developing a healthy skepticism—asking, in effect, "That might be what happened, but what else could it be?"

Though essential, this question could lead to an almost endless string of answers. For instance, after noticing that democracy and Islam seem related, we could check for connections to region, or history of colonial rule, or vitality of civil society, or income, or dependence on natural resources, or . . . So many possibilities. Too many. We need to find some way to balance our professional skepticism with the realization that we typically can't test all possible sources of spuriousness in our descriptions.

This is another place where a good literature review comes in handy. By introducing not just one hypothesis but rival hypotheses in the lit review, we may be able to conclude later that "the relationship is between *A* and *B*, not *A* and *C*." Sure, we haven't examined factors *D*, *E*, and *F* (not to mention *G* and *H*), which might complicate or undermine our account. At least we considered two strong alternatives, *B* and *C*, and found enough evidence to rule out one of them. Given the page limits of journal articles or class assignments, this could be the best we can do.

There is a silver lining. Once we realize that the complexity of political life creates many chances for spurious relationships, we can gain a healthy dose of humility. We start using verbs like *suggests* and *indicates* rather than *proves* to describe the relationships we are analyzing. We qualify our claims with terms such as *probably* and *likely*. We seek out help from other scholars who may have found good ways of eliminating some sources of spuriousness. In other words, we might not need to look for a relationship between *A* and *D*; it does not exist. Maybe we conclude our project by calling for more research on factors that could be related, but we didn't have time to test.

The process of ruling out rival descriptions or explanations is integral to the search for truth in political science. The formal name for this process is falsification, and we will encounter it again in the next chapter. One way political scientists grow more confident that a relationship between *A* and *B* exists is by finding evidence to reject alternative factors (*C*, *D*, *E*, . . .) that may be related to *A* and *B*. For a variety of reasons, though, including the almost limitless supply of confounding factors, we can never be 100 percent confident in our own research findings or anyone else's. But that doesn't mean we stop trying. With hard work and some creativity, scholars can gradually develop a better grasp about what happened with ethnic conflict, democratization, and many other important political puzzles. Falsification is, by necessity, a collective enterprise, one that requires a substantial commitment of time and energy.

BOX 2.1

CREATING AN INDEX

Let's think ahead for a minute. Chances are good that we are measuring concepts carefully in order to incorporate them into a descriptive or causal hypothesis. We realize that most of the "big" concepts in politics will require multiple measures. Nevertheless, as a practical matter, it could be really cumbersome to work with each measure individually. Imagine, for instance, that our concept of democracy has seven measures, and that we want to analyze the relationship between democracy and literacy. We might have to report results for regular elections and literacy, for party competition and literacy, for adult suffrage and literacy, for freedom of the press and literacy, for . . . ugh. It would be much simpler for us, as authors or as readers, if all those measures could be combined into one overall indicator of democracy.

Political scientists do this all the time. Their usual tactic is to create a summary index. By now social scientists have created indexes for democracy, failed states, human development, gender empowerment, global firepower, party competition, cultural diversity, trust in government, trade openness, and many other concepts.[1] Thus, it would behoove us to know how an index is built. In practice, some are put together quickly and easily (maybe too easily), while others are more elaborate. Still, the five basic steps are the same:

1. Define a general concept.
2. Identify key attributes or dimensions of that concept.
3. Identify at least one measure for each attribute or dimension.
4. Select a common unit of analysis and convert each measure into that unit.
5. Decide on an aggregation rule for combining the measures into a summary index.[2]

Although the first three steps look familiar, there's a wrinkle to steps 2 and 3 that I want to introduce. When building an index, some political scientists use statistical techniques such as factor analysis to make sure that all their measures are truly correlated with the general concept. If some measures are not, they could be dropped from the index. These same techniques may also identify individual measures that are highly correlated with each other, which could be a sign that one of them could be dropped as well. Finally, these techniques can help determine if our concept has one underlying dimension or more.

Steps 4 and 5 require some explanation. Many indexes are expressed as interval- or ratio-level measures, as are the components. If some of the components were ordinal, the author would probably convert the values for each label into a number in order to facilitate aggregation. For example, the American National Election Studies has developed a Trust in Government Index, with possible scores ranging from 0 to 100. One part of this index is based on a question about trust in the federal government in which the possible answers are Just About Always, Most of the Time, and Only Some of the Time. For the purpose of the index, these categories are assigned the values of 100, 67, and 33, respectively (and anyone who volunteered the answer None of the Time is scored a 0). An index of gender empowerment might include questions about attitudes toward women in a given country. Suppose one question asked whether women were just as capable as men in running the country, and the possible answers were Strongly Agree, Agree, Disagree, and Strongly Disagree. These responses might be converted to the numbers 1, 2, 4, and 5 (we might leave a space for 3 that would correspond to a middle option, Neither Agree nor Disagree). In both examples, we have made certain assumptions about the spacing between each value of the measure.

The usual practice in political science is to count each part of the index the same (step 5). We just add or average the values to produce a total score. Some indexes depart from this practice. The author may feel that certain parts of the index are more important than others and thus deserve greater weight. In building a democracy index, someone might argue that party competition matters more than the transparency of the budget process, and thus should count more. Exactly how much more will likely be subjective (twice? three times? 1.5?). Implicitly, the Glasgow Coma Scale gives more weight to motor response, where the maximum score is 6, compared with 5 for verbal and 4 for eye response. That represents another kind of judgment call. Regardless of how an index is aggregated, readers should expect some justification for the weights given to each component, even when they are equal weights.

The final point is the difference between an index and a scale. The two terms are sometimes used interchangeably, but they aren't the same. "Scales are also multi-item measures, but the selection and combination of items in them is accomplished more systematically than is usually the case for indexes."[3] In other words, creating a scale takes more work and forethought than creating an index. Students of political behavior often use scales to measure the intensity of some attitude or feeling. Better-known techniques include the Likert scale and Guttman scale.

NOTES

1. Of course, creating an index is no cure-all. Any index could have structural problems: see, e.g., Dan Hough, "Here's this year's (flawed) Corruption Perception Index. Those flaws are useful," *Washington Post* (January 27, 2016), available at https://www.washingtonpost.com/news/monkey-cage/wp/2016/01/27/how-do-you-measure-corruption-transparency-international-does-its-best-and-thats-useful/; Munck and Verkuilen, "Conceptualizing and Measuring Democracy." And some indexes could conceal as much as they reveal: Joe Soss, Sanford F. Schram, Thomas P. Vartanian, and Erin O"Brien, "Setting the Terms of Relief: Explaining State Policy Choices in the Devolution Revolution," *American Journal of Political Science* 45, no. 2 (April 2001): 378–95.

2. These steps are similar to Munck and Verkuilen, "Conceptualizing and Measuring Democracy."

3. Janet Buttolph Johnson and H. T. Reynolds, *Political Science Research Methods*, 7th ed. (Thousand Oaks, CA: CQ Press, 2012), p. 152.

PRACTICE: INSPECTING

1. Moving from concepts to measures in everyday life. In the following articles, identify the core concept(s), their main dimensions, and their specific measures. If the author created an overall index, is each measure weighted equally or unequally?

   Malcolm Gladwell, "The Order of Things," *New Yorker*, February 14, 2011; available at http://www.newyorker.com/reporting/2011/02/14/110214fa_fact_gladwell?currentPage=all;

   Randy Nelson, "Meet the New Vegas: The 10 Most Sinful Cities in America," available at http://www.movoto.com/blog/top-ten/sin-cities/;

Ryan Nickum, "The United States of Fear: Which American States Are the Scariest?" (July 15, 2014), available at http://blog.estately.com/2014/07/the -united-states-of-fear-which-american-states-are-the-scariest/.

2. Moving from concepts to measures in political science. In the following articles, identify the core concept(s), their main dimensions, and their specific measures. If the author created an overall index, is each measure weighted equally or unequally?

Sarah Binder, *Stalemate: Causes and Consequences of Legislative Gridlock* (Washington, DC: Brookings Institution Press, 2003), chapter 3;

Michael Coppedge and John Gerring et al., "Conceptualizing and Measuring Democracy: A New Approach," *Perspectives on Politics* 9, no. 2 (June 2011): 247–67;

Michael P. McDonald and Samuel L. Popkin, "The Myth of the Vanishing Voter," *American Political Science Review* 95, no. 4 (December 2001): 963–74;

Jeffrey Mondak and Mitchell Sanders, "Tolerance and Intolerance, 1976–1998," *American Journal of Political Science* 47, no. 3 (July 2003): 492–502;

Gerardo Munck and Jay Verkuilen, "Conceptualizing and Measuring Democracy: Alternative Indices," *Comparative Political Studies* 35, no. 1 (February 2002): 5–34;

Robert D. Putnam, *Making Democracy Work: Civic Traditions in Modern Italy* (Princeton, NJ: Princeton University Press, 1993), chapter 3;

Taylor B. Seybolt, Jay D. Aronson, and Baruch Fischoff, eds., *Counting Civilian Casualties: An Introduction to Recording and Estimating Nonmilitary Deaths in Combat* (Oxford, UK: Oxford University Press, 2013), multiple chapters;

Deborah Stone, "Making the Poor Count," *American Prospect* 17 (Spring 1994): 84–88;

Craig Volden and Alan E. Wiseman, *Legislative Effectiveness in the United States Congress: The Lawmakers* (New York: Cambridge University Press, 2014), chapter 2.

3. Describing relationships in politics. What do these authors see as the main patterns? Do they consider or rule out any alternative descriptions?

Jack Citrin and David O. Sears, *American Identity and the Politics of Multiculturalism* (New York: Cambridge University Press, 2014), chapter 3;

Christopher Howard, *The Welfare State Nobody Knows: Debunking Myths about U.S. Social Policy* (Princeton, NJ: Princeton University Press, 2007), chapter 2;

Arend Lijphart, *Patterns of Democracy: Government Forms and Performance* in *Thirty-Six Countries* (New Haven, CT: Yale University Press, 1999), chapter 12;

Alfred Stepan with Graeme B. Robertson, "An 'Arab' More Than 'Muslim' Electoral Gap," *Journal of Democracy* 14, no. 3 (July 2003): 30–44.

PRACTICE: BUILDING

1. How would you complete the following table?

Concept	Conceptual definition	Operational definition
Trust in government	The level of confidence that individuals have in public officials and institutions.	*(handwritten) I want to look at what has caused the public to lose confidence.*
Child-friendly	The extent to which countries provide basic levels of income, food, and medical care for residents under the age of sixteen.	*(handwritten) I want to look at how policies on ... the ... on the ... steps taken*
Bureaucratic capacity	*(handwritten) Is the ability of the legislature or agency to agree on policy change at the impact.*	Reflects the size of the agency's budget, the number of full-time agency employees, and the average length of tenure at the agency among senior officials.

2. How would you improve this attempt to operationalize the concept of political knowledge?

Concept	Political knowledge	
Definition	"The factual information citizens need to participate in politics"	
Dimensions	Domestic affairs	Foreign affairs
Specific measures	Can name vice president, chief justice, and House Speaker.	Can name UN Secretary-General and chancellor of Germany.
	Can define *civil liberties*. How often reads domestic magazine/newspaper.	Can define *authoritarianism*. How often reads foreign magazine/newspaper.

CHAPTER TWO

(handwritten notes at bottom of page) First I would give a more detailed conceptual definition, eg. Political knowledge is one of the primary variables in political communication research. Then I will add an operational definition using domestic affairs and foreign matters by taking part in ...

3. For each of the following, indicate whether the level of measurement should be nominal, ordinal, interval, or ratio.
    (a) Per capita income   *ratio*
    (b) Views toward abortion (Never Permitted; Only in Cases of Rape, Incest, or Danger to the Woman; Yes if Need Clearly Established; Always Permitted)   *ordinal*
    (c) Party identification in Britain (Conservative, Labour, Liberal, Scottish National, Social Democratic, Green, Other)
    (d) Percentage of Muslims   *interval*
    (e) Ideology of members of Congress, ranging from −1 (most liberal) to +1 (most conservative)   *nominal*
    (f) Belief that providing health insurance is an essential function of government (Strongly Agree, Agree, Disagree, Strongly Disagree)   *ordinal*
    (g) Index of ethnic diversity, ranging from 0 to 100   *interval*
    (h) Number of nuclear missiles   *interval*
    (i) Marital status (single, married, divorced, separated, widowed)   *nominal*
4. For each of the following concepts, create an index (see box 2.1 for details). Be prepared to explain why you made certain choices at each step in the process.
    (a) Teacher quality
    (b) Quality of life in a community
    (c) Presidential greatness
    (d) Military power
    (e) Support for environmental protection
5. Suppose you read an article or book claiming that the following concepts were directly related. Name at least one other concept that might render each relationship partly or completely spurious.
    (a) Per capita income and voter turnout
    (b) Number of major language groups within country and chances of civil war
    (c) Education level and support for racial equality
    (d) Number of countries contributing soldiers to UN peacekeeping mission and success of that mission

how these 2 are part of political knowledge & will score down on the amount of specific measures?

3
WHY?

March 26, 2010, should have been one of the highlights of Veronique de Rugy's career. Not many social scientists are invited to testify before Congress, yet there she was, presenting her research to the House Committee on Transportation and Infrastructure. The main objective of the hearings that day was to assess the initial impact of the American Recovery and Reinvestment Act of 2009, better known as the Recovery Act or the stimulus. This act was supposed to help pull the US economy out of a deep and painful recession. Some of the speakers at the hearing discussed specific highway or mass transit projects. Among them were local officials and representatives of organizations that stood to benefit from these projects. De Rugy, the lone academic on the panel, was there to explain why some parts of the country had received more stimulus funds than others. She identified party politics as the most important factor responsible for these differences. Congressional districts represented by Democrats received considerably more money than districts represented by Republicans.[1]

De Rugy's day on Capitol Hill seems to have gone fairly smoothly. She read a brief statement summarizing her research, and submitted her entire report to the committee. The committee chair, Rep. James Oberstar (D-MN), asked de Rugy to clarify her sources of data and repeat her main findings. At his initiative, they even conversed a bit in French.* He did question whether politics truly mattered more than economic need in determining the allocation of aid, and de Rugy replied that she had measured unemployment in different ways and used different statistical tests, and economic need failed to explain the outcome every time. Rep. Oberstar asked whether de Rugy had any evidence of deliberate intent to channel funds to Democratic districts, and she stated clearly that she was explaining the effects of decisions, not their intent. No one else on the committee challenged her analysis. Judging from the transcript of these hearings, most of the attention of those present

---

*According to a translation printed in the *Washington Post* (March 27, 2010), Rep. Oberstar told de Rugy that "the oysters of Normandy are the most delicious in the world." Which sure beats talking about wastewater treatment plants in Minnesota.

was focused on other speakers, who discussed the impact of specific projects in their home states.

A few days later, de Rugy's professional reputation took a serious hit. Her research attracted the attention of Nate Silver, a prominent analyst who uses statistics to analyze politics (and sports). He was, shall we say, not impressed. In a posting to his website, FiveThirtyEight.com, Silver referred to her study as "manifestly flawed." De Rugy's biggest mistake, he said, was so "obvious" that it was "mind-boggling." Fixing it would have taken "literally five minutes." At a loss to explain how a PhD could err so badly, Silver raised the possibility that her study was "deliberately biased" from the start.[2] Jonathan Chait of the *New Republic* quickly picked up the story and posted a brief item, "A Case Study in Hackery."[3] In less refined company, de Rugy might have been called an unscrupulous fraud.

What in the world had she done wrong? Her data came from the Bureau of Labor Statistics, the Census Bureau, and other agencies of the federal government, all of them credible sources. De Rugy made it clear that her findings applied to contracts and grants, not the tax cuts that were also part of the stimulus. (It would have been nearly impossible to allocate those tax cuts by congressional district.) To be transparent, she posted her dataset to a publicly available website at George Mason University, where she worked. She used Stata, a well-known software package, to generate correlations and multiple regressions, which are standard statistical techniques.

Like a good social scientist, de Rugy tested rival explanations. She considered the hypothesis that economic need influenced the distribution of funds, which the architects of the Recovery Act had said would happen. Nevertheless, her measures of unemployment and income were nowhere near statistically significant. Districts that had suffered badly during the recession were receiving no more help than districts that were hit lightly. De Rugy also tested whether seniority or a leadership position in Congress might have influenced the direction of federal monies, with longtime members and committee chairs winning more aid for their districts. She found no relationship between stimulus funds and these measures, either. And she carefully qualified her conclusions by stating that the exact magnitude of the effect was hard to pinpoint; what she knew for sure was that the partisan slant of the congressional district had an effect on the distribution of stimulus funds, in favor of Democrats. Although her results may have been politically embarrassing for the Obama administration and congressional Democrats, that doesn't make them wrong.

Unless . . . unless she forgot to control for some really important factor that might have been involved. That was the essence of Nate Silver's argument.[4] De Rugy failed to notice that the districts receiving the largest amount of aid had one thing in common: a vast majority of them contained state capitals. The top two recipients were California's Fourth Congressional District, which included Sacramento, and New York's Twenty-First, which included Albany. Number three on her list came from Texas—Austin, Texas. Number four was Tallahassee, Florida. And so on down the list.[5] There was no great mystery or conspiracy here, according to Silver. Federal aid for many programs is sent initially to state capitals, which then distribute the monies across the state. Moreover, state capitals are often urban areas with more racial minorities, higher levels of education, or many government workers. Districts encompassing state capitals are thus likely to elect Democrats to Congress. In Silver's view, anyone with a basic understanding of American politics would have known that state capitals might be related to federal aid and to political party.

This episode offers some lessons about how to explain political outcomes and how not to, and I will come back to de Rugy and Silver later in this chapter. The most obvious lesson involves the potential threat of spurious relationships. This threat looms over both descriptive and causal arguments, and it can be quite serious. On the face of it, the state capital–federal aid–political party relationship sounds suspiciously like the summer–ice cream–deaths by drowning example mentioned in the previous chapter. Another lesson, as we shall see, concerns the difference between correlation and causation.

This episode also illustrates a few general lessons about political research. In particular, it shows how visible and contentious our work can be. I seriously doubt that de Rugy expected to be skewered so publicly by someone like Nate Silver when she woke up on the morning of March 26. Not based on testimony to the Transportation and Infrastructure Committee. Not during the same week that Congress passed and President Obama signed the historic Affordable Care Act, when everyone in Washington was still buzzing about health care. Nevertheless, she was skewered. Politics is serious business for many people, more than just a game, and everyone conducting research should expect their work to be challenged.[6]

CREATING A CAUSAL HYPOTHESIS

As mentioned in chapter 2, causal hypotheses are the bread and butter of political science. Most political scientists focus on asking why things happen the way they do. "Things" is deliberately plural; political scientists seek explanations for patterns in the political world. Even single case studies are typically analyzed in the context of some pattern (discussed in chapters 4 and 5). These explanations are often called **theories**, and they range from grand theories that cover a broad range of phenomena (e.g., realist theories of international relations) to more modest theories (e.g., Supreme Court decision making). A theory in political science doesn't really qualify as a theory unless it contains at least one general statement about cause and effect.[7]

Creating and testing causal arguments are therefore essential skills to develop. Let's start with some basic vocabulary. At some point in elementary school, our science teachers introduced us to **independent variables** and **dependent variables**. You might remember the school science fair where a kid planted identical seeds in identical pots of soil and gave them the same amount of water, but put one pot in a closet and one by a window to see which seeds would grow faster. Her independent variable was sunlight, and her dependent variable was plant growth. She would probably expect the seeds exposed to more sunlight to grow more. And she would expect sunlight to cause that growth, not vice versa.

Political scientists think about independent and dependent variables in much the same way. The dependent variable is some outcome we hope to explain. It is the effect in a cause-and-effect relationship. When we ask, "Why are some countries more democratic than others?" then our dependent variable would be something like the extent of democracy.* When we ask, "Why are some UN peacekeeping missions more successful than others?" our dependent variable would be the level of success of peacekeeping mission. The dependent variable in de Rugy's study was based on the stimulus dollars awarded to each congressional district.

Independent variables are the factors thought to cause some change in the value of our dependent variable. Because we are still trying to ask good questions at this point, we aren't sure if our independent variables will in fact have some effect on our dependent variable. Students of comparative politics might ask what influence natural resources, income, religion, or education (the independent variables) have on the extent of democracy around the world. Students of international relations might examine the number of countries contributing personnel, indigenous support for the local government, or other factors when explaining the relative success or failure of those peacekeeping missions. Like the child in the science fair, political scientists might be able to manipulate the values of their independent variables, which is one of the hallmarks of a true experiment (discussed

---

*The dependent variable should be expressed in general terms and not as a specific value of that variable. Here, we would use "extent of democracy" rather than "more democratic."

in chapter 4). More likely, political scientists will have to work with whatever values they can observe.

A **path** or **arrow diagram** can be a useful way to simplify and clarify a causal argument. The most basic form of a causal hypothesis can be drawn as $A \rightarrow B$, with A as the independent variable and B as the dependent variable. This diagram would be improved by indicating whether the relationship is believed to be direct or inverse. By writing,

$$(+)$$
$$A \xrightarrow{\hspace{3cm}} B$$

we are making an educated guess that more of A leads to more of B. Perhaps more income leads to higher voter turnout. Or, maybe less education contributes to lower levels of political tolerance. Either hypothesis reflects a direct relationship between A and B. On the other hand, if I change the sign from $+$ to $-$,

$$(-)$$
$$A \xrightarrow{\hspace{3cm}} B$$

then I would hypothesize that more of A results in less of B, an inverse relationship. According to the resource curse hypothesis, greater dependence on oil usually leads to less democracy.

In reality, published research seldom involves a single independent variable and a single dependent variable. De Rugy's statistical regression model featured several independent variables and one dependent variable because she wanted to know which causes were most responsible for the outcome. Sides and Citrin considered a variety of influences on immigration attitudes among Europeans (see chapter 1). Other scholars might have a single independent variable and two or more dependent variables. Someone studying the Fukushima nuclear disaster might want to investigate how it affected public opinion toward nuclear energy in Japan, and how it affected the behavior of Japan's Atomic Energy Agency. As we add more variables, naturally our path/arrow diagrams will become more complex.

If you watch as much television as I do, you might remember a series of commercials for Direct TV. The ads start with a regular guy having trouble with his cable television company. Then his problems spin out of control. In one ad, his anger leads to an accident on a racquetball court that lands him in a hospital, where he gets an eye patch, which later triggers a confrontation with thugs on a bus, eventually leaving the guy facedown in a roadside ditch. The moral of the story is to switch from cable to Direct TV. I seem to be immune to this message, because all I see are **intervening variables**. Everything in this ad between the guy's anger with the cable company and his lying in a ditch qualifies as an intervening variable. These are the steps linking independent and dependent variables, and they are quite important in building a causal argument. "Why do we see variations in the value of *B*? Because of *A*. How? How does *A* lead to *B*?" Intervening variables help us figure out how, for example, huge reserves of oil, located deep underground, inhibit democracy. There must be some other steps along the way.[8]

Figure 3.1 illustrates a simple and a more complex way to diagram a causal argument. In both cases, the hypothetical objective is to explain why some people are more supportive than others of same-sex marriage. Support for same-sex marriage would be our dependent variable, and it could be measured at the ordinal level (maybe four values ranging from very supportive to very opposed) or at the ratio level (perhaps from 0 to 10). A simple version of this argument might focus only on education as the independent variable, and posit that more education leads to more support. That would be a direct relationship. The more complex version in this figure incorporates three independent variables—age, education, and religiosity. Our new hypotheses are that age and religiosity are both inversely related to our dependent variable, so that older people and those who attend religious services more often are less likely to support same-sex marriage. In addition, the more complex diagram introduces a couple of intervening variables to indicate how education might influence support for same-sex marriage. More education might lead to more tolerance in general, which could enhance support for same-sex marriage. More educated people might also have more daily interactions with "out" gays and lesbians (e.g., at work), which could boost their support for same-sex marriage. Most of these hypotheses would emerge from our literature review, and all would be, at this stage, educated guesses. We would still need to gather evidence for every hypothesis, that is, for every pair of variables connected by a causal arrow.

It would be easy to make figure 3.1 even more complicated by adding more independent variables (partisanship? income? race/ethnicity?) and more intervening variables. We could easily find any number of published studies in which political scientists have created more complex diagrams for their explanations than the ones shown here. Likewise, we could draw a diagram somewhere in between the two shown in this figure, perhaps with age and education as the independent variables and just one intervening variable. Our explanations could take on myriad forms.

There is no widely accepted standard for how simple or complex our causal explanations should be. Many political scientists believe that analytic "leverage" is a virtue; the best explanations use a few independent variables

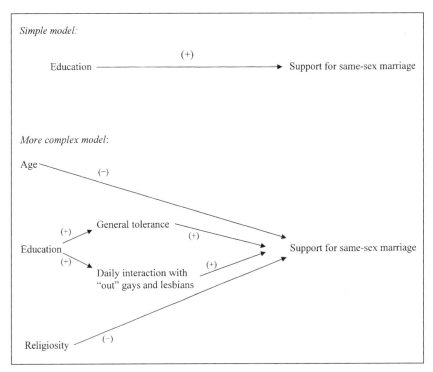

Figure 3.1. Diagramming a causal argument.

to explain much of the outcome.[9] If three factors account for one-half the variation in the dependent variable, focus on them and ignore all the lesser influences. Other scholars prefer their explanations to be more complete, even if that adds complexity. They don't want to settle for half the story. If we need to consider six, seven, eight influences on a given outcome, so be it. At some level, these differences reflect subjective judgments about the characteristics of a good explanation, which make those differences hard to resolve.

Practical considerations of time and space may force us to make choices. Students routinely tell me they plan to investigate all kinds of complicated, cause-and-effect relationships in their own research papers. While I may applaud their ambition, I will likely ask, "Really? In seven to eight pages? Before Thanksgiving?" For example, the more complex argument depicted in figure 3.1 would be very hard to analyze well under such constraints. Each arrow signifies a causal relationship, and we would need to provide good evidence for all six. That's going to take some work. Of course, we could finesse this problem by focusing on a few of these relationships, and calling on other researchers to help complete the argument. But we have to be mindful of promising more than we can deliver.

TESTING A CAUSAL HYPOTHESIS

Once we have identified one or more causal hypotheses worth investigating, we need some criteria for accepting or rejecting them. With descriptive hypotheses, we ask two questions, one about covariation and one about spuriousness, in order to figure out whether A and B are related (discussed in chapter 2). Determining whether A actually caused B would seem like a tougher chore, and it is. However, political scientists disagree over how much more work is required to establish a causal relationship.[10]

According to some scholars, a causal hypothesis of the form $A \rightarrow B$ will need to pass three tests. Researchers will need to establish covariation between the values of A and B. The pattern could be direct or inverse, and the degree of covariation will rarely if ever be perfect. The simplest way to flunk this test will be if A is a constant and B is a variable, or vice versa. Second, researchers should, as much as possible, demonstrate that their relationship is not spurious. And they will have to establish that A happens before B.[11] However, other scholars include a fourth test: researchers must identify a "credible causal mechanism" linking A and B.[12] These differences of opinion are important, but they should not be overstated. When defining causation, most political scientists would agree that "a cause raises the probability of an event occurring."[13]

Personally, I believe that four tests are required, and I will explain why in a minute. A number of political scientists (especially those who conduct experiments) favor three tests, and they have good reasons for doing so. From this perspective, a good explanation is one that provides a reliable guide to future action. We may not know the exact causal mechanism, but we can say with confidence that changes in A usually lead to changes in B. Moreover, that knowledge may enable us, as a society, to change B in desirable ways.

For many, many years, people understood that sunlight helps plants to grow. Even though they had no clue how photosynthesis works, they knew enough about sunlight to plant their crops. Had they refused to act until they fully understood the biological and chemical changes that translate sunlight into plant growth, they would have starved. In more recent times, psychiatrists have found that certain antidepressants seem to help people with obsessive-compulsive disorder (OCD). Doctors have prescribed the medicines without understanding exactly how these reduced the symptoms of OCD, other than having some effect on serotonin levels in the brain. For them, seeing a regular pattern of cause and effect was enough to justify a prescription.

One of the more famous experiments in political science was conducted during the New Haven, Connecticut, mayoral election of 1998.[14] The researchers, Alan Gerber and Donald Green, tested different ways of boosting voter turnout. One of their strongest findings was that face-to-face canvassing worked better than direct mail or phone calls. Personal contact was more effective than impersonal contact. The experimental design made Gerber and Green very confident that they had identified one influence on voter turnout. At the end of their article, they admitted they did not understand the mechanism(s) linking personal contact to turnout. They offered a few plausible suggestions, such as boosting voters' interest in politics or sense of obligation, but tested none of them. Still, the authors claimed their results were "of great practical significance for those who seek to reverse the declining trend in voter turnout."[15] In other words, someone didn't need to know how personal contact works in order to appreciate that it works.

In contrast, many social scientists believe that good explanations must also pass a fourth test—the identification of a credible causal mechanism.[16] Without this test, correlation would be established more than causation. Political scientists differ, however, on what counts as "credible." For some, a credible causal mechanism just has to sound reasonable (akin to establishing the face validity of measures, discussed in chapter 2). That was to some extent what Gerber and Green did in their study of voter turnout, and we will read more about experiments like theirs in the next chapter. Other scholars believe that causal mechanisms have to meet a higher standard. They need to be backed with empirical evidence. Informed speculation is not enough. Put simply, it's the difference between telling a dean that a prolonged illness might have been the cause of your lousy semester, and actually producing a note from a doctor who diagnosed you as having mononucleosis.

If we subject causal arguments to just three tests, we could end up accepting some pretty bizarre explanations. Those of you who follow professional football may have heard of a remarkable connection between the Washington Redskins and US presidential elections. If the Redskins win their last home game before Election Day, the party currently in the White House will stay in power. If the Redskins lose, the incumbent party will lose. Between 1940 and 2012, this pattern held true in seventeen out of nineteen presidential elections.[17] That's not a perfect record, but in the world of social science it is a very strong correlation. Spurious? Although the state of the economy or the partisan leanings of the electorate could be influencing the election results, it seems far-fetched to think they are also affecting the Redskins' offense. Or even their kicking game. I have tried and tried, and I can't think of a single factor that might be causing both the Redskins and a certain political party to win during a two-week period in the fall, every four years. Timing? Well, the key game is right before Election Day, so we aren't worried about the causal arrow pointing in the wrong direction. Three tests of causation taken, three tests passed. Thus, we can be confident that the Washington Redskins are helping to decide the outcome of presidential elections.

Except that's crazy.

There are, in fact, a large number of Incredible Coincidences in life and in politics. Between 1990 and 2009, the correlation between honey-producing bee colonies and juvenile arrests for possession of marijuana was almost perfectly inverse. Each year that bee colonies decreased by a certain increment, juvenile arrests increased by a similar increment. How about that. And did you know that the number of people who drowned after falling out of a fishing boat was almost perfectly and directly correlated with the marriage rate in Kentucky between 1999 and 2010?[18] The connection between the Redskins and presidential elections is yet another example. Incredible Coincidences can be funny, and they can be weird, but they don't qualify as causal relationships.

These examples are, of course, rather absurd. But even when we are working with more typical relationships, such as between natural resources and democracy, or public opinion and public policy, our explanations should include a causal mechanism. Otherwise, we are put in the awkward position of claiming that changes in our independent variable somehow, as if by magic, produce changes in our dependent variable. Political science, which is built on a foundation of empirical evidence, cannot rely on magic.

Consequently, when we ask why in politics, our answers should clear four hurdles, not three:

- covariation between values of the independent and dependent variables;
- careful checks for spuriousness;
- proper sequence of cause, then effect;
- credible causal mechanism(s).

We will need evidence to clear each hurdle; sometimes that will be simple, but many times not. The first two hurdles are the same ones we face when asking what happened (see chapter 2). The latter two are new and help us make the sizable jump from correlation to causation. Before we take a closer look at these additional hurdles, I want to expand briefly on the first two.

Even though we learned about covariation and spuriousness in chapter 2, the stakes are higher here. Descriptive generalizations simply require that *A* and *B* be related. Somehow. Causal generalizations, in contrast, imply responsibility. Changes in *A* may be responsible for changes in *B*. With that responsibility comes the potential for credit and blame. Things don't just happen; someone or something makes them happen. As a result, interested parties may take notice of our explanations. Our research will receive tougher scrutiny. So before we start pointing fingers at responsible parties, we would be smart to consider alternative explanations.

Imagine that you performed poorly for an entire semester at college, or for six months at a job. You were then summoned to meet with a dean or supervisor. Before you even had a chance to explain what happened, you were told, "I bet you're not the sharpest knife in the drawer." That would hurt. True, being dumb would explain your performance, but so would other (and less damning) factors. You would hope that this person might consider the possibility that falling ill, dealing with family problems, or being overwhelmed with other assignments was the main reason why you did a poor job. Likewise, before de Rugy started pointing fingers at Democratic officials, she probably should have looked harder to find alternative reasons for the allocation of stimulus dollars. I suspect this is why Silver suggested that her study was deliberately biased. Maybe once she found the answer she was looking for, she stopped asking questions.[19]

What de Rugy did next was commendable. She took Silver's criticisms seriously and analyzed the data again, incorporating several new independent variables. State capitals was one of them. And she published her results just a week later, which is lightning-fast by academic standards.[20] In this second version, de Rugy found that Democratic congressional districts still received more stimulus funding than Republican districts, although the gap was considerably smaller than the one she had reported to Congress. Two new variables, for state capitals and poverty, also mattered. Districts with state capitals received much more than other districts, which is what Silver had argued. Moreover, the positive relationship between poverty rates and stimulus funding meant that economic need did seem to have an influence; in the previous version, de Rugy tested the impact of unemployment and found little relationship with the allocation of aid. Finally, it's clear from her statistical analysis that the partisan makeup of the district had a relatively modest impact compared with other factors, such as whether it was a state capital. Her newer model, by the way, accounted for much more of the variation in stimulus funding than had her original model. These improvements, however, meant that de Rugy could no longer tell such a simple story about partisan influence.

At first glance, the search for spurious relationships seems never-ending. We may always be left wondering what else is out there that could be affecting our relationships. That dose of humility and caution mentioned in the previous chapter applies here as well. Nevertheless, we might be able to winnow down the number of unseen variables that could create trouble. Because we are now trying to establish causal relationships, we need only worry about variables that occur before our dependent variable(s), and that have a credible causal connection. If we were trying to describe the factors associated with support for same-sex marriage, I suppose the list could include how often people play miniature golf. To explain that support, however, we can strike miniature golf from the list, because no credible causal mechanism exists. We can strike many, many variables from the list on the same grounds. This is one reason why the four hurdles mentioned above are not ordered 1, 2, 3, 4. In practice, we might start testing explanations by looking for causal mechanisms or the right sequence of cause and effect even before we looked for covariation.[21]

To see the process of testing causal hypotheses at work, try reading one of the more important studies of the resource curse, "Does Oil Hinder Democracy?" by Michael Ross.[22] This article is challenging, because Ross employs statistical techniques that most undergraduates (and perhaps some of their teachers) haven't been trained to use. His general approach, though, is pretty straightforward. A central question he poses is whether oil has a causal relationship with democracy, even after other influences are factored in that could be important. In addition to oil, Ross considered the influence of other minerals, Islam, income, geography (measured a couple of ways), and prior history of democracy. Although this list was certainly incomplete—he did not consider who owned the oil, for example—Ross did include several likely suspects. He wasn't hunting blindly for Incredible Coincidences; he tested only those variables which might reasonably influence the level of democracy in a country. To make his list, each variable had to come with a credible causal mechanism.

For each of his independent variables, Ross had a clear set of expectations: "if A indeed causes B, then we should be able to observe . . ." Building off previous studies (i.e., the lit review), we would expect oil, other minerals, and Islam all to have inverse relationships with democracy. Income and prior history of democracy, however, should be directly related with democracy. Ross's statistical analysis found that all these factors covaried with democracy in the expected directions. He also suspected that oil would exert a negative influence on democracy, even after controlling for other relevant variables. That turned out to be true, which makes us more confident that the relationship is not spurious. Finally, Ross expected that this relationship would hold not just in the Middle East and Africa, which were the usual focus regions of the resource curse literature, but around the world. It did hold, based on evidence from over one hundred countries. (Ross did even more to test his causal hypotheses, which I discuss below.)

For an example that avoids highfalutin statistics, take a look at Robert Putnam's explanation for the decline of civic engagement in the United States during the second half of the twentieth century.[23] Putnam considered a number of potential causes and used the same approach as Ross: if *A* truly leads to *B*, then what should we be able to observe? Residential mobility was one possibility that Putnam considered. Maybe Americans were moving more often and thus less able or inclined to become involved with their communities. That would be a credible causal mechanism, and we would expect the relationship to be inverse. However, data from the US Census Bureau revealed that Americans were a little less likely to move in the 1990s, when civic engagement was lower, than in the 1950s, when engagement was higher. Because the independent and dependent variables did not vary in the expected direction, Putnam ruled out residential mobility as a cause.*

Growth of the welfare state was another possible cause. That growth might have diminished the need for ordinary citizens to become involved in their communities. If government is taking care of the sick, the poor, the hungry, and the homeless, then the rest of us can just worry about ourselves. If that were true, Putnam reasoned, then we ought to see a clear pattern in which American states with larger budgets for social welfare had lower levels of civic engagement, while states with smaller budgets had more engagement. Putnam found no clear pattern, direct or inverse, between these variables at the state level. He tried a second approach, comparing the United States to other affluent democracies. If anything, the evidence indicated that larger welfare states had more civic engagement, not less. He then eliminated growth of the welfare state as a cause. Putnam was engaged in falsification, trying to move us closer to a good explanation by ruling out plausible alternatives. For both residential mobility and growth of the welfare state,

---

*Thus, the process of creating and testing hypotheses often involves a combination of inductive reasoning and deductive reasoning.

CHAPTER THREE

the decisive test was whether these independent variables covaried in the expected direction with civic engagement, his dependent variable.*

The new tests discussed in this chapter involve causal sequence and causal mechanism. Many times, it will be fairly easy to figure out whether our independent variable *A* truly happened before some dependent variable *B*. If we are trying to explain the outcome of a process, such as enactment of a law or treaty, we would expect the influences to appear before the law or treaty took effect. Any public official who voiced support only after enactment would not normally be viewed as a causal influence. A more extended process might incorporate some type of feedback loop. An interest group could push for passage of a law at one point in time, and its enactment could boost the power of that group later on, which might then enable the group to preserve the law it originally fought to enact. In that scenario, we would carefully trace out the initial sequence of cause and effect, with effect later turning into a cause. In general, we would think like historians or detectives and pay close attention to exactly who did what, and when.

Alternatively, if we are comparing cases at a single moment in time, such as an opinion survey, we might include independent variables that could not possibly be caused by the dependent variable. The hypothetical explanation in figure 3.1 features age as one independent variable, and it would be hard to imagine how support for same-sex marriage might cause someone to become younger or older. The causal arrow would have to point in just one direction. When Sides and Citrin examined attitudes toward immigrants in Europe, one of their independent variables was gender. Whether a man prefers more or less immigration will not change him from a man into a woman. Some statistical techniques, such as the use of time-lagged variables, may also help us to distinguish cause from effect.

However, there will be times when the direction of the causal arrow is ambiguous. Returning to figure 3.1, the connection between education and general tolerance raises an important question: does more education make people more tolerant, which is how the path diagram currently reads, or do more tolerant people seek out more education? We could imagine the arrow pointing in either direction, and maybe even both, which means we might need evidence for more than one direction. A researcher (or reader)

---

*Readers familiar with the TV medical drama *House* will recognize this process. Faced with a difficult case, Dr. House considers a number of possible diagnoses. Each one comes with a certain set of classic symptoms. If the patient does not exhibit most or all of these symptoms, then the diagnosis is ruled out.

shouldn't blithely assume that the only possible relationship is more education causing more tolerance.[24] Another example would be foreign aid. Some studies have found that foreign aid boosts economic growth in the recipient country. That sounds hopeful. Yet other studies suggest that economic growth enhances the odds that a country will receive aid in the first place; donors prefer to bet on good performers.[25] The impact of that aid depends in part on which way the causal arrow is pointing. Neither of these debates is purely academic. We can imagine a whole host of governments and nongovernmental organizations that would want to promote tolerance or economic development. To do so, they would need to know which factors cause tolerance and development and which are caused by them.

In everyday conversation, we call this the chicken-and-egg problem (as in "Which came first . . . ?"). Political scientists, especially those with a statistical bent, call it **endogeneity**. In our line of work, endogeneity ranks right up there with spuriousness as a Big Problem That Can Mess Up Your Research. In a causal argument, an **endogenous variable** is one whose value is influenced by other variables in the overall model. The values of **exogenous variables**, on the other hand, are determined by factors outside the model. In figure 3.1, we have a model that might explain why some people are more supportive than others of same-sex marriage. Here, age would be an exogenous variable. Nothing connected to education, religiosity, or support for same-sex marriage will trigger changes in someone's age (nothing, that is, this side of science fiction). Support for same-sex marriage in this model would be an endogenous variable. Education and general tolerance, as I suggested earlier, could conceivably be exogenous or endogenous. We would need to devise some tests to determine which came first. If we suspected that causation ran both ways, we could amend our path diagram by adding an arrow leading from tolerance to education. All this means, of course, is that as we add independent and intervening variables to our causal hypotheses— whether they involve same-sex marriage, democratization, the allocation of federal aid, or any other topic—and as we sort out the direction of cause and effect, we increase the number of connections that must be tested and verified. That reality affects us as builders and as inspectors of arguments.*

The last hurdle for explanations involves causal mechanisms. As John

---

* The problem of endogeneity is not limited to politics. In many sports, it's not hard to find reserves whose playing time correlates directly with their team's success. Before we credit those bit players with leading their team to victory, we might ask whether they enter the game only after the starting players have secured a large lead. The reserves may be playing because their team is winning, and not vice versa. Similarly, Grammy Award–

Gerring points out, social scientists have become quite enamored with causal mechanisms in recent years—so enamored that they may not have noticed the multiple and sometimes conflicting meanings of this concept.[26] Resolving these differences is beyond the scope of this book. For now, the main question that needs to be asked is, how? How do changes in my independent variable, over here, routinely lead to changes in my dependent variable, over there? In essence, we are asking about intervening variables and the links that connect them to our independent and dependent variables.

Medical researchers grapple with the How question all the time. For instance, doctors have suspected for years that chronic stress increases the chances of a heart attack or stroke, but they haven't known exactly how stress affects the body. One recent study points to white blood cells as a key link in the causal chain. Chronic stress may cause the body to produce more of the hormone noradrenaline, which then binds to the surface of a specific protein located in the bone marrow. That change seems to trigger an increase in the production of white blood cells. When too many of these cells circulate through the body, they can cause inflammation in the blood vessels. When that happens, fatty plaques may break loose from the vessel walls and cause blockages of blood flow to the heart or brain. Not good.[27] (And yes, this whole sequence does sound remarkably like the ad connecting a regular guy's anger with his cable TV provider to his winding up facedown in a ditch.) Knowing the full causal chain and causal mechanisms could enable researchers to develop drugs that would break the chain and thus reduce the number of heart attacks and strokes. Without this knowledge, doctors are left telling people to reduce the stress in their lives, which would certainly be helpful, but may be less feasible than taking a daily pill.

When Ross analyzed the negative impact of oil on democracy, he considered at least three possible causal mechanisms. In one, countries that are rich in natural resources might be able to finance their governments without imposing significant taxes on the general population. People who are taxed lightly might not expect their government to be accountable or transparent. They might not push hard for democratic institutions. Ross found evidence for this mechanism; he didn't merely offer it as a possibility. As mentioned in chapter 1, Luong and Weinthal believe that government ownership and control of oil, not the oil itself, lead to problems in the economy and the government. In their view, the path leading from point A to point B goes through the government's fiscal policies, including its choice of taxes. Their

---

winning singers might owe their success to great songwriters, or their success might lead others to write great songs for them.

mechanism thus bears some resemblance to the one Ross tested. Ross also examined whether substantial resource wealth may enable governments to finance a repressive military that periodically cracks down on anyone who calls for democratic reforms. That is a very different kind of mechanism and it, too, seemed consistent with his data.[28]

The hypothetical example in figure 3.1 suggests that greater levels of education could boost general tolerance, which would then lead to more support for same-sex marriage. To offer a complete explanation, we would still need to determine how education fosters tolerance. Now we face two challenges. First, we need to operationalize the concept of tolerance, which raises issues of concepts and measures we encountered in chapter 2. Intervening variables can be just as abstract and challenging to work with as our independent and dependent variables. Second, we need to identify the causal mechanism(s). Do certain courses in high school or college consciously promote tolerance? Do certain assignments, such as arguing for and against a given position, make students more open-minded? Maybe the general college experience exposes individuals to a wide variety of people, which challenges their old stereotypes and prejudices. Surely other pathways are possible.

In my judgment, de Rugy's study of stimulus funding is lacking in the causal mechanism department. She can't really tell us how districts represented by Democrats managed to receive so much more money than districts represented by Republicans. She didn't have records of any meetings in which congressional Democrats agreed to shortchange their Republican rivals. She didn't mention whether state-level Democratic officials lobbied hard for relief. Nor did she interview congressional leaders or members of the Obama administration to inquire about their intent. None of those options may have been feasible. Still, without some sort of credible causal mechanism, what de Rugy found may not qualify as an Incredible Coincidence, on a par with the Redskins and presidential elections, but it might be closer to a Provocative Correlation than a Genuine Explanation. And a Provocative Correlation could simply be masking a spurious relationship. We will come back to this issue in the next chapter when we talk about the strengths and limitations of different research designs. In general, statistical comparisons like hers can have trouble pinpointing a causal mechanism.

Several months after the contretemps between de Rugy and Silver, two political scientists from Georgia State University provided more insight into the causal mechanisms.[29] Looking back at the written record, Jason Reifler and Jeffrey Lazarus found that congressional Republicans were generally opposed to the spending side of the stimulus bill. They much preferred tax cuts, which were included in the stimulus but—and this is important—were excluded from de Rugy's analysis. Thus, it makes sense that Democrats had a lot of input into the design of the spending portion of the stimulus, and that Democrats figured prominently in de Rugy's analysis. In addition, a careful reading of the bill revealed that it directed spending toward certain policies such as health care and K–12 education, which Democrats often support. What's more, many major health care facilities and large public school systems are located in urban areas that tend to elect Democrats to Congress. Aha. Now we understand better how political parties influenced the allocation of stimulus monies, and the explanation doesn't seem quite as underhanded or sinister.

By this point, your mental checklist for building and inspecting causal arguments should include several items. The independent and dependent variables always need to be identified, with a clear direction to their relationship. Determining the validity of that relationship requires four separate tests. Passing two of those tests, covariation and spuriousness, is enough to establish correlation but not causation. To prove the latter, we must also test for causal sequence and causal mechanisms. Those tests will help us understand how some influence A led to some outcome B. When testing for causal mechanisms, we will have to decide how much evidence is required to prove that one is truly "credible." However we decide, we should keep an eye out for one or more intervening variables.

PREPARING FOR CAUSAL COMPLEXITY

Some people gravitate toward simple stories of cause and effect. They want to find the one food or one pill that will help them lose thirty pounds quickly. They want to know the three easy steps to becoming a millionaire. They believe that Soviet communism collapsed because of Ronald Reagan. They insist that the country's domestic problems would largely disappear as soon as illegal immigration was stopped. They blame Yoko Ono for breaking up the Beatles.

By and large, political scientists aren't these kinds of people. Their explanations seldom boil down to a single cause. They are fully willing to believe that patterns of political behavior have multiple causes, and that the connections between cause and effect will often be elusive or complicated. However, few political scientists would maintain that everything is equally connected to everything else, making the number of potential causes almost infinite. They tend to believe that some causes will be more important than others, and that collectively researchers need to figure out which ones matter the most. Even if only one cause emerged from their research, they would usually concede that other factors, which they had not yet examined, might also contribute to the outcome in question.[30]

As we test causal hypotheses, we should therefore be prepared for answers more complicated than $A \to B$. When Ross analyzed the impact of oil on democracy, he found that oil did have a negative effect, controlling for other possible causes. He also found that several of those other causes mattered as well, controlling for oil. More income in a country was associated with greater levels of democracy. Putnam's explanation for the decline in civic engagement put most of the blame on television. In addition, he felt that rising divorce rates "were an accessory to the crime, but not the major villain."[31] And he remained open to the possibility that greater female participation in the labor force could have contributed to the decline. To me, Putnam's ability to rule out some causes and then rank the remaining ones in rough order of importance is a pretty good model to keep in mind when conducting your own research.

The complications go beyond having two or more distinct causes. It is quite possible that interactions among our independent variables will be important. Sunlight helps plants grow—as long as those plants also receive a certain amount of water. Without water, or with just a tiny amount, it doesn't matter how much sun most plants get; they're going to shrivel up and die.[32] The impact of sunlight on plant growth thus depends partly on water. In the hypothetical example of support for same-sex marriage, more education might foster greater support, but its impact could be conditioned by gender. Going to college might have a bigger impact on men than women if, say, men entered college with more stereotypes and prejudices.[33] Sides and Citrin found that the interaction of identities and information exerted a significant influence on attitudes toward immigration in Europe. Instead of a simple $A \to B$ relationship, we have something that looks like this:

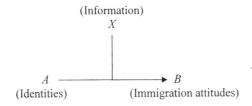

Interactions like these are common in politics, which means that the explanations we read and build on our own may be context specific. When Ellen Immergut tried to explain differences in health policy across three European countries, she found that the interaction of the medical profession with institutional design was decisive. Doctors were better able to block national health insurance in Switzerland than in France or Sweden, because Switzerland had substantial "veto points" built into its political system. In particular, Swiss doctors relied on public referenda, which are unusually common in their country, to minimize the scope of government involvement. Through referenda, they could overturn or threaten to overturn any major expansion of government involvement that had been endorsed by Swiss officials. Doctors in Sweden, by contrast, operated in a political system with fewer veto points. When elected officials there proposed greater government involvement in health care, doctors had more difficulty stopping them. Doctors in France operated in a system where the veto points were more powerful than in Sweden but less so than in Switzerland. Thus, the power of doctors depended on the political context in which they operated.[34] As you can imagine, interactions such as these will motivate researchers to qualify their causal arguments. *A* may lead to *B*, but the effect could be larger for some cases than others.

An equally vexing problem, analytically, is when multiple and often distinct paths lead to the same outcome. In other words, different combinations of independent and intervening variables could have similar effects on the same dependent variable. The formal name for this state of affairs is **equifinality**.[35] We see this problem in everyday life. While some sports teams are successful because they sign or trade for established stars, other teams do just as well by drafting and grooming young talent. Some college students could fail two courses in a semester because they were battling a chronic illness, while a different group of students could fail two courses because of serious problems at home (e.g., parents divorcing). These factors need not interact in order to be powerful. If a college wanted to help these students, it would need to be aware of both causal paths. Taking steps to reduce the spread of mononucleosis on campus wouldn't help students who needed counseling services.

Equifinality can occur in politics, too. In their study of war termination, Elizabeth Stanley and John Sawyer discuss two different causal paths. The first is the one most scholars recognize: "Interstate wars can only end once all belligerents develop similar expectations about the war."[36] Typically, this happens when a power imbalance develops between the combatants, and the outcome of continued fighting becomes clear. In other words, at least one incumbent leader has to change his mind about the benefits of continued fighting. The authors propose a second causal path based on changes in leadership during a war, what they call a domestic coalition shift. Such a shift might result from a coup, a death, or an election. They tested these two theories, using some fairly sophisticated statistical techniques, with evidence from twenty-seven wars since World War II, involving seventy-eight separate countries. Long story short, Stanley and Sawyer found that a power imbalance did help to shorten the length of wars, as most scholars would expect. The best-known causal path was the most common path. Domestic coalition shifts during wartime had a similar, albeit smaller effect, meaning there was a second causal path. The more general lesson here is that simply because we manage to identify one causal path that leads to a given political outcome, we can't assume that we have found the only path.

USING EXPLANATIONS TO MAKE PREDICTIONS

Compared to philosophy and mathematics, political science is a relatively young discipline. Its age is better measured in decades, not centuries. Nonetheless, political scientists have been researching and writing for a long time, and much of that effort has been directed toward building better explanations. One would think, by this point, that some of these explanations should be well established. Some pieces of conventional wisdom should explain how certain factors lead to a certain political outcome—not always, but often.

Understanding why things happen could enable us to make some intelligent forecasts of what will happen. We might be able to predict the future. To the rest of the world, this is where academic research becomes relevant, interesting, maybe even important. Reporters start asking us who will win the next election. Investors want to know which countries are most likely to be politically unstable in the coming years. Government officials want help figuring out where the next terrorist attack will come from. For once, political scientists truly feel wanted.

The reality is that most political scientists hesitate to predict the future. Or at least, they hesitate to predict outcomes. They might predict some process; those tend to change pretty slowly. For example, although political scientists might not predict which American states will be the next ones to raise the minimum wage, they might predict that party politics will be decisive. (Which, when you think about it, doesn't exactly qualify as a bold forecast.) There are exceptions. Some political scientists do forecast elections, picking not only the winners but also the winning margin.[37] Organizations as diverse as the US Department of Defense and the Peace Research Institute Oslo (Norway) devote considerable energies trying to predict future conflicts around the world. For the most part, though, political scientists do not believe that predicting outcomes is part of their job.

Predicting the future seems a bit disreputable, because any fool can make good predictions. Imagine that you were living in the United States in the fall of 2000. At the annual meeting of the American Political Science Association that September, several scholars had predicted the outcome of the upcoming presidential election, and all of them said that Al Gore would win the White House. Their statistical models gave the popular vote to Gore, with anywhere from 52.8 to 60.3 percent of the two-party vote—more than enough to win the Electoral College.[38] But you had a special gift for forecasting. Once the Washington Redskins lost their home game versus the Tennessee Titans on October 30, you were positive that George W. Bush would take the White House. Your prediction was based on a pattern that has held true in every election since 1940. And you would have been right, and those esteemed political scientists would have been wrong—proof that good predictions can emerge from Incredible Coincidences. Or, imagine a local meteorologist who predicted that a major storm was imminent because the barometric pressure was dropping, but who couldn't explain how or why changes to his barometer were related to changes in the weather. This relationship is no coincidence, and we would expect a professional weather forecaster to understand each step in the causal path. In short, while someone can predict what will happen without knowing why, most political scientists really want a good explanation.

Predicting the future seems somewhat hopeless considering the state of our explanations. Many of them, in a statistical sense, account for only a fraction of the total variation in the dependent variable. The analysis that de Rugy submitted to Congress accounted for less than 5 percent of the variation in the allocation of stimulus monies. Other, more accepted explanations might account for a quarter or a third of the variation in some political pattern. In many cases, much of the outcome is produced by systematic factors we don't understand, or by random chance. When we know so little, it's hard to make good predictions. Other explanations in politics depend on interactions among variables, making them highly contingent: "X may happen soon, as long as the value of factor A goes up at the same time that C goes down, the values of D and E increase together, and factor G remains more or less constant." This problem probably explains why so few political scientists predicted the collapse of Soviet communism or the coming of the Arab Spring, two developments of enormous import.[39] And the threat of equifinality means that we may think that only one combination of variables could lead to a given outcome when it fact two, three, or more combinations could produce the same result.

Predicting the future also seems hopeless because of human nature. The audience for our predictions often wants to know the outcome of specific events, yet our explanations are designed for general patterns. If an explanation fails to generate an accurate prediction on the first try, people might discard it too quickly. Furthermore, the act of making a prediction public may lead key actors to change their behavior. If someone predicted that the next terrorist attack on the United States would originate from Yemen, certain well-armed individuals might move from Yemen to a different country. If someone predicted that Rep. Eileen Pharr-Wright would lose her next election, she and her supporters might redouble their efforts to win. Scientists who predict solar and lunar eclipses don't have this problem.*

Given these difficulties, political scientists are much more comfortable predicting the past. In fact, we do this all the time. To outsiders, this may sound like cheating, but political scientists define the verb *predict* in two ways. It can mean "to forecast the future," which is how most people think of predictions. It can also mean "to declare in advance." When political scientists test hypotheses, they declare in advance what they expect to find. If hypothesis *X* is true, then it would predict the following results. For instance, a literature review might establish that economic factors often influence US elections, based on evidence from 1960 to 2000, and then predict that economics were also important in the 2008 election, which has already happened. The idea would be to extend an existing theory to cover a new case or cases. A different literature review might introduce two competing explanations for the causes of civil war, and then trace out what each explanation would predict to occur in a particular set of civil wars that have already started (and may have ended). One advantage of predicting the past is that we can evaluate the accuracy of those predictions right away. When someone predicts the future, it might take awhile before we know if she was correct.

It could be inferred from this discussion that political scientists should never try to predict the future, or that readers should always dismiss such predictions. I don't believe this is the right approach. Predictions could be quite useful to society at large, and they offer one way to test our explanations. The advice here, once again, is to proceed with a healthy dose of humility and skepticism. At a minimum, credible causal mechanisms ought to be evident, and predictions about the future should come with some measure of confidence. In other words, an election forecaster might predict that candidate *X* will win the upcoming election, and state that he is 70 percent

---

* So, while political analysis might not be as complicated as brain surgery, it can be harder than astrophysics.

sure of that prediction. Or an analyst might predict that country *Z* has a small chance of experiencing a civil war in the next five years, but its chances are greater than for most other countries. These kinds of statements help convey a degree of uncertainty, which is appropriate for predictions about politics.

Part I of this guide is designed to help readers ask good questions about politics. Curiosity certainly helps, but much more is needed. By now you should have the beginnings of a thorough checklist, one geared toward asking three fundamental questions—Who cares? What happened? and Why?—intelligently and systematically. As the many and varied examples demonstrate, these questions are asked by specialists in comparative politics, American politics, international relations, and public policy. In part II of this guide, we move from questions to answers. Chapters 4 and 5 will introduce alternative research designs and alternative methods of picking cases to analyze. Readers hoping to find the One Right Way will be disappointed. My view is that all research designs and all case selection methods have their advantages and disadvantages. In chapters 6 and 7, we will look carefully at the main kinds of evidence, words and numbers, used by political scientists. No matter how elegantly we design a research project, a shortage of high-quality evidence will undermine our efforts.

PRACTICE: INSPECTING

1. The following articles and chapters cover a wide range of subjects, and you might not be deeply familiar with any of them. Some rely heavily on statistical evidence and some do not. Nevertheless, you can still identify the independent, dependent, and any intervening variables, and indicate whether the relationships among them are direct or inverse. And you can evaluate the main strengths and weaknesses of their causal arguments. In other words, how well does each one clear the four hurdles discussed in this chapter? (Note: if you want to reinforce lessons from chapters 1 and 2, you can also describe how this research builds on past studies, and analyze how key concepts are measured.)

    Alan Abramowitz, "Forecasting in a Polarized Era: The Time for Change Model and the 2012 Presidential Election," *PS: Political Science and Politics* 45, no. 4 (October 2012): 618–19;

    Frank R. Baumgartner and Bryan D. Jones, *Agendas and Instability in American Politics* (Chicago: University of Chicago Press, 1993), chapter 4 (regarding nuclear power);

    Stephen Biddle, Jeffrey A. Friedman, and Jacob N. Shapiro, "Testing the Surge: Why Did Violence Decline in Iraq in 2007?," *International Security* 37, no. 1 (Summer 2012): 7–40;

Dara Kay Cohen, "Explaining Rape during Civil War: Cross-National Evidence (1980–2009)," *American Political Science Review* 107, no. 3 (August 2013): 461–77;

Omar G. Encarnación, "International Influence, Domestic Activism, and Gay Rights in Argentina," *Political Science Quarterly* 128, no. 4 (Winter 2013/2014): 687–716;

Michael C. Horowitz and Allan C. Stam, "How Prior Military Experience Influences the Future Militarized Behavior of Leaders," *International Organization* 68, no. 3 (June 2014): 527–59;

Ellen M. Immergut, "The Rules of the Game: The Logic of Health Policy-Making in France, Switzerland, and Sweden," in *Structuring Politics: Historical Institutionalism in Comparative Analysis*, ed. Sven Steinmo, Kathleen Thelen, and Frank Longstreth (New York: Cambridge University Press, 1992), pp. 57–89 (this is a much-condensed version of the book by Immergut mentioned in this chapter);

Cindy D. Kam, "Risk Attitudes and Political Participation," *American Journal of Political Science* 56, no. 4 (October 2012): 817–36;

Robert D. Putnam, "Tuning in, Tuning Out: The Strange Disappearance of Social Capital in America," *PS: Political Science and Politics* 28, no. 4 (December 1995): 664–83. A shorter version of this article appeared as "The Strange Disappearance of Civic America," *American Prospect* 24 (Winter 1996): 34–48;

Michael Ross, "Does Oil Hinder Democracy?," *World Politics* 53 (April 2001): 325–61.

PRACTICE: BUILDING

1. Translate each of these path/arrow diagrams into three or four sentences of plain English:

(a)

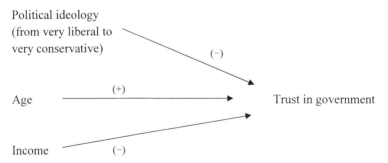

(b)

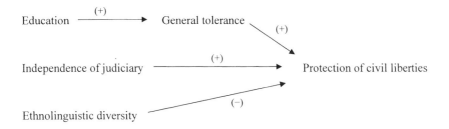

2. Create a path/arrow diagram for each of the following causal arguments:
   (a) "The model that we develop of the process by which citizens come to
   be active in politics is similarly comprehensive. . . . Our conception of the
   participatory process rests upon two main factors: the <u>motivation</u> and
   the <u>capacity</u> to take part in political life. . . . We consider a third factor as
   well. Those who have both the motivation and the capacity to become
   active are more likely to do so if they are asked. Therefore, we consider
   the <u>networks of recruitment</u> through which requests for political activity
   are mediated." Source: Sidney Verba, Kay Lehman Schlozman, and
   Henry E. Brady, *Voice and Equality: Civic Voluntarism in American Politics*
   (Cambridge, MA: Harvard University Press, 1995), p. 3.
   (b) "In this paper, we argue that the greater accountability of democratic
   leaders to their citizens creates powerful pressures on leaders to reduce
   the human costs of war. In an analysis of a new dataset of fatalities in
   interstate wars (1900 to 2005) we find that highly democratic states
   suffer significantly fewer military and civilian fatalities. We argue that
   democracies limit their war losses primarily by adopting four specific
   foreign and military policies. First, democracies generate higher military
   capabilities than nondemocracies in times of war. Second, democracies
   are more likely to augment their national capabilities by joining more
   powerful coalitions of states during war. Third, democracies are more
   likely than other states to utilize battlefield military strategies that
   minimize their fatalities. Finally, democracies are more likely to fight
   wars on battlefields that are not contiguous to their home territories,
   thereby shielding their civilian populations from the fighting." Source:
   abstract of Benjamin A. Valentino, Paul K. Huth, and Sarah E. Croco, "Bear
   Any Burden? How Democracies Minimize the Costs of War," *Journal of
   Politics* 72, no. 2 (April 2010): 528–44.

3. For each of the following pairs of independent and dependent variables, suggest a plausible causal path with one or more intervening variables (the first one is done for you). In every case, assume that the independent variable is directly related to the dependent variable:

Independent variable	Intervening variable(s)	Dependent variable
Income	*Perceived stake in outcome; free time*	Voter turnout
Age		Political knowledge
Education level		Support for the United Nations
Power of organized labor		Size of welfare state
Number of languages in country (spoken by >1000 people)		Chances of civil war
Extent of democracy		Level of economic development
Level of economic development		Extent of democracy

PART TWO

GENERATING GOOD ANSWERS

4

CHOOSING A RESEARCH DESIGN

In the introduction to this guide, I offered the metaphors of the home inspector and the home builder, and I compared the research design for a piece of political analysis to blueprints for a house. The parallels hold true up to a point. Homes often require multiple blueprints for the exterior frame, the electrical system, and the plumbing. Typically, different specialists are then hired to put up the walls and roof, wire the entire house, and install the pipes needed for water and sewage. Building a house requires a team effort. Political scientists work in a similar fashion to the extent that each researcher tends to specialize in a particular design. Some of them are quite skilled at running experiments. Others are adept at statistical comparisons or detailed case studies. Some researchers can execute two designs, much as some contractors can handle the electrical and plumbing systems. Once in a great while you hear about someone who can build an entire house by himself, or a political scientist who has mastered multiple designs. Most times, though, solving a political puzzle requires teamwork and a division of labor.

Home builders and political scientists both work under practical constraints. They don't enjoy unlimited budgets, which means they can't afford perfection. In many instances they will need to make trade-offs between what they would love to accomplish and what they can accomplish. The physical contours of the lot or the standards of the neighborhood may rule out some home designs, much as certain political puzzles may not lend themselves to every possible research design. Moreover, the size of the final product—a journal article, a chapter, a book, or a house—is determined largely by what others will accept or pay for.

Those are the similarities. However, unlike home building, political science lacks a single architect or an authoritative general contractor. No one is in charge. Nor are definitive blueprints available for the study of the democratic peace, the resource curse, the American welfare state, voter turnout, or any other political puzzle. Instead, different researchers harbor distinct and often competing visions for the final product (and some may have no vision at all). The irony is that power and authority are two of the most fundamental concepts in political science, and yet no one is responsible for organizing our research. No one. The lack of top-down control could lead to some truly original insights; it could also produce redundancy, gaping holes, and a certain measure of chaos. Another basic difference between home building and political science concerns the professional egos of those involved. Rarely would a plumber insist that plumbing is by far the most important element of a house—that all a good home needs is a sink, a tub, and a couple of toilets. By contrast, some political scientists believe that their research design is clearly the best way to solve political puzzles. If you encounter one of these True Believers, my advice is to imagine how it would feel to live in a house with terrific indoor plumbing and nothing else.

In this chapter, I adopt more of a live-and-let-live attitude toward research design. (The fancy name for this stance is methodological pluralism.) No single design is likely to produce a complete answer to any significant question about politics. Different research designs have characteristic strengths and weaknesses. Consequently, a good portion of this chapter will be devoted to highlighting the pros and cons of the most common designs. Fortunately, the strengths of one design can often help compensate for the weaknesses of another.

Despite their differences, all these designs rely on comparisons. This is perhaps the most important way that political scientists acquire knowledge: we compare. When we work with descriptive or causal hypotheses, we analyze relationships between two or more variables. We figure out whether these variables covary, which means comparing the values of one with the values of the other. To check for spuriousness, we see if our initial relationship between *A* and *B* still holds true after controlling for other variables. Questions about causal sequence and causal mechanisms require comparisons over time. Periodically, we compare the results of our analysis with previous studies of the same or a similar question. Even the authors of single case studies find ways to make comparisons. With apologies to Julius Caesar, political scientists live by the motto *veni, vidi, compari* (I came, I saw, I compared).[1]

CHARACTERISTICS OF A GOOD RESEARCH DESIGN

At the risk of stating the obvious, we want to select a research design that helps us answer the Who Cares, What Happened, and Why questions. Traditional textbooks tell us to pick a design that maximizes the internal validity and external validity of our study, which sounds like a different piece of advice but really isn't.[2] A research design with high levels of **internal validity** gives us confidence that the results are accurate and true for the case(s) under study. In other words, internal validity refers to our ability to figure

CHAPTER FOUR

out what happened, why, or both. If the relationship between *A* and *B* is descriptive, then we would need to be confident that the values of *A* and *B* covary, and that we can rule out confounding variables. If our hypothesis is causal, then an internally valid design allows us to clear the four hurdles discussed in the previous chapter, including causal order and causal mechanism.

Imagine that we were analyzing the relationship between gun ownership and crime in the American states. Simply as a descriptive proposition, this relationship would be hard to believe if crime were measured by the number of arrests for shoplifting and excluded violent crimes. Likewise, our audience would be skeptical of any alleged relationship if we failed to control for other, potentially relevant factors such as poverty rates or the number of police officers in each state. A causal relationship, perhaps stating that wider gun ownership led to fewer crimes, would be hard to believe if based on evidence from one state in a single year. A better design might track a state over many years, allowing us to see changes in the values of our key variables and to figure out whether an increase in gun ownership preceded a drop in the crime rate. Or, we might track all fifty states over many years, making comparisons across states and over time. Either way, we'd also need to show how more guns led to less crime. For example, do we have evidence that would-be criminals worry more about being shot by their victims, and therefore initiate fewer crimes, when guns are more widely available?

External validity refers to our ability to extend the findings to some larger population of cases. The results would hold true outside the confines of our particular study. In a sense, external validity is related to the Who Cares / So What questions raised in chapter 1. One common way of establishing the larger significance of a study is to claim that the findings can be extended to additional cases. When Robert Putnam wrote about the performance of regional governments in Italy (first discussed in chapter 1), he claimed that governments all over the world faced similar challenges. Understand why Emilia-Romagna is working so well, he implied, and you may be able to help Cairo and Moscow.[3] Returning to the example of guns and crime, a historical case study of a fairly typical state like Ohio might have more external validity than one focused on a highly unusual state like Alaska. We might reasonably infer that what happened in Ohio also happened in other states. External validity is all about making inferences, with confidence, but those inferences need not be limited to additional countries, states, or cities. A well-designed study of attitudes toward gender equality might apply just as well to attitudes toward racial equality. A study analyzing the organization of labor strikes might also apply to social movements.

Most political scientists believe that trade-offs exist between internal and external validity. A lab experiment could be well designed to promote internal validity. We might come away from the experiment convinced that changes to an independent variable triggered changes in the dependent variable. However, ensuring internal validity might require so many artificial conditions that we doubt the results would hold true in the real world of politics. Medical researchers face this problem all the time. They might demonstrate that a new drug managed to kill cancer cells in one-third of the mice they tested. But they are unsure whether that same drug would work equally well in human beings. Internal validity, yes; external validity, who knows? By the same token, a large-scale study of the resource curse, covering many countries and many years, might be based on so many cases that we feel confident about its external validity. Yet that same study could test a relatively small number of hypotheses, depending on what comparable data can be collected from every case. Key variables might be omitted from the study, calling into question its internal validity.[4]

This isn't the only trade-off to keep in mind. Establishing the internal validity of a causal hypothesis requires four separate tests, and few research designs are capable of passing all those tests with flying colors. This is particularly true of observational studies. Large-n comparisons might excel at detecting covariation between variables and at checking for spuriousness, while small-n case studies could be better suited for identifying causal mechanisms.* It's usually easier to dismiss rival hypotheses when working with one hundred cases than with one or two cases.

These trade-offs are a big reason why mixed-methods/multimethod research is all the rage among political scientists. Increasingly, published research is based on two or more research designs, executed by the same scholar or team of scholars. The idea is to play to the distinctive strengths of each design and compensate for the weaknesses of each. Practically speaking, few college students will have the time or skill needed to use multiple designs in their own research. Graduate students and professors are more likely to do so. Nevertheless, all of us are likely to read examples of multimethod research, and as budding inspectors we need to understand how and why such projects are designed. Toward the end of this chapter, I will provide a few examples.

---

* The letter n is a common shorthand for the number of cases in a sample. N refers to the entire population of cases (though some studies refer to sample size as N). We will learn more about populations and samples in the next chapter.

When I was being trained as a political scientist, way back in the twentieth century, the main choice was between quantitative and qualitative research designs. Basically, this meant large-n statistical studies versus small-n case studies. The differences between these designs seemed quite large at the time, and some political scientists worried that the discipline was dividing into two hostile camps. Those frictions have subsided, and those categories no longer seem helpful (if they ever were). For one thing, they don't illuminate problems of covariation, spuriousness, endogeneity, and causal mechanisms as well as other ways of categorizing research designs. Moreover, they create a misleading impression that political scientists use either numbers or words, when in fact they routinely do both. A so-called quantitative design might convert portions of written documents into numbers through a technique called content analysis (see chapter 6). A supposedly qualitative design might rely on numbers to measure the extent of public support for a certain policy, or to track changes over time in spending on a social program. I can't tell you how many times students have asked me if it was okay to include numbers in their case study. (Pained look on my face, followed by "Yes, of course.")

For a better approach, we can turn to the world of motivational speakers, those well-dressed folks who tell us we can Make Life Happen or Let It Happen. We can be Drivers or Passengers. Order-Makers or Order-Takers. Architects or Minarets (for some reason this slogan never caught on). All these folks are exhorting us to take more control of our lives. And control is what distinguishes experimental research designs from the observational ones.[5] Using an **experimental design**, researchers have considerable control over what happens in their study. They're able to randomly assign subjects to two or more groups, one of which becomes the control group. They can also manipulate the values of one or more independent variables. Both of these steps are necessary to isolate the effect of some independent variable A on some dependent variable B. Done properly, such experiments score high in internal validity. Those motivational gurus were right: more control is a good thing, a very good thing.

With an **observational design**, researchers lack such control. They must work with whatever cases and observe whatever variation the world of politics gives them. Political scientists are often in this position, because much of the political world does not lend itself easily, or at all, to experimentation. As mentioned in chapter 1, various studies of the resource curse in comparative politics have focused on a single country, a handful of countries, or over one hundred. Those scholars simply can't manipulate the amount of oil in a given country, or randomly assign countries to public versus private owner-ship of key resources. Instead, they must observe existing differences among countries in their oil revenues, the percentage of Muslims in their popula-tion, public versus private ownership of their resources, and any other inde-pendent variables, and then try to connect these to observed differences in economic development or democracy. Likewise, we have no way of randomly assigning people to different genders, ethnicities, religions, or ages as part of some experiment. We must observe these characteristics. Although some ob-servational designs can approximate the level of control in true experiments, they will always fall short. On the plus side, observational designs might have good external validity, because they are based on real-world behavior.

Another useful way of thinking about our options is to distinguish be-tween **variable-oriented designs** and **case-oriented designs**. The main dis-tinction here is analytic breadth versus depth: knowing a few things about many cases, or knowing many things about a few cases.[6] You might think of this as the difference between the high school guidance counselor and the psychiatrist. While the former may be responsible for three hundred students and meet with each one for twenty minutes per year, the latter will meet over and over with a smaller number of patients. The typical guid-ance counselor might know your name, grade, and plans for college, but not much else. The psychiatrist might know how overprotective parents limited someone's ability to rebound from failure, or how the death of a beloved grandparent cast a pall over someone's teenage years.

Political scientists who run experiments are oriented toward variables. They want to know how much a deliberate change in independent variable A affects the value of dependent variable B. In their experiment about voter turnout discussed in chapter 3, Gerber and Green (and their many research assistants) made no effort to become acquainted with any of the potential voters. No long discussions about family, school, work, or world affairs. That would have been impractical given the thousands of people included in their study. Gerber and Green were mostly interested in knowing whether each person had been contacted by mail, by phone, in person, or not at all, and whether they had voted. Researchers who compare many cases, using obser-vational data and statistical techniques, are also variable oriented. Ross (also from chapter 3) didn't want to get bogged down in the details of every single country in his study. He just wanted to know a few things about each one, such as their reliance on oil and their level of democracy.[7]

Those who produce case studies favor analytic depth over breadth. (These scholars probably never learned much from those brief meetings with their guidance counselor.) In the world of politics, such researchers expect to find interactions among variables. They believe that causal chains can have many links, and that documenting them can take time. They won't be surprised by endogeneity or equifinality. Not surprisingly, this kind of research lends itself more to 250-page books than to twenty-page journal articles. In her book *Health Politics*, Ellen Immergut analyzed policy making in three countries over several decades (chapter 3). Because she was showing how institutional veto points can shape policy, and because those veto points differed across countries and sometimes varied over time (e.g., in her French case), she had to immerse herself in the history of all three countries.[8]

When it comes to internal validity, variable-oriented designs have certain advantages in testing for covariation and spuriousness. These advantages can be rooted in the extensive controls available through experiments, or the greater number of potentially confounding variables that can be analyzed statistically. The variables in these studies are typically expressed as interval or ratio-level measures, such as per capita income or percent voter turnout.[9] Thus, the results are often quite precise. We might learn, for example, that a one-unit increase in the independent variable is usually associated with a 5 percent drop in the value of the dependent variable. For their part, case-oriented designs can be quite useful in determining the causal order of variables and identifying the causal links connecting them (e.g., any intervening variables). To some extent variable-oriented designs are good for determining causal effects, while case-oriented designs are good for causal mechanisms. These are general tendencies, not hard-and-fast rules. If you read Ross's statistical analysis of the resource curse, you know that he tested three different causal mechanisms.[10] Read Immergut's book and you will see how she rejects a few alternative explanations for differences in health policy among her three country cases.

The rest of this chapter provides more detail concerning three research designs—experiments, large-*n* statistical comparisons, and small-*n* case studies. Thus, we have one experimental design and two observational designs, one of which is variable oriented and the other case oriented. Each one actually represents a family of designs, and readers will meet the main members of each family. These are definitely not the only designs used by political scientists, but they're probably the most common in the literature.[11] As much as I might like to discuss additional research designs, I am operating under serious constraints. My book contract limits me to eighty-five thousand words; if I exceed that limit, all my royalties will be automatically donated to the University of North Carolina–Chapel Hill. Having grown up near the University of Virginia and graduated from Duke, I must not let that happen.

Experiments

Practically everyone who reads this guide will have conducted an experiment at some point, maybe involving plant seeds, fruit flies, or simple chemical reactions. The basic idea was to figure out what happened to some outcome *Y* (like plant growth) if you manipulated some factor *X* (like sunlight). More and more political scientists are using experimental designs in their research, for similar reasons.[12] Experiments are appealing because they can test causal hypotheses more decisively than observational designs can. (Seldom are experiments used to develop or test descriptive hypotheses.) To some people, experiments are also appealing because they constrain researchers' ability to rummage through observational data, looking for certain patterns and perhaps ignoring others. Once an experiment is set up properly, researchers are supposed to carry it out and report whatever results emerge. There is, in short, a certain machinelike quality to experimental designs.

Although the details vary, a typical experiment starts with recruitment of participants.[13] These individuals might be more or less required to participate, as happens in some college courses, or they might be volunteers. They would then be randomly assigned to one of two or more groups (e.g., via a coin toss). **Random assignment** is crucial, because it helps ensure that the groups are alike in all respects. Depending on the study, "alike" might mean that all groups have a similar mix of men and women, liberals and conservatives, employed and unemployed, or many other factors.[14] To make sure that random assignment worked properly, researchers might administer a survey to all participants before the experiment began, asking them a variety of demographic and opinion questions. The results could then be compared across groups.

Once participants have been assigned to different groups, the researcher administers a treatment to one group but not the other.[15] That treatment is the independent variable. In medical drug trials, that treatment is usually delivered by needle, pill, or drink. Political science experiments work a bit differently (though it might be more fun if they did work the same). The treatment could involve watching news stories about a specific issue or reading about a hypothetical family in need. Participants might be exposed to certain appeals encouraging them to vote, or given rewards for correctly answering questions about politics. Lots and lots of possible treatments. The group that doesn't receive the treatment is called the control group. If the experiment is administered more than once, the process must be standardized so that every participant is given the same instructions, every step in the experiment is taken in the same order, and so on. Toward the end of the experiment, researchers would then measure some dependent variable for the treatment and the control groups: it could be opinions toward climate change, willingness to spend on social programs, voter turnout, or what have you. Whatever differences were observed between the treatment and the control groups would then be attributed to the treatment.[16] After all, random assignment assured us that but for random chance, the only relevant difference between the groups was the treatment variable. Thus, experiments solve what Gerber and Green call "the problem of unobserved confounders."[17] Now you can see why experiments, done the right way, have such high internal validity.

The experiment described above is called a between-subjects design, because it allows us to compare groups of subjects. Another type of experiment relies on a within-subjects design. In this version a single group of subjects is usually given two or more treatments. Suppose the dependent variable involves willingness to spend money on foreign aid, and the independent variable is information about the recipients. An experimenter might initially give participants no information about the recipients and measure how much of the national budget participants were willing to give other countries. The second iteration would provide these same participants information about average life expectancy in the recipient countries, and then measure how much participants were willing to give. In the final iteration, these same participants would be told about a specific needy individual in one of those countries, and then asked what share of the budget they would give. The experimenter could thus determine whether information had much impact on one's support for foreign aid, and if so, what kind of information. In a sense, the same people would serve as the control group and the treatment group in this type of experiment, which helps ensure that the two groups are alike.[18]

Experiments sound authoritative, beyond reproach. Experts in white lab coats can't be wrong. Nevertheless, experiments have potential weak spots. The conventional wisdom is to question their external validity, and that's a smart move. Sometimes their internal validity is suspect, too. Given the fundamental importance of random assignment, we might start there by inspecting for problems. Especially when we are working with numerically small treatment or control groups, we should make sure that those groups are indeed equivalent. If you have ever dealt playing cards randomly from a deck, five to one pile and five to another, you know that occasionally one pile will have all red cards or all black cards. The same result could happen with liberals and conservatives, men and women, or other politically relevant attributes during a small-scale experiment.[19]

Other kinds of problems could surface. If an experiment extends over a period of time and some members of the treatment or the control group drop out along the way, then attrition poses a threat to internal validity. Those who remain could be systematically different from those who left, thus distorting the causal effect.[20] An extended experiment also creates the possibility for some extraneous development to affect participants. This problem is known generally as the threat of history. Imagine a within-subjects design in which participants are sent specific kinds of scientific information about climate change once a week for six weeks. If the United Nations happened to release a major report about climate change during that six-week period, researchers would not know if any change in participants' views toward climate change stemmed from that report or from their carefully scripted messages. For even longer-running experiments, such as those measuring the effects of charter schools or Head Start on educational achievement, we might worry about maturation. Maybe the subjects got smarter simply because they got older, and not because they attended a better school. Any experiment that includes a pretest runs the risk of tipping off participants to the larger purpose of the study, which might lead them to modify their behavior.[21] Most of these problems are less common with between-subjects designs than within-subjects designs. It helps to have a control group alongside a treatment group in order to detect threats to internal validity such as history and maturation. In effect, the control group helps us answer the counterfactual question, what would have happened without this treatment?

Threats to external validity come primarily from two directions. Just because an experiment uses random assignment is no guarantee that the subjects involved represent a random sample of a larger population. The most obvious example would be experiments conducted by all kinds of social scientists on their college students. Just how far can we generalize from a bunch of twenty-year-olds at State U? Other kinds of samples are suspect as well. One of the more famous experiments concerning the media relied on a few dozen volunteers who replied to a newspaper ad in New Haven, Connecticut.[22] Even though the participants weren't college students, it takes a big leap of faith to believe they represented a typical slice of Americans. A number of experiments designed to analyze conflict and cooperation create games for ordinary citizens to play; we might legitimately wonder whether elected officials and seasoned diplomats would approach these games the same way, and their behavior is what ultimately interests us.

Second, the design of experiments may not come close to mirroring the real world of politics. The treatment may be contrived. In the media experiment discussed above, participants were paid to watch the news in a special room on the Yale University campus, surrounded by strangers. Just like we all watch the news. In a different experiment, researchers were trying to determine if traditional surveys of political knowledge were faulty because they gave respondents little incentive to think before answering. Those surveys might be underestimating how much people really know. During the experiment, some people were therefore paid a dollar for every question they answered correctly.[23] Personally, I would love to live in such a world, but in my experience the rewards for knowing which party controls the US Senate aren't quite so tangible or immediate. Perhaps more important, many experiments are designed to isolate the effect of a single variable when much of political life is determined by the interaction of multiple variables.[24]

The setting can have a big influence on these threats to external validity. A **laboratory experiment** is probably the most vulnerable. The participants usually come from the immediate area, and they may share other characteristics, such as attending the same university or needing whatever money the experimenters are paying for their time. The sheer number of participants is often low. The whole design of a lab experiment can be pretty artificial, from its physical location to the treatment to be administered. Participants know they are being watched, which may lead them to behave in atypical ways. Thus, some researchers use lab experiments to test out their ideas before undertaking a different kind of study. Lab experiments may still be preferred, however, to answer some research questions. Recent experiments, for example, have used functional magnetic resonance imaging machines to observe how the human brain reacts to certain hypothetical situations or visual cues. For instance, what kinds of racial images activate the amygdala, a small region of the brain that is central to emotion and memory?[25] Such experiments are very expensive to run, and the number of test subjects is usually in the double digits. Experiments relying on electroencephalograms to measure brain activity can be a cheaper alternative.

Survey-based experiments, in contrast, are based on a larger and more representative sample of participants. These experiments can be embedded in traditional nationwide surveys so that, for example, five hundred people can be asked their opinions about climate change while five hundred other people are asked to read a short scientific article about climate change before giving their opinion. Or, half the sample can be told about a hypothetical white mother in need, and the other half about a hypothetical black mother, in order to determine if participants blame one mother more than the other for her situation, or if they favor more government help for one than the other. Because of random assignment, we can be confident that any differences between the groups were due to the availability of information in my first example or to race in the second. One real advantage of this design is that participants are less aware of being tested, because they aren't given both scenarios. Advances in survey software and easier access to national samples (e.g., through Time-Sharing Experiments in the Social Sciences, funded by the National Science Foundation; the YouGov market research firm; or Mechanical Turk, sponsored by Amazon.com) have made these types of experiments much more feasible. Some survey experiments are, in my professional opinion, pretty cool.[26] Nonetheless, they remain vulnerable to the criticism that whatever people may say to a polling organization isn't really an accurate measure of how they will behave. (This is a common concern about survey research in general.)[27]

Field experiments are supposed to overcome both of these threats to external validity. These experiments are conducted in more natural settings such as campaigns, elections, bureaucracies, and a variety of public programs. We don't have to make huge inferences from what happens in a carefully controlled lab or opinion survey to what would happen in the messy world of politics. We are now in that world. Not only is the setting more realistic, but so are the treatments, the participants, and the outcomes.[28] Compared to lab experiments, participants are less aware of being watched.*
If you wonder whether face-to-face canvassing is more effective than direct mail or phone calls in boosting voter turnout, then run an experiment during an election in which potential voters are contacted in different ways. If you wonder how to empower women in developing countries, then run an experiment in which actual development projects in some villages require female participation, but comparable projects in comparable villages do not.[29] With many of these field experiments, researchers are able to work with a large number of villages, voting precincts, registered voters, and so on, drawn from a representative sample of that population. The n in these studies usually numbers in the hundreds or thousands, not the tens. Field experiments therefore have unusually good external validity and internal validity, which helps explain why many political scientists are finding new ways to employ this research design.

What's not to like? Well, for one thing, researchers might not control how the treatment is administered in field experiments. They might rely instead on third parties, such as election observers provided by a nongovernmental organization (NGO). We then have to trust those third parties to act the same

---

*Thus, field experiments might generate something that political scientists value highly—unobtrusive measures of political phenomena.

way as one another for the duration of the experiment. If not, the internal validity could be compromised. Likewise, conducting a field experiment might require cooperation from some host organization or government. This creates the possibility that those entities will allow only those treatments they believe will work, or will allow experimentation only in areas known to be receptive to change. For instance, in development projects, perhaps only the more educated or stable regions of a country will be deemed suitable for a field experiment. Such "prescreening" of treatments or test subjects could compromise the external validity of the experiment.[30] Finally, field experiments are often quite expensive, and researchers will usually need financial support from a university, foundation, NGO, or government. Those organizations don't have the ability or the desire to fund every good idea political scientists might have for a field experiment.

Keep in mind that all experiments—lab, survey, or field—face ethical constraints as well. They must respect principles such as "do no harm" and win the approval of institutional review boards. Although we might be curious to know how different health care systems respond to epidemics, we should not be randomly assigning high-quality and low-quality systems to different countries. To unravel the relationship between guns and crime, we shouldn't randomly distribute .457-caliber Magnum handguns to citizens in certain states. Perhaps a more realistic example is in order. While political scientists are fond of experimenting during elections, they shouldn't undertake research that might influence the winner of that election—a warning that three scholars from Stanford and Dartmouth recently failed to heed, much to their embarrassment.[31]

Large-n Statistical Comparisons

As mentioned earlier in this chapter, many parts of the political world are not amenable to experimentation. We have to work with whatever data, qualitative or quantitative, we can observe. But we still want our research designs to have as much internal and external validity as possible. We still want to figure out what happened and why, and we still want our findings to shed light on some larger set of issues, be they theoretical or practical. We might search for "natural experiments," in which someone besides the researcher has already assigned subjects randomly to different treatments. For years California has listed the order of candidates for statewide office based on a random draw of alphabet letters, allowing scholars to study whether placement on the ballot had an impact on the share of votes won.[32] Potentially, we might discover "quasi experiments" (that, strictly speaking, aren't experiments), in which observed values of the independent variable appear to be arbitrarily assigned without any conscious intent. Posner's study of the Chewas and Tumbukas from the introduction is one example, in which some members of each group live in Zambia and other members of the same groups live in neighboring Malawi.[33] Such instances could allow us to control for the influence of many (but not all) confounding variables. Most of the time, however, nature and circumstance aren't so considerate.

For decades, the dominant research design in political science has involved statistical comparisons of many cases, using observational data. This is particularly true in the study of American politics, where statistical analyses of public opinion, campaigns and elections, legislative behavior, and public policies are abundant. A large and growing share of journal articles in international relations relies on this design.[34] Among comparativists who study political behavior (providing they have access to opinion surveys or credible voting data), this design is common. The same is true for cross-country comparisons of social and economic policies. In some instances the statistics are as basic as percentages and averages; more often, researchers employ some variant of multiple regression analysis.

Like experiments, large-n statistical comparisons come in different flavors. A **cross-sectional design** compares a number of cases at a single point in time. An opinion poll is a classic example. Most polls give us responses from hundreds and hundreds of people, and each individual would be considered a separate case. We could search for relationships between an individual's income and trust in government; gender and views toward international trade; formal education and partisanship; or any number of other variables. For a study about guns and crime, we could collect data about gun ownership, poverty rates, size of police force, and homicide rates from all fifty US states for a given year. We would therefore compare across fifty cases.

The conventional wisdom is that large-n statistical comparisons are stronger on external than internal validity. What, specifically, does this mean for cross-sectional designs? When working with a descriptive or causal hypothesis, we need evidence that the values of our variables change in some regular pattern (i.e., a direct or an inverse relationship). With hundreds and hundreds of individuals, and even with fifty states, we can detect covariation using some of the statistical techniques discussed in chapter 7. The problem is clearing the second hurdle, where we check for spuriousness and confounding variables. In the hypothetical study about guns and crime, we might have the data needed to analyze a few alternatives such as poverty. Lacking true experimental controls, we can substitute statistical controls to hold the influence of these other variables in check. Put more generally, we can estimate the relationship between A and B, controlling for C. It wouldn't take too much effort to identify more factors (hello, lit review) that might vary by state and be related to crime: unemployment; share of the population between the ages of eighteen and thirty years; maybe severity of punishment. Unfortunately, even assuming that we collected data for these additional variables and used the right statistical techniques, our study would remain vulnerable to those dreaded "unobserved confounders."[35]

Now we have two options—give up, or proceed with caution. The first option is actually defensible as long as we find a different research design or a different puzzle and don't just curl up in a ball under the desk. Proceed with caution means controlling for as many other variables as we can and not overstating our findings.* This is also a decent option, especially when working with descriptive hypotheses.

For causal hypotheses, cross-sectional comparisons are not very satisfactory. It's inherently difficult to determine the causal order of variables based on a single snapshot. We can overcome this problem if some of our variables refer to more or less fixed characteristics such as race and gender. We would not argue that an individual's views about international trade caused them to be male or female. Attitudes toward international trade would have to be the dependent variable here. But in many cases the causal sequence could go either way. More unemployment in a state might lead to more crime as people became more desperate to survive; more crime could lead to more unemployment if businesses closed down. Someone's party affiliation might lead that person to be more trusting of government, or vice versa. In other words, endogeneity (discussed in chapter 3) is rearing its ugly head.

A **time-series design** can help remedy this problem. Researchers collect data at regular intervals for a given case and compare those observations over time. Thus, we might track gun ownership, crime rates, and a number of other variables for the state of Ohio between 1970 and 2010, giving us forty potential cases (i.e., state-years) to observe. That way we could observe whether any increases in gun ownership preceded any declines in the crime rate, and do the same for trends in Ohio's poverty rates or number of police officers. With enough statistical training we could build multiple regression equations in which some independent variables were time lagged. Immigration is a pressing issue in many countries, and some scholars believe that public opposition to immigrants increases when the economy sputters. To test this hypothesis, we could pick a country with a reasonably long history of polling its citizens about immigration, and see if inflation or unemployment regularly got worse before public opinion turned more negative. We

---

* Lo and behold, another call for humility.

would probably examine other trends that might be connected to public opinion as well. In both scenarios, we still haven't eliminated the problem of unobserved confounders, but we have at least taken a step toward proving cause and effect.

An interesting variant on this design is the interrupted time series. The basic idea is to pick a period of time that is interrupted by some major change. Starting in 2004, for example, the State of Ohio allowed adults to carry concealed weapons under certain conditions. To determine the impact of this law on crime, we might gather data from several years before 2004 and several years after. Did crime drop after 2004? For a different project, if we noticed that a country experienced a surge in immigration, we might track public opinion for several years before and after. In some ways this design approximates a within-subjects experiment.

Sticking with a single state or country, however, can limit the external validity of our design. As a result, political scientists increasingly rely on **time-series cross-sectional research designs**. Comparisons over time and across space are now made.[36] This is what Ross used when testing the resource curse: he collected annual data from 113 countries between 1971 and 1997 (which means that the n in his statistical analysis was greater than 2000). Similarly, when Cullen Hendrix and Wendy Wong analyzed the impact of regime type and "naming and shaming" (by the media and NGOs) on respect for human rights, they collected data from 157 countries over three decades. *Unequal Democracy* is one of the more powerful analyses of inequality in the United States. At a number of points the author, Larry Bartels, pooled together opinion polls conducted every two years by the American National Election Studies.[37] Many, many other published examples of this design could be cited. (And they require more sophisticated techniques than what is taught in an introductory statistics course.)

To proponents of experiments, all these large-n observational designs fall short, because statistical controls don't work as well as true random assignment. For instance, researchers might be able to conclude that higher unemployment rates diminish public support for immigration, even controlling for the actual number of immigrants and their country of origin. But researchers won't know for sure if something they failed to include in their statistical analysis, such as the individual's party affiliation, might negate or mitigate that relationship. The study's internal validity is therefore compromised. To proponents of case studies, most of these large-n statistical comparisons are lacking because they pay too little attention to causal complexity and causal mechanisms (a criticism they extend to experiments as well). It is often unclear from a statistical regression model how changes in some independent variable regularly produce changes in the dependent variable. That, too, is a problem of internal validity. (As discussed in chapter 3, the force of this criticism depends on whether one believes that a clear causal mechanism is essential for a good causal argument.)

*Small-*n *Case Studies*

Historically, case studies have been the Rodney Dangerfield of research designs (as in "I don't get no respect"). Scholars who use this design are sometimes looked down upon as storytellers or, worse, journalists. The lowly status of the case study is puzzling given how many famous works in political science were based on this design.[38] Perhaps for every great work, we could point to examples of poorly crafted case studies that somehow managed to get published. I wouldn't be surprised if the shaky quality of case studies performed by undergraduate and graduate students also hurts the reputation of this design. Nevertheless, prominent scholars continue to publish case studies, and professors keep assigning case studies for their students to read and research, so we ought to take this design seriously and learn what it can and cannot do well.

As John Gerring points out, scholars don't always agree on what a case study entails. His definition, though, strikes me as quite reasonable: "A **case study** may be understood as an intensive study of a single case where the purpose of that study—at least in part—is to shed light on a larger class of cases (a population). *Case study research* may incorporate several cases. . . . However, at a certain point it will no longer be possible to investigate those cases intensively."[39] Several pieces of this definition are worth noting. The importance of intensive study is what I meant earlier about analytic depth. Case study scholars would rather dig a hole a foot wide and ten feet deep than scrape an inch of dirt off an entire ball field. In other words, they would rather know a lot about one substantively important case than know a little about many cases, some of them trivial or only mildly interesting. Scholars using this design may conduct **single case studies** or **comparative case studies**, typically involving two or three cases.[40] Gerring leaves open the possibility that case studies could answer descriptive or causal questions. And he encourages us to consider the wider significance of our findings. In other words, the case study design can help us figure out what happened, why, and who cares.

The easiest problem to spot with case studies concerns their external validity. To be blunt: how can we possibly generalize from one or two cases? Could we understand the Beatles just by listening repeatedly to "Love Me Do"? Part of my answer is, wait until the next chapter. There we will see how careful case selection might allow us to make modest but important inferences. For now, though, it's worth noting that not all case studies are designed first and foremost to apply to other cases. Some scholars hope their case studies will enhance our understanding of general theories of politics.[41] By identifying a new intervening variable, or by clearly tracing two different paths connecting independent variable *A* and dependent variable *B*, a case study might enrich subsequent work by scholars using a variety of research designs on a variety of political puzzles. You can imagine something similar happening in medical research. Scientists might develop a new drug to fight a very specific form of cancer affecting a small part of the population. That drug might not work on any other cancer. However, the way that drug works, by targeting certain proteins, could provide important clues for researchers who are investigating other cancers, which would be a very valuable insight.[42]

On the surface, case study designs don't seem likely to foster internal validity, either. You would be hard-pressed to demonstrate any sort of relationship between guns and crime if your case was Ohio in the year 2000. (As in geometry, one political data point could lie on an infinite number of trend lines.) One way to get around this problem is to distinguish between a case and the observations within that case. This distinction is crucial to grasp. Those who create case studies sometimes find ways of maximizing the number of observations within each of their cases. In the case of Ohio, that strategy could mean collecting relevant data at the city or county level for the year 2000. That way, we could mimic a cross-sectional design among larger-*n* studies. With more time and effort we could gather the same data for several years, thus approximating a time-series cross-sectional design. More observations would give us greater ability to test for covariation, spuriousness, and causal order. By sticking with a state like Ohio, we may be able to (more or less) hold constant a variety of relevant factors such as the state's political culture, whether judges are appointed or elected, and the formal powers of the governor. We might be able to rule them out as possible influences on crime. In short, more observations would improve the internal validity of our design.

"Unpacking" a case could be done for geographic entities such as countries, regions, provinces, or states. It could be done for a single piece of legislation, perhaps by analyzing the debates and votes in multiple committees. Not every case, however, is suitable for unpacking in this manner. The needed data may be unavailable, or the key decisions may not be made at lower levels of analysis. We could end up asking a different and less interesting question. In those situations, increasing observations by building in

a historical dimension to the case study could still be helpful. And researchers might add in another case or two for comparison. We might pair Ohio
with another state that was similar in many respects but had a considerably
higher or lower crime rate, and then try to explain why the two states had
such different outcomes. Immergut's analysis of health policy in three European countries is a clear example where comparing two or three cases can be
quite illuminating. In the next chapter I will offer some guidance on picking
a single case versus a few cases for intensive study.

One of my favorite case studies is called "Testing the Surge."[43] Granted, I
know precious little about the Middle East or US foreign policy, but I think
I can recognize a good case study when I see one. The authors wanted to
explain why violence in Iraq declined so sharply after 2007. Some analysts
believed that the military surge, largely supplied by the United States, was
responsible. Others pointed to the "Anbar Awakening," a more indigenous
cause involving local Sunnis. A few observers suggested that by 2007, most of
the key regions in Iraq were ethnically homogenous, which reduced the need
to fight. To test these competing explanations, the authors collected evidence from multiple regions within the country for a few years before 2007
and a few years after (i.e., a time-series cross-sectional design). What they
found was that the interaction of the military surge and the Anbar Awakening was instrumental. Regions with both of these factors experienced much
larger declines in violence than regions with one or the other. One case,
many observations.

A case study design can do more than imitate its larger-n cousins. This
design is also well equipped to uncover causal mechanisms, which is not
exactly a strength of statistical comparisons. Many case studies rely on **process tracing** to identify and test the ways in which some independent variables might influence some outcome. Process tracing is all about answering
the How question that is embedded in our mission to figure out the Why
question.

> The hallmark of process tracing . . . is that multiple types of evidence
> are employed for the verification of a single inference. . . . [P]rocess
> tracing usually involves long causal chains. Rather than multiple in-
> stances of $X_1 \to Y$ (the large-N cross-case style of research), one exam-
> ines a single instance of $X_1 \to X_2 \to X_3 \to X_4 \to Y$. (Of course, this causal
> path may be much longer and more circuitous, with multiple switches
> and feedback loops.)[44]

Process tracing is intrinsically historical; just as politics unfolds over
time, so too does political analysis. Seldom if ever do our independent vari-

ables lead instantaneously to our dependent variables. Process tracing therefore requires careful analysis within each case. Any break in the causal chain, any missing link threatens the validity of the causal hypothesis. In contrast, when we test for covariation and spuriousness, we typically compare across cases, and a few exceptions aren't necessarily a big deal.

In my experience, case studies written by undergraduates are often weak in process tracing, which is a serious flaw. A typical case study might try to examine whether interest group J (e.g., the financial industry, gun owners) was instrumental to the passage of law Z, a causal argument. The main evidence offered in the paper compares what group J said it wanted, maybe a year or two before law Z was passed, and the eventual content of that law. So far, so good—but two snapshots aren't nearly enough to prove causation. In addition, it would be important to demonstrate that members of group J spoke as one voice on this issue; that J worked hard to have its preferences enacted, perhaps via campaign contributions, legislative testimony, or efforts to shape public opinion; that J did not change its position and embrace Z once J recognized that the law was likely to be enacted; that legislative staff asked J for help in drafting significant parts of the bill that became Z; that important members of the legislature changed their mind in response to the efforts of J; or that other interest groups with similar preferences weren't lobbying nearly as effectively as J. Connecting the links in the causal chain would take more than a position paper posted to J's website and the text of law Z. We could also need secondary studies by historians and political scientists, newspaper and magazine articles, government documents, personal interviews, public opinion polls, records of campaign donations, and material from other interest groups' websites.[45] Sound like a lot of work? Welcome to process tracing. Put on a good pair of work gloves and start digging.

Case studies definitely have their limitations. Like any observational design, they can't fully address the problem of unobserved confounders as well as experimental designs can. If the number of observations within or across cases is fairly small, then the case study design won't be able to detect covariation and confounding variables as well as most large-n statistical comparisons will. Poor case selection could be devastating, which makes the next chapter essential reading for those who plan to write or read case studies (i.e., most of us). In the right hands, however, a case study can help us understand what happened and why.

I offer one last point in defense of this design. For most of their professional lives, political scientists worry about testing descriptive or causal hypotheses. Much of this guide is oriented toward these same objectives. Yet these hypotheses aren't sent by divine messenger; someone has to come up with them. That someone is often the case study scholar, whose careful and sustained digging uncovers relationships that weren't previously visible. Once other scholars investigate further, those relationships could turn out to be weak or atypical, but at least we have a plausible starting point and direction for our research. Case studies can help us to generate hypotheses, and they can provide the descriptive evidence essential for testing hypotheses.[46]

COMBINING RESEARCH DESIGNS

One of the main messages of this chapter is that different research designs have both strengths and weaknesses. It follows that we should be prepared to read widely if we truly want to understand any important puzzle in politics. The democratic peace literature offers a good illustration. A number of classic studies are based on large-n statistical comparisons. They cover many countries and many years. The authors examine a number of factors—such as form of government, affluence, international trade, geographic contiguity, military capabilities—that might affect conflict between countries. One standard result is that democratic governments do not go to war with each other.[47] In reviewing this literature, Andrew Bennett and Alexander George noted that "statistical studies have proved more capable of addressing *whether* a non-spurious democratic peace exists than of answering *why* it might exist."[48] A related stream of research, often based on historical case studies, emerged to sort out the causal links.[49] If democratic institutions matter, exactly how do regular elections reduce the chances of democracies fighting each other? If democratic values are crucial, which ones, and how? Although it might seem impossible to conduct experiments regarding the democratic peace ("Sorry, Canada, but you have been randomly assigned to be an authoritarian regime"), there are a few examples. A recent survey-based experiment found that ordinary citizens in the United States and the United Kingdom were less supportive of military strikes against democracies than nondemocracies, even controlling for other considerations such as military alliances and military power. Thus, democracies might not fight each other because elected leaders are heeding the wishes of voters.[50] In short, to make sense of the democratic peace and many other literatures in political science, we need to become familiar with different research designs.

An emerging trend among political scientists is to employ two or more designs in a single research project. This strategy is known as **multimethod research** or, less commonly, methodological triangulation. Adopting a second or third research method can help test the findings of the original method, or address questions that the first method is not well equipped to answer.[51] Combining methods is probably easier to accomplish in books than journal articles, if only because authors need more time to introduce their data and methods and to develop their arguments. For instance, Edward Mansfield and Jack Snyder used statistical comparisons and case studies to show that while established democracies might not fight each other, newly democratizing countries are prone to war. In her study of policy diffusion, Katerina Linos combined statistical comparisons of many wealthy democracies with case studies of Greece, Spain, and the United Kingdom. Nicholas Winter conducted original experiments and performed statistical analysis of polling data in order to analyze how certain issue frames can activate racial and gender attitudes.[52] Scholarly journals contain examples as well. In a pathbreaking study of rape during wartime, Dara Kay Cohen conducted a statistical analysis of eighty-six major civil wars over a three-decade period, followed by a case study of Sierra Leone. Why? Because, in her words, "although the statistical analysis demonstrates a correlation between extreme forms of forced recruitment and rape, the nature of the relationship between these variables is best established through a case study."[53]

Practically speaking, the growing interest in multimethod research could be a mixed blessing. While it probably benefits us as readers by generating more nuanced and complete answers to scholarly questions, it also raises the bar for us as researchers. Taking a few semesters of statistics courses will no longer be enough; now we need to add expertise in running experiments or conducting case studies. Fortunately, no one really expects a middle-aged political scientist like me to add new skills. So good luck, kids!

PRACTICE: INSPECTING

1. While reading some of the studies listed below, determine which features of political life the authors are comparing, and how (e.g., over time, across countries, across individuals). Then evaluate the internal and external validity of the research, noting strong points and weak points. Finally, what might you do next to build on this line of research?

EXPERIMENTS

Andrew Beath, Fotini Christia, and Ruben Enikolopov, "Empowering Women through Development Aid: Evidence from a Field Experiment in Afghanistan," *American Political Science Review* 107, no. 3 (August 2013): 540–57;

Alan S. Gerber and Donald P. Green, "The Effects of Canvassing, Telephone Calls, and Direct Mail on Voter Turnout: A Field Experiment," *American Political Science Review* 94, no. 3 (September 2000): 653–63;

James L. Gibson and Amanda Gouws, "Making Tolerance Judgments: The Effects of Context, Local and National," *Journal of Politics* 63, no. 4 (November 2001): 1067–90;

Shanto Iyengar, Mark D. Peters, and Donald R. Kinder, "Experimental Demonstrations of the 'Not-So-Minimal' Consequences of Television News Programs," *American Political Science Review* 76, no. 4 (December 1982): 848–58;

Mona Lynch and Craig Haney, "Capital Jury Deliberation: Effects on Death Sentencing, Comprehension, and Discrimination," *Law and Human Behavior* 33, no. 6 (December 2009): 481–96;

Markus Prior and Arthur Lupia, "Money, Time, and Political Knowledge," *American Journal of Political Science* (January 2008): 169–83.

LARGE-*N* STATISTICAL COMPARISONS*

Jack Citrin and John Sides, "Immigration and the Imagined Community in Europe and the United States," *Political Studies* 56, no. 1 (March 2008): 33–56;

M. Steven Fish, "Islam and Authoritarianism," *World Politics* 55, no. 1 (October 2002): 4–37;

James L. Gibson, "The Truth about Truth and Reconciliation in South Africa," *International Political Science Review* 26, no. 4 (October 2005): 341–61;

Rodney E. Hero, *Faces of Inequality: Social Diversity in American Politics* (New York: Oxford University Press, 1998), especially chapter 5;

Edward D. Mansfield, Diana C. Mutz, and Laura R. Silver, "Men, Women, Trade, and Free Markets," *International Studies Quarterly* 59, no. 2 (June 2015): 303–15;

Pippa Norris, "Does Television Erode Social Capital? A Reply to Putnam," *PS: Political Science and Politics* 29, no. 3 (September 1996): 474–80;

Vesla M. Weaver and Amy E. Lerman, "Political Consequences of the Carceral State," *American Political Science Review* 104, no. 4 (November 2010): 817–33.

SMALL-*N* CASE STUDIES†

Frank R. Baumgartner and Bryan D. Jones, *Agendas and Instability in American Politics* (Chicago: University of Chicago Press, 1993), chapter 4 (regarding nuclear power);

Stephen Biddle, Jeffrey A. Friedman, and Jacob N. Shapiro, "Testing the Surge: Why Did Violence Decline in Iraq in 2007?," *International Security* 37, no. 1 (Summer 2012): 7–40;

Justin Crowe, "The Forging of Judicial Autonomy: Political Entrepreneurship and the Reforms of William Howard Taft," *Journal of Politics* 69, no. 1 (February 2007): 73–87.

---

* None of these articles requires a high level of statistical sophistication to comprehend.

† Many excellent case studies are book length. These suggested journal articles and book chapters have the virtue of being shorter.

Ellen Immergut, "The Rules of the Game: The Logic of Health Policy-Making in France, Sweden, and Switzerland," in *Structuring Politics: Historical Institutionalism in Comparative Politics*, ed. Sven Steinmo, Kathleen Thelen, and Frank Longstreth (New York: Cambridge University Press, 1992), pp. 57–89;

Sarah Elizabeth Parkinson, "Organizing Rebellion: Rethinking High-Risk Mobilization and Social Networks in War," *American Political Science Review* 107, no. 3 (August 2013): 418–32;

Daniel N. Posner, "The Political Salience of Cultural Difference: Why Chewas and Tumbukas Are Allies in Zambia and Adversaries in Malawi," *American Political Science Review* 98, no. 4 (November 2004): 529–45;

Kurt Weyland, "The Arab Spring: Why the Surprising Similarities with the Revolutionary Wave of 1848?," *Perspectives on Politics* 10, no. 4 (December 2012): 917–34.

PRACTICE: BUILDING

1. Suppose you wanted to investigate the relationship between media exposure and political tolerance. How might you design (a) an experiment, (b) a large-*n* statistical comparison, and (c) a small-*n* case study to provide some insights? What would be the main trade-offs for each design?

2. Now imagine that your interest lies in the relationship between economic conditions and immigration laws. Could you design a good experiment to shed light on this question? Briefly explain.

3. In writing a case study about tax reform enacted in the year 20XX, you plan to make the following causal argument:

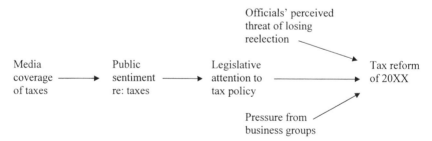

What would be the independent and intervening variables in this argument? What kinds of evidence would you need for each step in the causal chain?

5

CHOOSING CASES

One of my regrets is never seeing Ricky Jay perform live. The video clips of him on YouTube are amazing (go see for yourself), and I own a DVD of the documentary film, *Deceptive Practice*, based on his career.* Yet watching him in person would be even better, because Ricky Jay is one of the greatest magicians of all time. He doesn't use smoke and mirrors to make elephants disappear onstage, and he doesn't saw women in half. Jay specializes in close-up magic, especially card tricks. After shuffling and reshuffling the deck, he can make cards appear in virtually any combination—all queens, all spades, ace-king-queen-jack-10. He can riffle through a deck, cards facedown, and produce an ace anytime someone in the audience yells, "Stop." Ricky Jay is the last person in the world you'd want to play poker with, but one of the first people you'd like to sit next to for an hour, just to watch a master at work. To top it off, he has developed a stage patter that is literate, funny, and self-deprecating. Ricky Jay is truly a wonderful performer.

Context matters. When Ricky Jay shuffles the deck several times and then deals himself four aces, we enjoy the trick and marvel at his skill. However, when political scientists choose a specific case or group of cases to test an argument, we might worry that they have somehow "stacked the deck" in their favor. Much like Ricky Jay and his cards, these experts generally know far more about their subject (e.g., elections, terrorism, judicial decision making, trade policy) than the rest of us do. They might be able to trick us into accepting or rejecting a hypothesis by consciously picking certain cases and ignoring others.[1] It's also possible that researchers could unwittingly choose cases that bias their results. Whether deliberate or accidental, poor case selection can compromise the validity of research in political science.

The purpose of this chapter is to point out some good and bad ways of choosing cases. By this stage we have identified general hypotheses to investigate and picked a research design; now we need to analyze some specific cases. We might choose one civil war, a handful of financial crises, all members of the European Union, 1348 individuals, thousands of roll-call votes in Congress—virtually any number of possibilities. Some of the better discus-

---

* Yes, I recognize that anyone who still collects DVDs is by definition "old."

sions of case selection offer readers a list of strategies.[2] While these lists are a good start, it might help to group these strategies into a few meaningful categories. In this chapter, I will discuss different ways of choosing cases in order to promote the external validity of a study, such as analyzing the entire population or a random sample of cases. I will then discuss strategies to boost internal validity, such as deliberately picking cases with sizable variation in the dependent variable. These are not the only strategies available, and scholars often mention more than one when justifying their choice of cases. As we shall see, some of these strategies make better sense for one research design than another. The key point is, everyone in this line of work realizes the importance of selecting cases openly and intelligently. Otherwise, the audience might believe they are dealing with a card shark.

CHOOSING CASES TO BOOST EXTERNAL VALIDITY

You might not know it by the way we dress, but political scientists can be a pretty ambitious group. We want our research to shed light on important features of the political world, clearly and accurately. We would rather go big than go home (well, at least before 5 p.m.). Logically, the most direct way of ensuring that our findings apply broadly would be to analyze the entire **population** of cases. Study every single voter, or every single war, or every single change to civil rights law. That sounds daunting, and it is. Practical considerations of time, money, and energy usually prevent us from analyzing an entire population. Could I really ask every adult in Denmark about their attitudes regarding the next election? No. Even in a relatively small country with modern infrastructure, the costs of doing so would be prohibitive. Could I figure out all the causes of every single interstate war since the emergence of the nation-state? Not without a much bigger brain and a much longer life span. Instead, I would interview a **sample** of Danish adults or analyze a sample of wars, and then make inferences from that subset to some larger population of cases.

Making inferences is risky; our generalizations could turn out to be wrong. One way to work around this problem would be to define our population so narrowly that we can analyze every case. Identifying the population of cases, then, hinges on how we define core concepts (see chapter 2). Choosing cases becomes as much a conceptual exercise as a practical one. Suppose we are interested in the role of political parties in communist countries. In particular, we want to know how these parties recruit and promote their leaders. If we believe that communist countries are fundamentally similar over time, then we have a fairly large population to work with. A certain amount of sampling seems inevitable. Nevertheless, a researcher might argue that communist countries in the twenty-first century are quite different from those of the twentieth century. Perhaps the fall of the Soviet Union marked a historic turning point. As a result, the total population of contemporary cases is just five (China, Cuba, Laos, North Korea, and Vietnam, as of 2016). Now we might be able to study party politics in the entire population. Likewise, a specialist in international security might argue that world wars are in many ways distinct from regional or border wars, and that wars fought with modern weapons are quite different from those fought with muskets or cannons. The concept of modern world war would therefore have a population of two cases, namely World War I and World War II. A study addressing the question, in the modern era, of how and why territorial boundaries were redrawn after a world war could incorporate evidence from the whole population of cases. Our ability to analyze these kinds of populations depends on convincing readers that we have defined the general concept properly, and that other potentially relevant cases don't belong. Chances are, some readers will disagree.

Figuring out whether we can work with the full population of cases also depends on the larger significance of our study (discussed in chapter 1). Let's return to the example of guns and crime in the American states. Conceivably, someone might analyze all fifty states for every year since 1960, when the FBI started publishing state-level crime figures. This researcher might conduct a large-n statistical study, using a time-series, cross-sectional design, to determine whether the availability of guns was linked to crime rates, controlling for other possible influences. That study might include the whole population of cases if the author intended to contribute only to the literature on US crime since 1960. And that study would have a receptive but somewhat limited audience. On the other hand, if the author placed this study in the context of state-level policy making more generally, the larger literature might include examples from education, taxation, and health care. Those studies would be referenced in the lit review. Crime would thus be a sample of a larger population of policy cases. Or, if the author intended to contribute to a cross-national literature regarding crime, then the United States could be one country case among many. Past research concerning those other countries would appear in the lit review. Either way, the audience for this project would be wider than if the cases were treated as the whole population.

Given the practical and conceptual issues discussed above, political scientists seldom analyze entire populations. They usually work with samples, and they must choose those samples with care. A bad sample could easily lead to erroneous conclusions. In medicine, drawing a blood sample is pretty straightforward. A small sample taken from the index finger will give us as good a picture of a person's health as one drawn from any other finger. Past research tells us that blood cells are quite uniform throughout the body. In cooking, a chef needs to taste only one or two spoonfuls of soup to know if it is ready to serve. But voters, environmental regulations, humanitarian missions, border wars, business lobbies—it's hard to find any feature of political life as uniform as blood cells or soup.

Ideally, we'd like our sample to mirror the larger population. For researchers who plan to work with many cases—perhaps by making statistical comparisons of observational data, or by conducting a survey or field experiment—the most common tactic is to choose a **random sample**. Researchers have different techniques for generating a random sample, but the basic intuition is that picking many cases indiscriminately will reduce the odds of a biased sample. This is a classic way to avoid the Ricky Jay problem: we don't allow the researcher to dictate which cases are chosen. Although a random sample will rarely look exactly like the larger population, it will often be fairly close as long as we have chosen a decent number of cases. For instance, a random sample of 1500 Americans should be accurate within a margin of error of +/− 3 percentage points. That group will likely include a representative mix of men and women, liberals and conservatives, less and more educated people, and so on. If 12 percent of the individuals in our sample believed that Barack Obama was born in Africa and raised a Muslim by radical lesbian vegans, then we can be quite confident that the true number in the entire population is somewhere between 9 and 15 percent.* Our sample might seem quite small, given that the United States is home to more than 300 million people. Nonetheless, a modest-sized sample chosen at random can usually tell us more than a much larger sample that isn't random. (You can trust me on this one, or you can take an introductory course on probability and statistics.)

In most walks of life, randomness is a source of frustration or a sign of danger. Imagine the reaction if teachers handed out grades randomly so that the best and worst papers had an equal chance of receiving an A. Imagine the mayhem if public buses were driven at random speeds to random

---

* "Quite confident" doesn't mean absolutely certain. In fact, given the laws of probability, we would be 95 percent sure that the true value in this example would lie somewhere between 9 and 15 percent. There is still a little chance that we picked a very unusual sample, and the true figure for the population could be less than 9 or more than 15 percent. Not likely, but possible. Note: a smaller sample than this would carry a larger margin of error (e.g., 400 people, +/− 5 points).

destinations. But political scientists find ways to use randomness to their advantage when they conduct research. We have already seen how random assignment helps the internal validity of experiments (in chapter 4). Here, random sampling of cases can enhance the external validity of experimental or observational research.

Some research projects rely on a **simple random sample**, in which each subset of the population has an equal chance of being selected. For instance, in a recent paper analyzing the behavior of lawyers appearing before the Supreme Court, the authors first identified a population of every legal case that had been argued orally before the court and decided by the court between 1994 and 2010. The total population numbered 1469 cases. They then invoked the Sample command in the Stata software package to select cases randomly for them. This command can be customized, and they requested 25 percent of the population, giving them 370 cases. For this sample, the authors collected detailed evidence concerning the Supreme Court decisions and the justices that had been cited in the lawyers' briefs. While the data collection process still required time and effort, it was a more efficient use of the researchers' time than gathering evidence for the entire population of court cases.[3]

Other projects rely on a **systematic random sample**. Someone wanting to survey students at a university might sample from the campus phone directory and contact every tenth or twentieth name in the book. This way the researcher is not targeting specific types of students, like classmates or close friends. The resulting sample should be a microcosm of the entire university. Multistage samples are also possible. A national exit poll, taken on Election Day, might start by randomly selecting a number of counties from across the country. From each county, researchers would randomly select a number of voting precincts. Pollsters would then be deployed to each precinct and instructed to survey a random sample of voters during the day.[4] We aren't limited to individuals, either; besides the court cases mentioned above, we could sample acts of Parliament, international conflicts, presidential speeches, campaign ads, municipalities, or practically anything with a large population.

Frequently, researchers want to be sure their sample includes certain elements that are relevant to their larger questions. They don't want to pick cases purely by chance; they want their hypotheses to inform their case selection. If we are testing the extent to which gender shapes policy preferences, it would help to draw a sample that was divided evenly between men and women. A simple random sample would usually come close to a 50/50 split, but not always. Or, researchers studying the behavior of interest groups might want to ensure that a decent number of economic and non-economic groups made it into the sample, as well as adequate numbers of organizations with a single national office versus those with a multiple offices across the country. In these kinds of situations, a **stratified random sample** would be useful. Researchers would define the relevant strata (e.g., men and women; interest groups of type A, B, C, and D), decide what fraction of cases should come from each stratum, and then collect a random sample from each.

Sam Whitt and Rick Wilson used this approach when recruiting subjects for an experiment about fairness in Bosnia. Their basic question was, "Once a multiethnic society has emerged from a period of violent conflict, civil war, and even genocide, can those who survive adopt norms capable of sustaining peace with former ethnic rivals and adversaries?"[5] To answer this question, the researchers used different versions of the "dictator game," in which individuals were given a sum of money and told to split it between themselves and a stranger who was a member of either their own ethnic group or a rival group. In other words, each test subject was allowed to dictate how the money would be divided. From the start, Whitt and Wilson insisted on a sample that included roughly equal numbers of Bosnjaks, Serbs, and Croats, the main ethnic groups in the country. Based on previous studies of conflict and cooperation, the researchers also realized the importance of including individuals of different ages, genders, and levels of education. Random sampling for each stratum stopped once the target number for each part of the population was met. A total of 681 individuals, selected at random from different regions of Bosnia, eventually participated in the experiments.

Random sampling is standard practice in experiments and large-n observational studies. For case studies, random sampling is a genuinely bad idea. When our sample size is large, maybe numbering in the hundreds or thousands, the occasional weird or trivial case won't exert much influence on the overall results. With an n of 1 or 2, which is common in case studies, every case is important.[6] For a single case study of guns and crime in the American states, am I really going to pick one state blindly and spend months of my life becoming intimately familiar with Arkansas? I don't think so. For a comparative case study of interstate conflict, am I going to pick two wars at random, knowing that I might end up with the Spanish-Moroccan War of 1859–60 and the four-day Football War between El Salvador and Honduras (1969)? *Claro que no.* Case studies should be selected deliberately and thoughtfully, and I'll explain how in a minute.

As a practical matter, it might not be easy to identify a random sample. First, we need to have a good handle on the entire population. A campus phone book, a complete list of voting precincts, or a directory of all registered lobbyists would make our lives much easier as researchers. Nevertheless, many times we don't know much about the entire population. A *Peterson's Guide to the Major Policy Innovations of North America* does not exist. The same goes for terrorists, environmental nongovernmental organizations (NGOs) in Africa, likely candidates for elective office, and a wide variety of political phenomena. Second, we might lack the time, money, or skill to collect a random sample, even if we do know the population. Only a handful of organizations are equipped to conduct a statewide or nationwide exit poll. Running an experiment in different parts of a country like Bosnia can't be done quickly or cheaply.

With some ingenuity and persistence, we might be able to estimate the size and shape of a population. Likely candidates for the US House of Representatives might include all current members of state legislatures, all governors, and all mayors of cities larger than fifty thousand people. Although that list would exclude business leaders, former professional athletes, and entertainers—some of whom will run for a House seat—it might be a reasonable starting point. Out of those thousands of state and local officials, we could randomly sample a few hundred cases to learn why some potential candidates are more or less interested in running for national office.[7]

For some projects, however, we may have to select a nonrandom sample. Perhaps the most common variant is the **convenience sample**. Journalists working under tight deadlines might sample this way, asking passersby what they think about the latest ethics scandal or foreign crisis. The "man on the street" is a convenient source of information. Lab experiments in politics sometimes use samples of college students who live nearby and take courses requiring their participation in an experiment. These students may be smart and energetic, but their main virtue for researchers is their convenience (sorry). While some lab experiments may advertise more widely for participants, researchers often take whoever happens to volunteer. Lacking a complete list of environmental NGOs working in Africa, we might sample from those mentioned in a database of newspaper and magazine stories over some period of time. By sheer luck, a convenience sample could turn out to be as representative as a random sample, but the odds of that happening are not good. The bottom line is that anyone who generalizes from a convenience sample should be very, very careful.

A **snowball sample** is a special type of convenience sample, and probably more reputable. Researchers use this approach when the population of interest is hard to find or unlikely to cooperate. A random sample simply won't work. Think "tax cheats," "members of hate groups," or "those who provide material support to armed rebels." These are important topics, and we need to find some way of studying them. Sometimes the best strategy is to develop rapport with one individual and then reach out to others in the group who trust that individual. Like a snowball, the sample gets bigger as it is pushed gently across the terrain. Kathryn Edin and Laura Lein used this approach when they were trying to pinpoint the sources of income and major expenses for poor single mothers living on welfare or working in low-wage jobs. Because few people are willing to share this kind of information with strangers, the researchers had to gain the trust of one or two women and ask to be referred to similar mothers in the community. Eventually, the researchers managed to conduct personal interviews with 379 single mothers in four different cities. Given the inherent difficulty of the study, it was an impressive accomplishment.[8]

Nonetheless, a convenience sample or a snowball sample will probably be biased. Most of these samples won't represent the full population of interest and thus could lack external validity. The kinds of environmental groups that are mentioned in newspapers and magazines will likely be national and international organizations. By sampling from this population, we could miss their local counterparts. Edin and Lein might have gained the trust of single mothers who felt they had nothing to hide. They could have missed women with substantial under-the-table income.

The generic name for this problem is **selection bias**, and it can affect random samples as well. Selection bias occurs when researchers fail to sample from the entire population. Important segments may therefore be excluded or underrepresented. The infamous 1936 *Literary Digest* poll is often cited as an example of selection bias. In order to predict the winner of the US presidential election that year, the magazine sent surveys to an astounding 10 million Americans. Over 2 million people responded, an unprecedented number. The poll showed that President Roosevelt would be defeated soundly—and yet he won in a landslide. The challenger, Alf Landon, carried a grand total of two states. The survey went terribly wrong because it unwittingly sampled from special segments of the United States: registered automobile owners, subscribers to the *Literary Digest*, and people with a home phone number. The pollsters failed to recognize that those groups tended to be more affluent and more conservative than the population at large in 1936. Given this sampling strategy, many of Roosevelt's supporters never had a chance to voice their opinion.[9]

Polling organizations are more sophisticated these days, but problems of selection bias remain. For example, phone-based surveys have traditionally sampled from a population of people with landline phones. Doing so omits people who rely entirely on cell phones. Currently, over one-third of American adults don't have a landline phone, and that number has been growing. Studies show that cell phone–only households are more common among racial minorities and young adults than the rest of the US population. If those groups are underrepresented in the sample, the poll results could be flawed.[10] Benjamin Page argues that many academic studies overestimate the impact of public opinion on policy because they sample primarily from policies the public knows and cares about. Less visible policies might be exactly where the influence of interest groups is strong and public opinion is not.[11] Researchers who conduct experiments worry about selection bias all the time. A lab experiment that relies exclusively on college students as subjects might not end up with a sample that looks like most adults, or even most young adults.* The scope of field experiments, particularly in remote or unstable parts of the world, might have to be limited to certain regions or groups.[12]

A related problem is **nonresponse bias**.† Researchers might succeed in distributing an opinion survey to a random sample of some population. Or, they might invite a random sample of the local community to volunteer for an experiment. They could avoid selection bias entirely and still end up with a biased sample. It depends on who responds. Researchers might not receive many surveys at all from political conservatives, or from union members. Most of the volunteers who show up for an experiment could be retired or out of work; employed individuals could be underrepresented in the sample because they are short on free time. Almost any website asking people to rate restaurants, hotels, movies, or even professors will be vulnerable to nonresponse bias. Those who feel indifferent will probably not take the time to access the website and record their views. The comments posted to the website will tend to be very positive, very negative, or both. Some scholars believe that the 1936 *Literary Digest* poll suffered from nonresponse bias as well as sampling bias. For some reason Roosevelt's supporters, even those who owned cars and telephones, were less likely to return that survey than were

---

*Even a lab experiment that recruited college students by placing flyers in random dorms might be prone to selection bias if most of the juniors and seniors lived off campus.

†Some methods textbooks refer to this problem as response bias. That term, however, has a different meaning to specialists in political psychology and public opinion. To them, response bias refers to individuals behaving in ways that aren't truly sincere, perhaps because they want to appear more open-minded or cooperative than they really are. Response bias does not refer to the composition of the sample.

Landon's supporters.[13] While selection bias is often the fault of researchers, nonresponse bias may be due to a certain measure of bad luck.

A biased sample is not necessarily a fatal defect. The sample could be biased in ways that are theoretically irrelevant, such as failing to include anyone who adores Ricky Jay in a study about foreign policy attitudes. The extent of bias, even if relevant, could be minimal. Moreover, a biased sample could produce valid results if the groups that are overrepresented and underrepresented are similar in important ways. Imagine that we were studying American attitudes toward abortion, and that somehow our sample turned out to be 90 percent male. This sounds like a terrible sample, a clear sign to start over. However, in the United States, men and women usually have fairly similar attitudes toward abortion. Asked whether women should be able to get an abortion for any reason, 40 percent of men and 43 percent of women agreed in 2012; in 2000, about 37 percent of both men and women agreed to this same question.[14] In this example, it might not matter for the aggregate results if our sample was 90/10, 33/67, or 50/50 male to female (with only 10 percent women in a sample, though, we might not be able to say much about female attitudes). Likewise, an experiment conducted solely with undergraduate political science majors could produce the same results as one with a more representative mix of majors.

Of course, we might not know in advance whether different parts of our sample are similar to each other. Even if we did know that American men and women have had similar views toward abortion in recent decades, we might want to know if those patterns still hold true. In other words, we might not want to assume what we originally planned to investigate. In that case, researchers might recalibrate the cases in their sample so that underrepresented segments are given as much weight as they have in the full population. Faced with a sample in which men happen to outnumber women 2:1, researchers might count each woman's response twice in order to achieve parity. The best strategy might be to choose a stratified random sample from the beginning. That way we could generate the right mix of men and women, different ethnic groups, old and new bureaucracies, resource-rich and resource-poor countries, or whatever characteristics are relevant to our study. At a minimum, we would expect researchers to be transparent about the process of generating their samples.[15]

We still need to figure out how to boost the external validity of case studies, which should not be selected randomly. It will be difficult to generalize from one case or a few cases, but we do have options. As mentioned above, one tactic is largely conceptual and definitional. If we believe that certain political phenomena are rare (e.g., modern world wars) or even unique (e.g.,

US presidential elections decided by the Supreme Court), then a case study design can cover much if not all of the total population. The external validity of our research should be good. For most research projects, however, the population is larger than a handful of cases. We will need to make inferences.

Intuitively, a comparative case study should have advantages over a single case study in this regard, if only because the *n* is larger. A comparative case study might boost external validity if the cases varied along some important dimension. In her study of health policy (see chapter 3), Immergut picked one country case (Sweden) in which the government was heavily involved in providing health insurance, regulating medical costs, and delivering medical care; one case (Switzerland) in which the government was much less involved in health care; and one case (France) somewhere between these two extremes.* Had she stuck with just Sweden or just Switzerland, we might have wondered if she picked an outlier that wouldn't tell us much about other countries. This would be like Ricky Jay showing us a queen of hearts and trying to convince us that his deck, which we cannot see, was full of queens. Had Immergut picked three countries that all resembled Sweden, we would have had similar concerns. That would be akin to revealing three cards, all hearts, and implying that the rest of the deck was mostly hearts. A clear pattern across three distinct cases, however, makes us more confident about health policy making in Europe or among affluent democracies.[16] This strategy can work whether we are trying to describe or explain patterns.

We can imagine many different projects using this same basic approach. To study the effectiveness of UN missions, a researcher might start by classifying missions into different categories. It could make sense to select one mission related to civil conflict and another related to natural disaster. When studying the durability of general interest reforms in the United States, Eric Patashnik chose cases from distinct policy domains such as taxation, transportation, and agriculture instead of limiting his cases to a single issue area. Melissa Nobles picked one country that emphasized race (the United States) and a second country that emphasized color (Brazil) in her book about the politics of census categories.[17] In these examples, some variety among the cases added to the project's external validity.

Although this strategy is not feasible for a single case study, researchers still have options. They might deliberately select a **typical case** for careful scrutiny. For this approach to work, previous research, perhaps based on statistical comparisons of many cases, must have already identified the

---

*We might think of this approach as stratified purposive sampling.

typical and atypical cases. Thus, the case is typical in light of many other cases. With the resource curse hypothesis, for instance, we know that Saudi Arabia is fairly typical—lots of oil, lots of inequality, not much democracy. We don't need a case study to show that these features coexist. A case study that carefully traced out the process by which oil impeded democracy, in contrast, could be quite useful. That causal path might also apply to other countries similar to Saudi Arabia. In the United States, presidential approval ratings often parallel the state of the economy. Demonstrating that approval dropped during a recession isn't exactly front-page news. Nevertheless, a case study that zeroed in on one such episode and tried to figure out what specific features of the economy (e.g., inflation, gas prices, unemployment, the deficit) worried most Americans; why individuals blamed the president for the downturn; and how the president tried to manage public expectations or deflect blame could be instructive. A typical case practically demands process tracing.

The external validity of a typical case study depends on how homogeneous the whole population is. The more cases are alike, the more readily one can generalize from a single case. But what if the relevant population is quite heterogeneous? Instead of tasting soup, we are facing an enormous buffet. In that situation, we could select an **intrinsically important case**, one that is more significant than most of the other cases in the population.[18] For students of terrorism, the attacks of 9/11 would certainly qualify. Anyone interested in understanding the rise of far-right political parties might well choose to study Germany's Nazi Party during the 1920s and 1930s. Many scholars who engage in descriptive research choose cases largely because of their intrinsic importance.

My research specialty is US social policy. Among programs aimed at the poor, Medicaid stands head and shoulders above the rest. It costs five times more than any other antipoverty program and a hundred times more than many of these programs. Medicaid helps more people in a given year than any public assistance or social insurance program, and that includes Social Security. Because Medicaid serves a diverse mix of poor people—children, adults, the elderly, the disabled; because it relies on powerful third parties such as doctors, hospitals, and nursing homes to deliver medical care; and because formal authority is shared between the national and state governments, the politics of Medicaid are fascinating. Although Medicaid is just one of over a hundred public assistance programs, I would argue that it is by far the most important case. Accurately describing and explaining its politics are essential to understanding public assistance programs. From this angle, the population that matters consists of analytic insights, not individual programs. Studying Medicaid is more likely to generate those insights than examining a dozen lesser programs would.*

Alternatively, a case could be intrinsically important because the author believes it has been widely misunderstood (in effect, challenging a piece of Conventional Wisdom; see chapter 1). Many observers have maintained that the recent Great Recession was unnecessarily painful because key institutions such as the World Bank and the International Monetary Fund performed so badly. Daniel Drezner's recent book, *The System Worked*, argues the opposite.[19] In his view, global economic governance prevented this recession from becoming a full-fledged depression and helped a number of economies to rebound quickly. Drezner isn't claiming that these institutions always work well, but in this one important case, contrary to conventional wisdom, they did.

Whether the population is homogeneous or heterogeneous, we could pick a **hard case** to analyze. "Hard" in this context doesn't mean that evidence will be tough to find. It means that the case seems unlikely to support a given hypothesis. If a hypothesis holds true in a hard case, then it ought to hold true in many other cases. This strategy should sound familiar, because we already use it in our everyday lives. To determine whether our clothes are ready to come out of the dryer, we feel the blue jeans first. Dry jeans probably mean that our T-shirts and socks are dry, too. To test whether meat is cooked through, we slice into the thickest portion. If that portion looks done, then the rest should be ready to eat.

In these mundane examples, the hard cases were chosen based on prior experience. In political science, a hard case is chosen in light of prior research. Charles Lipson points out that *Essence of Decision*, the classic study of the Cuban missile crisis, was a hard case for certain theories of bureaucratic politics. Sure, we may know that bureaucracies have a lot of influence over less visible or technically complicated policies, like agricultural price supports. The real test comes when the issue is visible to all, and elected officials hold very different views from bureaucrats about what should be done. The Cuban missile crisis showed that bureaucratic politics remained powerful even under these conditions: "Despite a presidential order and

---

*Among contemporary communist governments, China could seem more significant than the rest for almost any political question we might ask. Instead of studying the entire population of cases, we might focus on China to describe how party leaders are recruited and promoted. For a different project, one designed to inform current policy debates, an intrinsically important case could be one that closely resembles a contemporary problem.

close monitoring by the highest levels of American government, the US Navy still implemented the embargo according to its own internal procedures."[20] The implication is that if bureaucrats and operating routines were influential during one of the biggest foreign policy crises in US history, their power probably extends far beyond the price of soybeans. A hard test for theories of incumbency could involve a Republican senator from a state that routinely votes Democratic in presidential elections. If that senator can win reelection several times, then we would expect incumbency to benefit a wide range of politicians. Our case study would trace out the different ways this senator used his official position to enhance his chances for reelection.

An **easy case**, by contrast, is one in which the hypothesis is most likely to work. If it does not, then we feel confident that the hypothesis won't apply to many other cases. In the middle of the twentieth century, many political scientists believed that cross-cutting cleavages were needed to promote stability and comity within a country. The more that religious differences aligned with region, for example, or that language differences aligned with social status, the more likely that conflict would occur. Arend Lijphart's case study of the Netherlands cast serious doubt on this hypothesis. Here was a country with relatively few cross-cutting cleavages, and yet the level of political friction was quite low.[21] For an everyday example of an easy case, we can go back to the clothes dryer—if the T-shirts aren't dry, then the jeans must not be, either. When an easy case fails to support a hypothesis, we learn more than when it does offer support (dry T-shirts could still mean damp jeans).

A convenience sample is usually a poor way to choose a case study, for the same reasons as a random sample.* You simply do not know what kind of case will come walking through your door. A cautionary tale: Students in my Research Methods course are usually required to write a case study, with some evidence of process tracing, on a topic of their choice. A few years ago, one student wanted to investigate voter apathy in liberal democracies. His cases were Australia, Britain, Canada, Germany, Greece, New Zealand, and the United States. Put aside the question of whether anyone can analyze that many cases well in the six to seven pages I allotted for this assignment (the short answer is no). He picked these cases because they happened to be mentioned in newspaper articles about voter apathy that were published in the year 2009, which he found after spending two minutes with an electronic

---

* One exception to this rule might be exploratory research, where collectively we know very little about a certain population. A detailed study of a convenient case might generate insights and hypotheses that other scholars could analyze later using a larger set of cases.

CHAPTER FIVE

database. These cases bore no connection to previous studies of voter apathy; their selection was not informed by any theory. He did not argue that any of his cases were typical, intrinsically important, or hard. The real story here was researcher apathy, not voter apathy.

In a sense, external validity refers to the "exportability" of our research. Scholars hope their insights, whether descriptive or explanatory, will travel beyond their particular project. Picking the right cases will make that trip smoother. No one will be very interested in importing those insights, however, if the internal validity of the research is suspect. We also need to select cases in order to be confident that certain relationships do or do not exist within the confines of a given study.

CHOOSING CASES TO BOOST INTERNAL VALIDITY

The external validity of experimental designs depends in part on case selection (as well as the artificiality of the setting and the treatment). The internal validity of an experiment does not. As we saw in chapter 4, random assignment is the key. For that reason I will say little about experiments in this part of the chapter. The emphasis will be on choosing cases for observational research designs.

One basic element of internal validity, whether we are working with descriptive or causal hypotheses, involves covariation among our key concepts (technically, among the measures of those concepts). We need to figure out if our concepts are directly or inversely related, or if no relationship exists at all. It would help to have cases in which the values of our measures do indeed vary. Not all the measures have to be variables; some could be constants. A hypothesis involving the relationship between a constant and a variable will be rejected, which might be analytically useful. For example, when Putnam was trying to determine why some Italian regional governments performed better than others (see chapter 1), he eliminated institutional design as an explanation because all those governments shared the same basic design. Fortunately, his other explanatory variables weren't constant across the regions.[22] If we subscribe to the view that the United States has always operated within a Lockean liberal tradition, one that favors individual liberty and limited government, then it will be hard to establish any relationship between this constant political culture and some other feature of American politics that changes.

Most features of the political world do vary over time or space, and researchers try to take advantage of this fact when analyzing relationships. This is one place where large-n statistical comparisons have a decided advantage over small-n case studies. A deliberate sample of two or three cases could give us a good idea of the full range of values for an independent or dependent variable. We might interview one individual who strongly opposed sending troops to Syria and one who strongly supported the move. A random sample of one thousand people, on the other hand, would give us a much more refined picture of public opinion. We would encounter people whose views fell in between the two extremes, and we would have a better idea of whether the population was evenly split on the question (as the two-person sample implies), or whether the public leaned more to one side or the other. With more cases, our ability to detect the true direction of a relationship and its strength almost always improves.

Likewise, a large-n study is better equipped to check for spuriousness. We will be able to control for confounding variables if we have more cases. Scholars may have a number of explanations (e.g., political ideology, age, gender, education) for why people do or do not support military intervention overseas. A really small sample won't allow us to observe many combinations of factors, which we need in order to sort out their relative importance. We might talk with a conservative man, age fifty, who has a college degree, and with a liberal female, age thirty-two, holding a graduate degree. If we stopped there, we would have no clue as to which factors were linked to their opposing views toward military intervention. We might be forced to conclude that everything matters, which isn't much of an explanation. To give a more precise answer, we would also need to talk with conservative women, younger liberal men, older liberal men, moderates of both genders, high school graduates of different ages, and so on. We would need to talk with hundreds and hundreds of people, chosen randomly from the population. A large random sample thus provides a double benefit to researchers: it can help us generalize with more confidence, which is good for external validity; and it can supply useful variation in the variables we care about, which is good for internal validity.

The real challenge is figuring out how to test for covariation and spuriousness in small-n case studies. For comparative case studies, one smart move is to limit the number of rival hypotheses from the start. Although we can't control for many confounding influences, we can examine a few. With only three cases, Immergut could still make a strong argument that the power of doctors, by itself, was not a good explanation for national differences in health policy. Nor was the power of left-wing political parties. Institutions mattered more. Stated more precisely, she found that differences in institutional veto points enabled doctors to be more powerful in Switzerland than in France, and both were more powerful than doctors in Sweden. One might reasonably wonder about the impact of national values, economic crises, or any number of variables that she never tested. Fair enough. Immergut did not pretend to test for a large number of competing explanations, and wisely so.

Another smart move is to choose a few cases that differ on the variable of interest. If we are trying to explain some outcome, then our main interest is in the dependent variable, and we would pick cases with different values for that variable. That is what Immergut did. Richard Valelly did likewise when he contrasted the failed enfranchisement of blacks in late nineteenth-century America with their successful enfranchisement after World War II.[23] If instead we are interested in the impact of certain causal factors, then our main interest is in the independent variable. Someone studying the impact of ethnic diversity on public goods provision might select two communities, one with high levels of diversity and the other with low levels. Picking cases in this manner will make it easier for us to detect covariation.

To control for other confounding factors, at least to some degree, we would look for cases that differ on the variable of interest but are similar in other, theoretically relevant respects. Too many differences among our cases would leave us dazed and confused. Table 5.1 depicts several selection strategies for comparative case studies, and the first example (A) is definitely one to avoid. The values of the dependent variable do differ for our two cases, but so do the values for most of the independent variables. The second and third independent variables are directly related to the dependent variable, while the fourth independent variable is inversely related. To make this scenario more concrete, assume that the dependent variable is the traffic fatality rate, and our two states are Louisiana and Massachusetts. These seem like two great cases to analyze in depth, because Louisiana's fatality rate is much higher than that of Massachusetts. In addition, they share some factors in common (e.g., teenagers in both states are equally likely to ride in a car without wearing a seat belt). Unfortunately for our research, those two states also differ in the availability of public transportation, the number of doctors and hospitals, per capita beer consumption, population density, per capita income, and maximum speed limits—all of which might affect their traffic fatality rates.*

We would be better off, analytically, comparing states like Colorado and Montana, states that might not differ quite as much in their fatality rates, but otherwise are much more alike than are Louisiana and Massachusetts. In general, we should adopt the second strategy (B) shown in table 5.1. That

---

* In the language of social science, the differences between these two states will be overdetermined.

Table 5.1. Selection strategies for comparative case studies

	Independent variables				Dependent variable
	1	2	3	4	
(A) "METHOD OF CONFUSION"					
Case 1	Same	More	More	Less	More
Case 2	Same	Less	Less	More	Less
(B) METHOD OF DIFFERENCE					
Case 1	Same	Same	More	Same	More
Case 2	Same	Same	Less	Same	Less
(C) METHOD OF DIFFERENCE					
Case 1	A bit more	Same	A lot more	Same	A lot more
Case 2	A bit less	Same	A lot less	Same	A lot less
(D) METHOD OF AGREEMENT					
Case 1	More	Less	More	Same	Same
Case 2	Less	More	Less	Same	Same

Note: *More*, *less*, and *same* refer to values of each variable.

strategy produces a clear answer; we can eliminate several independent variables and focus on one that varies directly or inversely with our dependent variable. Political scientists often refer to this strategy as **Mill's method of difference**, after the philosopher and logician John Stuart Mill. The objective is to find cases with different values on the dependent variable, yet with similar values for as many independent variables as possible. In a sense, we're looking for a natural experiment in which we observe only one causal factor varying across our cases while the rest remain constant.

Finding real-world puzzles that correspond exactly to this scenario is rare. More often, we will need something like the third strategy (C) shown in table 5.1. This, too, is a version of the method of difference. Working with a few cases, we might be able to eliminate some causes, but a few will remain. Here is where it helps to pick cases that differ considerably on the dependent variable. We could have one independent variable whose values differ a little bit across our cases, and another independent variable whose values differ much more. We could reasonably infer that the latter was the main cause and the former was a minor influence. The assumption is that big changes in one independent variable are more likely than small changes in another independent variable to produce big changes in the dependent variable.*

The last strategy (D) for case selection in table 5.1 corresponds to **Mill's method of agreement**.[†] This is the opposite of the method of difference. Find cases that have identical (or very similar) values for the dependent variable but differ in all other relevant respects except one, and you will have found the cause. It turns out that Rhode Island and Utah have very similar rates of traffic fatalities. They also differ in their maximum speed limits, alcohol consumption, per capita income, population density, and doctors per capita. We would therefore rule out these explanations and keep searching for what these states do have in common that might account for their similar rates of traffic fatalities.

Political scientists tend to be skeptical of the method of agreement. By **selecting on the dependent variable**—in other words, by choosing cases with similar values for the dependent variable—we could be guilty of selection bias. Because we are sampling from only one part of the population, we might miss cases in which the dependent variable had a much different value, yet the independent variable looks much the same. What we thought was a key independent variable could be closer to a constant. In short, this kind of selection bias can compromise the internal validity of our research. Rhode Island and Utah both receive around forty inches of snow each year; maybe snow is the one thing they have in common that is connected with their similar rates of traffic fatalities. However, both states are below the national average when it comes to traffic fatalities. Had we included states that are above average in fatalities, we would have found cases (e.g., Pennsylvania, Idaho) with fairly comparable snowfalls to Rhode Island and Utah. Our independent variable would thus be associated with below-average scores and above-average scores on the dependent variable, which renders it pretty useless. Our snowfall theory quickly melts away.[‡]

---

* Large-*n* statistical comparisons are better able to detect covariation when the differences in values across cases are less pronounced.

[†] Given that Mr. Mill has already claimed title to examples B, C, and D in table 5.1, perhaps we can think of example A as "Howard's method of confusion."

[‡] Many authors writing about highly successful people try to discover what "secret ingredient" they have in common. Often the answer includes hard work and perseverance. But if you examine less successful people, many of them may be working just as hard.

Barbara Geddes is well known for her warnings about selecting on the dependent variable. She offers a particularly good illustration of this problem when discussing past studies of newly industrializing countries. Several of these studies focused on the same handful of cases—notably South Korea, Taiwan, Singapore, and Brazil—that all had strong economic growth. These same countries made it difficult for workers to organize. Hence, labor repression must have contributed to economic growth. That relationship looks far less convincing, however, once we include countries with lower levels of economic growth (i.e., once we create more variation in the dependent variable). Some of these additional countries feature just as much labor repression as Singapore and South Korea. So much for that explanation.[24] To avoid selecting on the dependent variable, many political scientists gravitate toward method of difference when comparing a few cases.

Some of the same selection strategies can be adopted for single case studies as for comparative case studies. Because variation is a good thing, individual cases that vary over time on key dimensions may be worth studying in detail. In the few years before 2007, hundreds of US soldiers and thousands of civilians were being killed annually in Iraq. By 2010, the death toll was one-tenth of what it had been. What changed over time that might account for this dramatic improvement?[25] Large variations like this one should make it easier for researchers to spot the causes; chances are slim that some small change could be responsible for such a big drop in violence. By the same logic, large variations within a country or bureaucracy or social movement (the list goes on) at a single point in time could prove analytically useful.

In some ways a single case study could help control for confounding variables more effectively than a comparative case study. Instead of comparing traffic fatalities between two states, we would track a single state over several years—perhaps a state that experienced a large or sudden change in its fatality rate. Certain features such as per capita income, the availability of doctors and hospitals, alcohol consumption, and population density would probably change little within that state over the chosen period. After verifying that this was true, we could eliminate them as explanations. We would look for something that had changed significantly, such as a change in the highway speed limit or drunk-driving laws. A related advantage of following a single case over time is that the researcher can more readily determine the causal order of variables. If the fatality rate rose two years before the state's speed limit increased from sixty-five to seventy miles per hour, the higher limit was probably not a decisive cause. In general, historical case studies have the potential to provide a decent dose of internal validity.

Choosing typical cases, I argued, can enhance the external validity of a study. Atypical cases, sometimes called **deviant cases** or **outliers**, can help with the internal validity in at least two ways.[26] If the claim is that *A* and *B* are <u>always</u> related (which is uncommon in the social sciences given our fondness for regularities, not iron laws), a deviant case refutes that wisdom by finding one instance where *A* was not associated with *B*. More often, deviant cases can help us to refine our thinking. In the resource curse literature, Norway is a clear outlier, an oil-rich nation with modest levels of inequality and a well-functioning democracy. Norway isn't Nigeria, and it's not Saudi Arabia. A careful study of that country might uncover other factors setting it apart from most resource-rich countries, which in turn might lead to a more nuanced understanding of how oil hinders democracy. Perhaps timing mattered, and Norway was fortunate to discover vast reserves of oil only after it had industrialized and democratized. For most other countries, that sequence was reversed. Another possibility is that a careful study of Norway could suggest a different kind of explanation that would work for other atypical cases such as Botswana.

Nevertheless, when we pick cases so carefully, hunting for just the right combination of similarities and differences in our key variables, we appear to be stacking the analytic deck in our own favor. We could be creating the illusion of internal validity. Once again we face a Ricky Jay problem. In working through the example of traffic fatalities, I have demonstrated an unusual and perhaps disturbing familiarity with death in the American states. Using a comparative-case or single-case design, I could support a variety of hypotheses. If I wanted to link alcohol consumption to traffic fatalities, I would contrast Utah to Montana. On average, people in Montana drink more than twice as much alcohol as people in Utah, and the traffic fatality rate in Montana is more than double as well. In many other respects, the states are quite similar. Therefore, alcohol must be the key factor. Alternatively, if I wanted to link population density or per capita income to traffic fatalities, I would pair Montana with Colorado. To debunk the impact of speed limits, I could conduct a historical case study of Nevada, whose fatality rate dropped by more than half in recent decades even though it raised the top speed limit on rural interstates from sixty-five to seventy-five miles per hour. Given the freedom to choose my cases, I can tell all kinds of stories. Cynical, but true.

But nobody wants to be known as the Ricky Jay of car crashes. The basic problem facing case study scholars is how to gain the trust of the audience when some suspect them of stacking the deck. One smart move is to demonstrate something that can't be rigged through deliberate case selection:

engage in process tracing, which is also essential in proving a causal relationship. As mentioned in chapter 4, process tracing is one of the real advantages of the case study design. Researchers analyze developments within each case in greater detail than is typically possible with large-n statistical comparisons.[27] Sure, I can pick a few states where traffic fatalities will vary directly with alcohol consumption. Immergut can pick a few European countries where the number of institutional veto points will vary inversely with government involvement in health care. Neither move requires a tremendous amount of skill. A good case study must do more. The real test is whether Immergut can establish clear links between the Swiss referendum and Swiss health policy, and between changes to the formal powers of the French executive and changes to French health policy. Once she does, the internal validity of her argument is in much better shape. Even if other scholars later examine additional cases and find different causes at work, the principle of equifinality says they could both be right. Moreover, skilled process tracing could redeem a method of agreement design as long as researchers (a) show precisely how their independent variable(s) led to a certain outcome, and (b) recognize the biased nature of their sample and don't generalize too broadly. In short, a method of agreement study with process tracing could have limited external validity but good internal validity.[28]

Effective process tracing usually requires different types of evidence from a variety of sources (see chapter 4). This is one reason why Van Evera recommends consciously choosing **data-rich cases**.[29] This advice is particularly sound for undergraduates and others who are working under tight deadlines. A nation, a war, or a piece of legislation that offers abundant evidence is a better choice than one where evidence is hard to come by. Researchers can then comb through government documents, party platforms, newspaper stories, policy briefs, biographies, and the like, trying to document each link in the causal chain that connects their independent and dependent variables. Between 1990 and 2009, the traffic fatality rate dropped by half in many US states, a truly impressive change. It would be good to know why. Using a historical case study, I might select New York or California over Oregon or Indiana. My strong hunch (which could be wrong) is that evidence would be more plentiful in the first two states. Essentially, I would go fishing in that part of the ocean where I believed many fish lived. Immergut could have picked Sweden, Andorra, and Switzerland to represent a range of health policies. Choosing France over Andorra made more sense given the evidence available for each country. On the other hand, a research project with a longer time horizon, such as a dissertation or book, might deliberately work with data-poor cases if one important objective was collecting new evidence.

A good question and a solid research design are not enough. Political scientists also need to choose their cases intelligently if they hope to produce a good answer. And they must do so transparently if they hope to convince their audience. The right strategy for choosing cases will often depend on the research design. As a general rule, random sampling is a smart move for variable-oriented designs (experiments, large-*n* statistical comparisons), while deliberate sampling works best for case studies. Some projects might combine elements of both strategies. For instance, of all the foreign policy attitudes, those toward military intervention could be considered intrinsically important. Such life-and-death issues deserve more attention than, say, goodwill ambassadors for the UN. Having deliberately chosen this set of attitudes, researchers could then survey a large random sample of adults to identify the conditions under which they would support sending troops into another country. A different kind of project might start with a deviant case and then devise an experiment to understand it more thoroughly.

This chapter has highlighted common problems in case selection, as well as ways to minimize or work around them. Even a large random sample, which has a number of analytic virtues, can be flawed. While random samples may be vulnerable to nonresponse bias, random and deliberate samples can be tainted by selection bias. Small deliberate samples, a staple of the case study design, are especially vulnerable to selection bias. Case study researchers should make sure they have picked each case wisely before investing considerable time and energy analyzing it in depth. Oftentimes it will be smart to invoke more than one justification. For instance, we might select Saudi Arabia as a typical case for the resource curse and then study the relationships among oil revenues, tax revenues, military spending, and democracy over a few decades. That approach could help both the external and the internal validity of the study.

More cases, or more observations within cases, will often be helpful. We want most of our measures to be variables, and perhaps all of them. Variation is essential to establishing the internal validity of a descriptive or a causal research project. Thus, while comparison lies at the heart of political research, many of those comparisons involve contrasting cases. To answer the Why question, we will also need evidence with respect to causal order and causal mechanisms. Cases that have a history and a rich pool of data are often good choices.

Having chosen a research design and one or more cases, we are now ready to gather evidence. (If we picked cases deliberately, we've already started collecting evidence; that's how I knew which American states would be good candidates for intensive study.) This is the point where some students ask, "How many sources do I need?" and some teachers say, "Raise your hand if you have used JSTOR." We can do better. The final two chapters of this guide offer suggestions for finding evidence and analyzing it as well. We start first with written documents, then numbers.

PRACTICE: INSPECTING

1. For each of the following readings, figure out first whether the case(s) represent a sample or a population. If the authors used a sample, did they choose it randomly, or deliberately? To what extent do you think the authors' selection of cases helped the external validity of their project? And the internal validity? Overall, what is your single biggest concern about the case selection strategy in each reading?

    Kevin Arceneaux, Martin Johnson, and Chad Murphy, "Polarized Political Communication, Media Hostility, and Selective Exposure," *Journal of Politics* 74, no. 1 (January 2012): 174–86;

    Andrew Beath, Fotini Christia, and Ruben Enikolopov, "Empowering Women through Development Aid: Evidence from a Field Experiment in Afghanistan," *American Political Science Review* 107, no. 3 (August 2013): 540–57;

    Michael C. Horowitz and Allan C. Stam, "How Prior Military Experience Influences the Future Militarized Behavior of Leaders," *International Organization* 68, no. 3 (June 2014): 527–59;

    Cindy D. Kam, "Risk Attitudes and Political Participation," *American Journal of Political Science* 56, no. 4 (October 2012): 817–36;

    Mona Lynch and Craig Haney, "Capital Jury Deliberation: Effects on Death Sentencing, Comprehension, and Discrimination," *Law and Human Behavior* 33, no. 6 (December 2009): 481–96;

    Edmund Malesky, Regina Abrami, and Yu Zheng, "Institutions and Inequality in Single-Party Regimes: A Comparative Analysis of China and Vietnam," *Comparative Politics* 43, no. 4 (July 2011): 401–19;

    Sarah Elizabeth Parkinson, "Organizing Rebellion: Rethinking High-Risk Mobilization and Social Networks in War," *American Political Science Review* 107, no. 3 (August 2013): 418–32;

    Steve C. Ropp, "Explaining the Long-Term Maintenance of a Military Regime: Panama before the U.S. Invasion," *World Politics* 44, no. 2 (January 1992): 210–34;

    Eleanor Singer and Mick P. Crouper, "The Effect of Question Wording on Attitudes toward Prenatal Testing and Abortion," *Public Opinion Quarterly* 78, no. 3 (Fall 2014): 751–60.

1. Imagine that you wanted to study attitudes in your community concerning the performance of the local schools. Your community is large enough and your time and money constraints are serious enough that you can't possibly include the entire population. Develop one or two good plans for sampling people from your community. Then describe a different sampling strategy that would be seriously flawed, and explain why.

2. Studies of voting behavior are quite common in political science, and voter turnout is probably the most prominent dependent variable in this literature. Suppose you were analyzing voter turnout on the continent of Lemuria, which comprises twenty-five countries but has seldom been studied. From your literature review of voting in other parts of the world, you learn that higher levels of income and education usually mean greater turnout. You find precise ratio measures of these variables for the year 2010. Tougher registration requirements, in contrast, usually mean lower turnout. You create an ordinal measure that combines factors such as whether voters need to register before Election Day, whether they face a poll tax or literacy test, and whether the registration places are easily accessible. The table below summarizes your evidence:

	Per capita income	Percent HS graduates	Registration requirements	Voter turnout (%)
Awkland	42,669	69	Medium	90
Bluebell	14,047	54	Very High	56
Bonquerres	49,754	84	Medium	84
Chinet	27,160	40	High	63
Colliestan	15,889	70	Low	63
Corazonia	5,626	32	Low	80
Drago	12,455	34	Medium	60
Flamboya	44,090	31	Medium	68
Fluoristan	29,709	79	Low	85
Huckland	15,697	63	Low	74
Joyrida	14,224	32	High	51
Laurelstan	29,713	50	Medium	64
Marginalia	17,636	64	Medium	57
Minaj	32,047	35	Medium	65
New Trenton	38,800	70	High	52

(*continued*)

	Per capita income	Percent HS graduates	Registration requirements	Voter turnout (%)
Peafunk	31,003	74	Low	83
Plaxico	19,584	42	Medium	58
Ronco	20,740	86	Medium	90
San Didunquen	45,726	76	Very Low	90
Slobovia	18,718	47	Medium	69
Uhuruguay	24,416	59	Medium	73
United Territories of Ostyo (UTOO)	43,115	78	Medium	77
Vietnaan	7,922	53	Low	66
Vuvuzela	15,189	60	High	44
Zischeln	13,875	49	High	87
Average	25,192	57	Medium	70

(a) If you wanted to conduct a comparative case study, which two or three countries would be good choices? Which would be bad choices? Either way, briefly explain why.

(b) If you wanted to analyze a typical case in depth, which country would you choose?

(c) If you wanted to study a deviant case (i.e., outlier), which country would you choose?

(d) What additional data would you want for any of these case studies?

6

USING DOCUMENTS AS EVIDENCE

When it comes time to start construction, all home builders go through the same process. First they purchase building materials from a trusted source. They might shop at a national chain such as Home Depot or Lowe's, or rely on local suppliers they know well. The types of materials they purchase will be quite varied, including wood beams and planks, metal joints and nails, asphalt or composite roof shingles, drywall, cinderblocks, cement, windows, and probably bricks or vinyl. At the construction site, the builders will deliberately make some parts of the home stronger than others. The corners of the house need to be much sturdier than the closet walls. Any wood that supports the roof should be thicker than the wood used to frame the windows.

Despite their fancy suits, trial lawyers work in much the same manner. When they call witnesses to the stand, lawyers begin by establishing the credibility of these persons. They will ask medical experts to state their academic degrees and professional experience. If someone is testifying as a character witness for the defendant, a lawyer will ask him how long he has known the accused, and in what capacity. In essence, lawyers want judges and juries to know if a given witness can be trusted. Few trials hinge on a single piece of evidence (the proverbial and sometimes literal "smoking gun"), and the process of piecing together different types of evidence consumes much of an attorney's time and energy. Lawyers in a murder trial might work with written reports from the medical examiner and the police, depositions from key witnesses, voicemails, text messages, photographs of the victim and, ideally, a weapon. A corruption trial might feature bank records, invoices, receipts, e-mail, secretly taped conversations, and photos of expensive gifts. And a good lawyer will know that she needs more evidence to establish the defendant's motive than, say, his home address.

Quality. Variety. A sense of proportion. These are important principles to keep in mind when assembling the materials needed to build a house or a court case. These principles apply with equal force to research in and writing about politics. As political scientists collect evidence, they search for the most credible sources of information available. They tend to think highly of peer-reviewed publications, and they realize that just about anyone can post just about anything on the Internet. Most use evidence from different sources in their arguments. Relying on a single scholar, think tank, or government agency could give a clear impression of what happened, but it might not provide a complete or a balanced impression. Moreover, political scientists realize that some parts of their argument will be common knowledge and therefore won't need to be documented, while other parts will require multiple sources of evidence. These principles hold true whether the evidence consists of words or numbers.*

Notice what attribute is <u>not</u> on this list—quantity. Quantity is much easier to measure than quality, variety, or a sense of proportion, which may explain why college students often want to know how many sources they need to cite in their research papers. This is the wrong question to ask. (Please. Stop.) In fact, it reveals a fundamental misunderstanding about evidence.[1] A lawyer who calls fifty unreliable witnesses to testify will not win her case. A smaller number of rock-solid witnesses would be much better.† Think instead about the types of evidence you will need. That's what good trial lawyers do. Calling close family members to serve as character witnesses might help the defendant; calling a mix of relatives, coworkers, and neighbors would help even more. And think about where the evidence is needed most. A house built with twenty-five hundred nails on the first floor and no nails on the second floor would fail inspection. Quality, variety, and a sense of proportion. If researchers abide by these three principles, they will end up with a substantial number of reference sources. But the sheer number is not the point.‡

The purpose of this chapter is to help readers understand the importance of quality, variety, and a sense of proportion when working with written records. For years I assumed that my students knew how to use documents as evidence in their research papers. They would have had plenty of practice in their history and government courses from high school and college. The

---

* Some undergraduates major in government / political science / politics as a logical step toward law school. They may even take courses about judicial politics or constitutional law. Nevertheless, the general ability to analyze and synthesize evidence from written documents is probably just as important as factual knowledge about the legal system. This helps explain how English, history, and philosophy majors are admitted to good law schools, even if they have never heard of the *Carolene Products* decision.

† Have you <u>ever</u> watched a courtroom scene—in person, on TV, or at the movies—where a lawyer asked the judge, "Your Honor, how many witnesses and exhibits will I need to win this case? I'm guessing the number is more than five, so . . . maybe eight? Ten?"

‡ Lenin is often quoted as saying that "quantity has a quality all its own." If we're talking about snow or dark chocolate, I would agree. But quantity is no substitute for quality when it comes to research.

hard part would be teaching them to work with numbers. Wrong. It turned out that some students had trouble finding good evidence from the written record, and many students had difficulty figuring how much and what kinds of evidence they needed at each step in their argument.[2] Simply introducing them to resources in the college library was not enough. Students needed more guidance in identifying and assembling the most useful sources out of the multitude potentially available to them. Otherwise, they might resort to a crude Google search and collect irrelevant or inadequate pieces of evidence. The general problem isn't limited to college students, either. Professional political scientists don't always handle textual evidence with care. As we read their books and articles, we should keep an eye on the kinds of written records they use to support different parts of their argument. This is particularly true for case studies, which depend more on documents for evidence than either experiments or large-n statistical comparisons.

Working with documents is an essential skill for political scientists because written records—for example, constitutions, laws, treaties, academic books and articles, court rulings, regulations, speeches, newspaper and magazine articles, legislative debates, party platforms, biographies, policy briefs—provide so much of the evidence in our research. When that evidence is lacking, some political scientists engage in field research to analyze or generate other types of written records. Working with documents requires a healthy skepticism, because some of them will be less credible or less helpful than others. It also requires a certain doggedness, a determination to dig and dig some more for the best possible evidence. Like so many elements of the research enterprise, working with documents takes training and practice.

QUALITY

Home builders have a decided advantage over political scientists. When builders go to buy their materials, they can rely on ASTM International (formerly known as the American Society for Testing and Materials) to set quality standards for everything from roof shingles and insulation to fasteners and gaskets. "ASTM" will often be printed somewhere on the product's container or packaging.[3] The American Political Science Association doesn't perform any function remotely close to this. It doesn't tell researchers which books are hazardous or unsafe, nor does it endorse newspapers that sustain a certain level of quality. Somehow, usually through trial and error, students have to learn for themselves what counts as high-quality evidence in the context of political research.

Many college libraries publish guides to help students identify credible sources of information. One of the top recommendations is to find authoritative sources.[4] This is sound advice, and I will discuss a few different ways in which a document can be authoritative. The extent of bias in a document, however, is distinct from its authority. A report from a think tank could be authoritative if a well-known expert wrote it, and yet that document could be biased if it presented only one side of an argument in the hopes of influencing policy. By the same token, a random blogger might skewer Democrats and Republicans equally with claims that alternated between the paranoid and the just plain wrong. Not very authoritative, but not particularly biased, either. Finally, the currency of a document is somewhat separate from how authoritative or biased it might be. Oftentimes we prefer the most recent research, but there are good reasons to use older documents. As readers and as researchers, we need to pay close attention to authority, bias, and currency in written records.

If you consult a dictionary, **authoritative** has at least three meanings, and all of them reflect the fact that *author* and *authoritative* share the same Latin root. To determine whether a document is authoritative, we focus on who wrote it. The first meaning, then, is "official." Government documents are considered authoritative sources of information, because they represent the official version of some event or process. We would usually consult the transcripts of hearings and floor debates in order to understand legislative behavior. In describing where political parties stood on the question of immigration (or any issue), we would read the official party platforms. These would probably not be the only sources we'd check, but a study of legislatures or political parties relying exclusively on newspaper accounts and omitting official documents would be sorely lacking. Other kinds of documents can also be authoritative in this sense. The official website of an interest group could give us an authoritative picture of its goals, activities, and policy preferences. It would be hard to imagine a satisfactory account of the National Rifle Association without some evidence from that organization's website. (Nevertheless, official documents like these can still be biased.)

The second meaning of *authoritative* refers more to the credentials and reputation of the author. The issue is whether the author is knowledgeable, maybe even recognized as an expert in the field. Frankly, this kind of authority is harder to evaluate than the official kind. A researcher might investigate the author's academic degrees, reasoning that someone with a doctorate in political science probably knows more about military coups than someone with a bachelor's degree in geology. That strategy works up to a point, but it will unfairly devalue authors with years of relevant experience (e.g., some journalists), and it could overstate the credentials of other authors. Even though I have PhD in political science, you should probably ignore anything I said about military coups, the European Union, international trade, democratization in Latin America, and a whole host of political topics.

Instead, I encourage students to examine the author's track record. Has she written a lot about this subject in the past? Someone studying the resource curse for the first time might come across an article by Michael Ross. A little more digging (which isn't hard; his CV is available online) reveals that he has been writing about the resource curse for more than a decade. Ross has published several articles about this topic in major political science journals, as well as two books with university presses. He certainly looks like an authority. Although Jody Williams lacks a PhD, she has written extensively about land mines and helped start an organization called the International Campaign to Ban Landmines, which was awarded the Nobel Peace Prize in 1997. Robert Pear has written scores of articles about US social policy over the years, primarily for the *New York Times*. Such impressive records make Williams and Pear authorities in their respective fields.

Nevertheless, the sheer number of publications or length of time spent studying a topic is no guarantee of an author's quality.* The Internet makes it cheap and easy for anyone to share his or her views about politics. Many advocacy groups and even some think tanks have in-house experts whose main qualification is their ability to repeat the company line over and over. Thus, when dealing with primary sources (which are created at the same time as the event or process under study), we might also ask whether the author was in a good position to observe. Historians refer to this as the "time and place rule": the closer a source is in time and place to the event, the more credible the source. A newspaper story explaining why the president withdrew from an arms control treaty would be more authoritative if it quoted the president's chief of staff than if it had quoted the Deputy Under Secretary for Food Safety at the Agriculture Department. Although both officials are members of the administration, the chief of staff works more closely with the president. Likewise, testimony from someone who personally witnessed Russian troops fighting in the Ukraine would be more authoritative than testimony from someone who read about these battles weeks later from the comfort of his Washington, DC, townhouse.[5]

---

* By analogy, consider the movies: the "comic actor" Rob Schneider has appeared in many films, yet seldom is he even close to being funny. He was nominated for a Razzie Award as Worst Actor of the Decade in 2010. The *Onion* once announced, tongue in cheek: "Rob Schneider Lands Role Originally Written for Chimp." Despite his long list of appearances, no one should look to Rob Schneider as an authority on comedy.

Newspaper and magazine articles are some of the most common primary sources cited by college students, and professional scholars routinely use them as well. The authority of these periodicals is often based on reputation. The *New York Times*, the *Wall Street Journal*, and the *Washington Post* are three newspapers generally held in high esteem for their coverage of US politics and international affairs.[6] Using evidence from these sources seldom raises concerns about quality. The *Economist* and the *National Journal* are two magazines that regularly provide trustworthy information about politics. Many other newspapers and magazines enjoy comparable levels of respect from professional researchers. Admittedly, these reputations don't reflect clear, objective standards of quality. They are conveyed more by word of mouth, and they can vary across subfields within political science. As a practical matter, it makes sense for college students embarking on a research project to ask their teacher for the names of trusted periodicals. And it makes sense for everyone to pay attention to the kinds of newspapers and magazines used in prior studies. The process of conducting a literature review (outlined in chapter 1) can tell us not only how previous scholars have asked and answered certain questions, but also what evidence they have used to substantiate those answers. While researching education policies in Texas, I might discover that past studies routinely cited evidence from the *Dallas Morning News* and *Texas Monthly*. I would be smart to look there for information.

Reputation matters a great deal when working with secondary sources such as books and journal articles, which are written after the event or process being examined. Generally speaking, publications that have been subject to **peer review** enjoy a stronger reputation for quality than those which have not. A lack of peer review isn't necessarily the kiss of death; it just means that the book or article should be treated with extra scrutiny.[7] Essentially, the objectives of peer review are to weed out bad or mediocre research and to improve the good stuff. Before publication, an article or book manuscript is typically sent out to two or three experts in the field. In a double-blind review, which is common with many academic journals, the reviewers are not told the name of the author, and the author does not know the names of the reviewers. Such anonymity is supposed to make the reviews more objective. (In a single-blind review, which happens with many books, the reviewers are given the author's name.) The reviewers are tasked with critiquing the work carefully, making sure that it is well constructed and represents a genuine contribution to the literature. They are expected to make a summary recommendation—for example, reject, needs major revisions, accept with minor revisions—and offer detailed comments to justify their verdict. Most submissions require revision, which then triggers a second round of peer review. The whole process can take from several months to a few years. The editors of these journals and university presses usually expect strong support from all the reviewers before agreeing to publish a new piece of research, which is one reason why most submissions are ultimately rejected.[8]

Figuring out whether a document has been peer reviewed is fairly straightforward. To my knowledge, all university presses use peer review for their books.[9] So do some other publishers, such as the Brookings Institution. Authors typically thank reviewers for their help in the acknowledgments section of their book. With academic journal articles, the first footnote or endnote almost always expresses some appreciation to the editors and "anonymous reviewers"; the latter are the peer reviewers. It's also common for authors of books and articles to name individuals who have provided useful feedback along the way, perhaps at a professional conference or departmental seminar. To the extent these individuals are well known and respected, their names provide readers with added reason to feel confident about the quality of the finished product.[10]

The peer review process isn't perfect, however. The most appropriate reviewers for a given project might not be selected by the editors, or they might be asked but decline due to other commitments. In some research communities it's fairly well known which people are working on which problems, making double-blind review more of an aspiration than a reality. Some reviewers are more careful and thorough than others. One negative review can carry a lot of weight, even if it might represent a minority view within the entire profession. Thus, good work might not be published. Sometimes the authors and reviewers fail to catch certain errors, eventually leading to an official correction. And once in a while, deeply flawed research manages to get published. In the summer of 2015, a minor scandal erupted over a study about public attitudes toward same-sex marriage, which had been published in *Science* and attracted considerable media attention. One of its authors appears to have misrepresented his procedures and faked some of his data, leading his highly embarrassed coauthor to request that the article be retracted.[11]

Peer review occurs before a piece of research is published, but it also happens afterward, more informally. Some research is published and essentially ignored; other work attracts more attention from scholars. With a little digging, we can see which authors and which studies have been cited often in subsequent work. Google Scholar is one handy tool in this regard; the Social Science Citation Index is another. While a high score is no guarantee of quality—I remember a teacher in graduate school who joked that he did very well by such measures because many scholars thought he was an idiot, and called him out by name—it can indicate whose work is important to consider. Alternatively, we can immerse ourselves in a literature and see which authors' names keep popping up.* Someone studying the politics of health care in the United States would probably come across references to work by Colleen Grogan, Jacob Hacker, the House Ways and Means and Senate Finance committees, Lawrence Jacobs, the Kaiser Family Foundation, Jonathan Oberlander, Jill Quadagno, and Theda Skocpol. Someone else studying the resource curse among developing countries would likely find repeated references to the work of Paul Collier, Terry Karl, Michael Ross, Jeffrey Sachs, and the World Bank. Through their citations, professional peers are indicating that these authors are some of the best-known (and maybe even best-informed) people in the field.† We now have input from dozens of experts rather than the small handful consulted before the research was published. Similarly, postpublication peer review can indicate which studies may be badly flawed. The main reason why the dubious study about same-sex marriage came to light was because other researchers were intrigued by the research design and the findings and tried to build on that study. When they encountered problems, they looked more closely at the article and found several troubling anomalies.[12]

There is a third definition of *authoritative* besides "official" or "knowledgeable." It can also mean "supremely confident" or "commanding," as in someone who speaks with an authoritative air. This is not—I repeat, not—a good way to assess the quality of a document. Like a judge or jury considering a witness, we want to know if each author of a document is credible. We ask, "How can we be sure that you know what you're talking about?" and not "Are you really sure that you're right?" Cable television, talk radio, and the Internet are filled with people who sound authoritative, who are very good

---

*These approaches could also help us figure out whether books and articles that didn't go through peer review before publication might still be important or well regarded. The journal *Foreign Affairs* publishes work by experts in and out of academia, without formal peer review. According to Google Scholar, several of their articles (e.g., by Francis Fukuyama, Samuel Huntington, Jessica Mathews) have been cited hundreds of times. Those might be worth a look to someone studying international relations.

†They should not be the only voices heard; a scholarly community mustn't operate like an exclusive club. Still, researchers would be smart to check in with well-known experts such as these and see if they can offer any relevant insights or point the way toward sources of evidence that would be useful.

at putting on airs. In the realm of political science, such confidence is not enough to be considered authoritative.

Deciding whether a document is authoritative, then, doesn't always entail a simple yes/no judgment. The same is true when we check for **bias**. As much as political scientists worry about biased sources of evidence, we don't always spell out what *bias* means. One common definition is "systematic error," which can be intended or unintended and can affect primary or secondary sources.[13] Bias is a problem for individual documents, and it can lead to erroneous conclusions. Someone studying foreign policy decision making in Country X could have access to an official government report. That document clearly indicates agreement among the relevant decision makers, whether the issue involves sending troops overseas, participating in a trade embargo, or signing a treaty. Nevertheless, it is quite possible that other documents, which are unavailable to the researcher (e.g., internal memos and e-mails), would reveal much more disagreement over these decisions. In addition, systematic error in the written record itself could lead us to describe the decision process incorrectly. A congressional hearing about welfare reform could include testimony from several witnesses, with most of them sympathetic to a bill sponsored by the committee chair. It's quite possible that the chair invited them precisely because he knew they would be supportive.[14] Anyone who read the official transcript of that hearing could underestimate the extent of opposition among interest groups and policy experts. The official website of the National Rifle Association includes a number of documents related to the Second Amendment. Not surprisingly, these documents support the view that gun ownership should be widely available and lightly regulated. More restrictive interpretations of the Second Amendment, which do exist, aren't exactly prominent on this site.[15] Researchers hoping to capture the constitutional debate over gun control could easily present a misleading portrait if all they consulted was the NRA website.

In these examples, some information is systematically excluded from the written record. These documents, though official and authoritative, are biased. The underlying sources of bias are not hard to imagine. Concerns about national security might lead government officials to make some foreign policy documents public while classifying others as top secret. Members of Congress might view hearings as a way to attract media attention and mobilize public support for a particular bill. They could feel that any genuine debate should take place elsewhere, such as the floor of the House or Senate. The NRA is an advocacy organization, one that attracts and keeps many of its members by taking a hard line against gun control. It's not in the business of being even-handed (and the same is true of most interest groups). For these and other reasons, political scientists aren't terribly surprised to find that many of the sources they work with are biased. The world of politics is filled with people trying to wield power and exert influence, and we cannot count on them to behave like dispassionate analysts. Put another way, official documents often reflect a combination of sincere and strategic motivations.

When the author isn't an official source—perhaps a journalist, biographer, historian, or political scientist—the potential for bias remains. Even the most neutral of these observers will have to make choices about what to include and exclude. That is how authors establish a theme, a narrative thread, a thesis statement. And they may not have complete access to all the relevant actors or primary sources of information. Before a deadline, journalists might be able to interview a few people who attended a protest march, but not the protest leaders. Biographers might have much more information about their subjects' time in office than their teenage years. Academics could lack the money needed to visit important archives overseas, making them highly dependent on secondary sources.

Moreover, many of these observers won't be neutral. Perhaps they work for think tanks and foundations with a clear political agenda. They could be pundits with a strong partisan or ideological leaning. They may be the kind of reporter or academic who seeks out evidence to support a favored theory: some scholars stress the role of culture in practically everything they write; for others, institutions are the dominant theme. Finally, there is the simple but powerful fact of human fallibility. Those who research and write about politics do make mistakes. They can misread a document, miss key steps in a sequence of events, or draw the wrong conclusions from the evidence at hand.

To historians, bias is pervasive because each of us has a point of view. An individual's ability to observe and record accurately will always be impeded by obstacles beyond his or her control. In the concert hall of life, every seat is "obstructed view." In addition, observations will be shaped by an author's own intellectual and emotional commitments. The documents produced will therefore be biased to a greater or lesser degree. To minimize the potential harm of bias, researchers need to approach each document carefully. Like a good trial lawyer, we should conduct a background check on every author or document we plan to introduce as evidence in our research. Does the author qualify as an authority on this subject? What was her or his larger objective in producing this document? How far can I trust this author to tell the truth, the whole truth, and nothing but the truth? We can ask the same questions when inspecting someone else's research. We should also look for ways to minimize or compensate for whatever bias we encounter (more on that in a minute).[16]

The last dimension of quality I want to emphasize is **currency**. The documents we read and the documents we cite in our own research should reflect the most up-to-date information available. That date will vary depending on the project; currency doesn't necessarily mean "published in the last five years." A literature review might cite studies published across several decades. A lit review about interest groups would likely refer to Mancur Olson's *The Logic of Collective Action* (1965) and Jack Walker's *Mobilizing Interest Groups in America* (1991). Both books have been highly influential, and each is a classic in its own way. However, if Walker's book were the most recent one cited in the literature review, readers would infer that political scientists have written nothing important about interest groups in over two decades. Really?[17] (While this may seem like an obvious flaw, I have read lit reviews from undergrads that would have been quite current had they been written thirty years ago.) For a project about the origins of World War I, currency of primary sources would involve documents written in the years leading up to 1914. The most current secondary studies, by historians and political scientists, would be published a century later. Research about more recent subjects, such as the Greek debt crisis, could be based almost entirely on documents written in the last decade.

By now it should be obvious why a simple Google search* is a poor way of finding evidence for a research project. Fast and easy, yes, but also inadequate. The pool of potential documents available on the Internet is immense, and their quality varies enormously. Any given search will produce some documents that are truly authoritative (i.e., official or knowledgeable); some documents that just have an air of authority; some that are irrelevant for our purposes; and a number of commercial advertisements. A simple example can illustrate the pitfalls.

Those who study comparative politics are familiar with "conflict diamonds," sometimes referred to more vividly as "blood diamonds." I am a simple Americanist by training and know little about the subject, but I would like to learn more. At one point in 2015 I typed in the phrase "conflict diamonds," and in 0.29 seconds Google gave me more than three hundred thousand results. My cup literally runneth over. No way would I read or even skim all those documents. Although Google does place the results in a certain order, its ranking algorithm is a closely guarded secret. The Web entries

---

* Or a search using Bing, Yahoo, DuckDuckGo, etc.

listed on the first few pages, which are the only ones that I and most people are likely to read, are there in part because they are the most popular, meaning that many other Web pages are linked to them. But popular isn't the same thing as authoritative. The algorithm is supposed to favor more established Web pages over newer pages, which might or might not promote the currency of information. Documents also achieve a higher rank depending on where and how often the keywords appear in the document. Apparently, the physical size of the keywords in the document's headings even matters. Google recently announced that mobile-friendly websites would move up in their rankings. That decision has nothing to do with the quality of information and everything to do with reaching consumers who have smartphones.[18]

The first item returned on my Google search was an ad for diamonds, sponsored by ritani.com. The second item was a *Wikipedia* entry for "blood diamond," whose collective authorship is unknown. On the first page I found documents from Amnesty International USA and Diamondfacts.org, which seemed to be connected to the World Diamond Council of manufacturers and sellers. The first news story dated from 2011 and focused on Africa. The next one was about Venezuela and Guyana, circa 2012. Page 2 of the results featured more ads for diamonds, a 2001 report from the World Bank, and a 2010 piece from the Mother Nature Network. The first news story from 2015 didn't surface until page 3. It all seemed pretty random. Almost nothing on the first three pages of my search appears to have been reviewed by outside experts. In short, looking for information this way is like shopping at the world's biggest yard sale: there's bound to be valuable stuff here and there, but also a bunch of useless junk. We would be smarter to search more specialized databases (perhaps even Google Scholar), library catalogs, and the websites of organizations that we know are authoritative.[19]

VARIETY

Part I of this guide showed how political scientists ask big questions. The first part of this chapter pointed out that political scientists trying to answer these questions routinely deal with documents whose quality is less than ideal. When you put these two pieces together, you understand why most political scientists employ a variety of documents in their research. The obvious example is the literature review (see chapter 1). As political scientists generalize about a conventional wisdom or ongoing debate, they incorporate evidence from a variety of prior studies. Not all those studies might receive equal attention, but it would be unusual (though not unheard of) for a lit review to focus solely on a single author or single piece of work.

Variety is just as essential when trying to figure out what happened and why. Think back to chapter 2, which started with concepts and their measures. Rich concepts have more than one dimension, and each dimension often requires more than one measure. We should expect to collect evidence from a variety of sources in order to create valid and reliable measures. Take for example the widely used measures of political rights and civil liberties generated by Freedom House. The general criteria are based on the UN's Universal Declaration of Human Rights, adopted in 1948. Country scores for the electoral process are based partly on current reports from national or international election monitoring agencies. Laws giving citizens the right to obtain information about their government help to determine the measure of accountability of each government. The scores for electoral process and accountability (and for other elements) then feed into the overall country score for political rights. Any regulations governing the construction of religious buildings are factored into the separate measure of civil liberties. The analysts at Freedom House review additional government documents as well as news stories and academic studies. Sometimes they interview experts on particular countries. What most of us see for each country is a simple Freedom House score, such as 4.5 or 7. Behind each number lies a sizable stack of written records drawn from a variety of sources.[20]

Teachers and employers sometimes give this assignment: "Tell me who is for and against current issue Z (e.g., legalizing same-sex marriage, easing the trade embargo with Iran), and summarize their main arguments." Teachers might ask their students the same basic question about a historical event, such as the Tax Reform Act of 1986 or the formation of the European Union. These are descriptive exercises, requiring students to figure out what happened. They are actually a close cousin of the lit review to the extent that competing sides of a debate need to be identified. As with the lit review, we would be smart to cast a wide net when looking for evidence. At least in American politics, elected officials, interest groups, think tanks and foundations, major media outlets, individual policy experts, and the general public could all be involved in these kinds of debates. In researching a current issue, we would start by hunting for different primary sources such as speeches, policy briefs, legislative hearings, newspaper and magazine stories (including op-eds), opinion polls, and probably the websites of elected officials and relevant interest groups. We could add a variety of secondary sources to this list if the event occurred long enough ago for scholars to have published their research about it.

Any study that tries to test competing hypotheses, descriptive or causal, will often require different types of evidence. The sources needed to document the influence of interest groups, for example, wouldn't be the same as those revealing the impact of institutional design.[21] Any study that relies on process tracing to explain why something happened will typically rely on different sources at different steps in the process. I return to John Gerring (see chapter 4): "The hallmark of process tracing . . . is that multiple types of evidence are employed for the verification of a single inference—bits and pieces of evidence that embody different units of analysis (they are each drawn from unique populations)."[22] Consider your basic story of How a Bill Became a Law. One step in that process could show how a certain interest group put pressure on legislators, directly and indirectly, to enact the law. We could then examine that group's website, congressional hearings, campaign finance reports, newspaper articles, and public opinion polls. If the bill passed long enough ago, we would add academic books and articles to the mix—just for this one step in the process.[23]

Of course, any one of these documents could be seriously biased. What a prime minister said about a trade embargo could differ depending on whether he was talking to a group of business executives or to Parliament. Americans are certainly accustomed to hearing their presidential candidates talk one way during the primaries and another during the general campaign. Should we rely solely on one speech made in February to determine a candidate's stance on any issue? Not if we're smart. In the same vein, the position taken by an interest group representative testifying before Congress might be more nuanced than what the group recently posted to its website. Consulting with a variety of documents would help us gain a more accurate picture of where any single individual or organization stood on an issue.

The core lesson here involves **triangulation of evidence**. Chapter 4 mentioned the strategy of methodological triangulation. Scholars who employ more than one research method are trying to enhance the validity of their study. They hope that the strengths of one method will compensate for the weaknesses of another, or that one research method will help to verify the findings of another. Even more common is the practice of triangulating evidence.

> Triangulation involves data collected at different places, sources, times, levels of analysis, or perspectives, data that might be quantitative, or might involve intensive interviews or thick historical description. The best method should be chosen for each data source. . . . Triangulation, then, refers to increasing the amount of information brought to bear on a theory or hypothesis.[24]

At the start of this chapter, I mentioned the different kinds of evidence that might be introduced at a murder or corruption trial—that is one form of triangulation, and it's the same form described in the quotation above. *Triangulation* can also mean "the checking of one source against another to reduce the danger of deception in the data sources."[25] This is what detectives, trial lawyers, and journalists do all the time. Having three people testify that they heard the accused threaten the plaintiff is better than relying on the plaintiff's word alone. Thus, the triangulation of evidence encompasses two related tasks, which for the sake of alliteration we can think of as diversification and double-checking. Triangulation helps us piece together answers to complicated research questions, and to ensure that each piece is credible. Done well, triangulation produces more valid descriptions and explanations of the political world.

Triangulation is a general strategy, not a specific formula. It can take on many different shapes. Knowing that political actors often behave strategically, political scientists will collect statements made at different times and to different audiences in order to establish why, for instance, a prime minister favored easing up on sanctions against Iran. We might supplement that evidence with information gathered from former government officials, academic experts, or respected journalists. These different strands could present a clear and coherent set of views, or they might reveal interesting variations. Either way, the results would be significant. Before I gave an interest group credit for influencing a certain law, I would look beyond statements from the group's leaders, who have incentives to exaggerate their impact if the law is popular and to downplay their impact if the law is controversial. It would help to find corroborating statements made by elected officials or opposing interest groups, or close congruence between what the group initially wanted and what the law eventually contained. I might search for evidence that ruled out competing explanations, such as public opinion or demographic pressures.

Though widely practiced, triangulation is no cure-all. For any given research question, there are potentially hundreds if not thousands of relevant documents. Constraints of time and space dictate that we can't use them all in our research; we have to make choices. An academic journal article might list fifty different sources in its bibliography. At key points in the argument, the scholar will cite two, three, maybe four different sources. It all looks and sounds impressive. Nonetheless, the author could have selected, intentionally or not, a very unrepresentative sample of documents.* In effect, the

---

* Unintentionally, several of my students have committed this mistake by relying exclusively on electronic databases to help find evidence for their research papers. Databases such as JSTOR and Cambridge Journals Online are wonderful if you're hunting for

Ricky Jay problem has reappeared in a new guise. Much as we worry that a skilled researcher could select only those cases that best support his argument (see chapter 5), we could fear something similar when he selected certain documents as evidence. He might not stack the deck as spectacularly as Mr. Jay, but even a little sleight of hand could be troubling. This practice, which Cameron Thies refers to as selectivity, can compound the problem of bias within individual documents.[26]

Robert Putnam's study of Italian regional governments, *Making Democracy Work* (1993), is one of the most cited and influential books in all of political science. At one point Putnam compressed roughly eight hundred years of Italian history into a single chapter, showing how and when the North developed differently from the South. Some specialists later questioned Putnam's choice of sources, arguing that his version of Italian history turned out to be far too simple and linear. They felt that he overlooked important developments and rival interpretations. He should have consulted more sources, or at least different sources.[27] If someone like Robert Putnam is vulnerable to criticism about his selection of documents, then we are all vulnerable.

That's the bad news. It's also the good news: we can add one more item to our mental checklist. As we inspect the work of others, we can always check the sources to see if some types of evidence are missing. While we may not be expert enough to verify the author's handling of each individual source (as in "Hey, that's not what Kenneth Waltz meant"), we can look for general patterns. Perhaps the argument was based on one kind of source to the exclusion of others. For a long time, Martha Derthick's *Policymaking for Social Security* (1979) has been considered the definitive study of that program's history between the 1930s and the 1970s. Read her footnotes carefully, and you will discover that she relied heavily on two types of sources—interviews with people who worked for Social Security, and congressional hearings. Not surprisingly, Derthick attributed much of the development of Social Security to the actions of bureaucrats and legislators. Her sources were authoritative. Nevertheless, we can legitimately wonder whether other types of sources would lead to a different interpretation of this history.[28] To take a more ob-

---

articles, but they're not very useful when looking for books. Why would this matter? The research featured in these databases may privilege experiments and large-*n* statistical designs, which fit more readily into a fifteen-page journal article. Detailed case studies often require an entire book to develop. For similar reasons, we might miss certain kinds of explanations, especially those rooted in historical processes, which are hard to condense into a standard journal article.

vious example, if you come across a report from a think tank or foundation that relies heavily on previous work by that same organization, you should triangulate the information in that report before you believe it.

As researchers and writers, we can take a few steps to show that we chose our documents in a reasonable manner. There will always be questions, maybe even serious doubts about our choices, but we can anticipate some of them. Step 1 is transparency. We must identify every source and cite it completely. We shouldn't leave readers wondering if we just made stuff up. Transparency is in fact a general virtue in this line of work. Political scientists should define and measure their concepts as clearly as possible; they should be equally transparent when it comes to their research design, case selection, and sources of evidence. Such transparency makes it possible for others to critique the work and to build on it. Transparency is essential for a research community to move forward.[29]

Step 2 is to triangulate from distinct perspectives whenever possible. We want to counter potential bias in documents, not reinforce it. That's why it would be better to invite a variety of people to testify as character witnesses at a trial instead of just the immediate family. By the same token, explaining a president's actions by quoting him, his vice president, and his chief of staff won't convince most readers. Three different sources, yes, but probably three similar perspectives. A better tactic could be to rely on evidence from the president, a respected journalist, and a historian. Citing several scholars who share the same basic theoretical orientation (e.g., neorealism, historical institutionalism) would be better than citing just one of them. However, if we could find places of agreement between these scholars and others who favor an alternative theory, our analysis could be that much stronger. For example, scholars who stress the role of interest groups and those who emphasize ideology both agree that the American Medical Association was instrumental in defeating President Truman's plan for national health insurance.[30] Referencing both camps would support that claim more effectively than only one camp.

Step 3 is to acknowledge the limits of our descriptions or explanations.[31] Some pieces of the written record may not fit with our analysis. Reasonable alternative interpretations of the evidence could be offered. Ignoring such problems is seldom a good strategy. Political scientists look for general patterns, not fixed laws of nature, and we expect our analysis to be bounded and imperfect. If we can refute a rival interpretation, or at least weaken it, then we should do so. Otherwise, it makes sense to note conflicting evidence or alternative explanations, perhaps in a footnote or endnote. I have also seen scholars use parenthetical references to accomplish this task, where they list several sources in their favor and one or two that are contrary, along the lines of (Brown 2011; Callaghan and Wilson 1998; MacDonald 2006; but see Cameron, Heath, and Macmillan 2009). That last reference probably would not support the author's argument. This is one important way in which political scientists do <u>not</u> operate like trial lawyers, who would be remiss if they presented evidence that cast doubt on their theory of the crime.

A SENSE OF PROPORTION

Home builders have one more advantage over political scientists. Before they start, builders can identify the key load-bearing points in a structure and figure out, for instance, how thick the roof truss and the flooring need to be. Those parts have to be strong. Other parts of the house won't have to withstand as much stress. Home builders can then buy enough of the appropriate materials to make a structurally sound dwelling. In contrast, political scientists usually have some idea about which parts of their argument will need the most support, though the exact requirements could differ depending on their audience. What one author views as an obvious point, needing little support, might strike some readers as questionable. More important, political scientists do not know in advance whether they will be able to find enough good evidence to support their argument and make it persuasive. Subjective judgment and improvisation will therefore be required during the process of research and writing.

If triangulation is such a smart strategy, then we might be expected to use it all the time. The teacher in me wants to advocate this practice, because few undergraduates are accustomed to triangulating their evidence. It would be better if they erred on the side of providing too much evidence than too little. Yet there are instances when triangulation isn't necessary. The first category is usually referred to as common knowledge, which needs no supporting evidence at all. The main examples are historical facts, which tend to be well known and uncontested (table 6.1): George Washington was the first president of the United States; World War II ended in 1945. Common knowledge also includes pieces of folk wisdom—"no risk, no reward," "better to be lucky than good"—that occasionally appear in political analysis. If we documented every single claim like these, our work would soon become larded with references. Readers could feel insulted that the author didn't trust them to know such basic facts.[32]

On the other hand, certain historical facts may be common knowledge in some circles but not others. How many people know that Barack Obama was the first black president of the *Harvard Law Review*? Most Americans probably do not (and others might guess that he led the *Review of Socialist*

Table 6.1. When to triangulate evidence (a rough guide)

Type of claim	Number of supporting sources
Well-known fact, not contested	0
Folk wisdom	0
Lesser-known fact, not contested	1
Direct quotation	1
Any contested fact	Multiple
Ideas or theories	Multiple
Actor's motive or intent	Multiple
Cause-and-effect	Multiple

Law). Besides participants in a Model UN club, how many people can name the permanent members of the United Nations Security Council? In these circumstances, one option is to play it safe and provide a citation. A single authoritative source could be sufficient. That option makes even more sense if the fact in question is integral to the analysis and not simply background information. Suppose that I am writing a paper about the Bosnian War. Any mention of specific provisions in the Dayton Agreement, which formally ended that war, should be referenced.[33]

Specific ideas, even those in wide circulation, don't qualify as common knowledge. The idea that democracies rarely go to war with each other ought to be supported with evidence, preferably from multiple sources. The idea that economic hard times trigger greater resentment toward immigrants would likewise require triangulation. Direct quotations, on the other hand, typically require a single source. In a few cases, a quote may be so well known that it qualifies as common knowledge. An example would be president John F. Kennedy's famous declaration, "Ask not what your country can do for you—ask what you can do for your country." It would be proper to credit Kennedy in the text, but we might not have to cite his 1961 inaugural address in a footnote or endnote.

Otherwise, triangulation is strongly recommended. Based on years of grading exams and papers, I can think of at least three general situations when the lack of triangulation is really damaging. The first is when the facts or their interpretation is in dispute. In many wars, for instance, the total number of deaths and injuries can vary widely from one source to another. Some documents might report only those deaths directly resulting from combat, while others might include war-related deaths connected to hunger, poor medical care, military suicides, and accidents. One combatant country might have incentives to exaggerate the numbers in order to gain more sympathy or aid. Researchers have to decide whether some sources are more credible than others, whether sources generally agree on a number, or whether it would be smarter to state a numerical range. Simply citing a number, uncritically, would make the author appear uninformed or biased. Similarly, the official accounts of how the conflict started could differ radically between the opposing sides. In another project, some sources might attribute passage of a law to the power of interest group lobbying, while other sources credit public opinion. If we take sides in this debate, then we need to produce multiple pieces of evidence showing why one side is more convincing than the other. Many times, reasonable people can disagree about features of the political world. These parts of our argument therefore have to be built to withstand added stress from members of our audience. We shouldn't expect a single piece of evidence to convince them.

In addition, we need to triangulate in order to distinguish involvement from influence—in other words, to separate correlation from causation. We might be studying an episode in which tobacco companies fought hard against an increase in tobacco taxes, and that tax hike was defeated. That's not enough evidence to prove that lobbying was decisive or even a contributing factor. We would still need to check for spuriousness (perhaps party politics was the real influence); to verify the timing and sequence of events; and to establish a causal path connecting what the tobacco companies did to the eventual outcome. Ideally, that causal path would be more than theoretically plausible. It would be supported with empirical evidence, even if circumstantial.

Finally, I strongly encourage triangulation when describing a political actor's intent or motivations. Such evidence can be essential in process tracing. Any statement from that actor could be biased. Of course public officials will claim they went to war only as a last resort, and only to promote the highest ideals. Of course business groups will say they were being responsive to public sentiment when they pushed for deregulation. Of course most people will deny that racism or homophobia affected their behavior. (Of course your little brother will swear that he ate your Halloween candy by accident.)* If our objective is simply to establish how actors explained their own behavior, then an official quote or two may suffice. To ascertain what

* As James Madison reminds us, "If men were angels, no government would be necessary" (*Federalist* no. 51).

really motivated an individual or group, we'll need evidence from additional sources. We might discover that the actor was speaking truthfully. And we might not.

BOX 6.1

WHEN THE PROBLEM IS TOO FEW DOCUMENTS, NOT TOO MANY

One unstated assumption running through this chapter is that the world of politics is teeming with written records. The main task of researchers is selecting the right ones in order to solve a given puzzle. This assumption doesn't always hold true. For certain topics, evidence can be genuinely scarce. We could be investigating something on the order of tax policy in Madagascar. After scouring the library and the Internet, we discover very few sources. We feel stuck. Alternatively, written records might exist, but we are unable to use them. Anyone trying to conduct sophisticated research regarding Soviet politics ought to be able to read Russian, but I can't. Key documents may reside in an archive that we lack the time or money to visit. Stuck again.

In these circumstances, we have two basic options: modify the original research question, or figure out how to acquire more evidence. Political scientists make these kinds of adjustments all the time. Research often involves a balancing act between the questions we want to ask and the evidence available to support our answers. Maybe in hunting for information about tax policy in Madagascar, we came across several interesting studies about tax policy in South Africa. We might switch to a different country and move forward with our research. Perhaps we found more evidence about environmental policy in Madagascar and decided to shift away from tax policy. Either way, we would endeavor to become unstuck. (Note: making these kinds of changes could also require reworking the literature review.) The intuition here comes straight from Crosby, Stills, and Nash: "If you can't be with the one you love, honey, love the one you're with."

Modifying the question is usually the more viable option. However, if researchers have the time and resources, they can try to generate new types of written records. Conducting field research, broadly defined, is the most common route. **Field research** entails "leaving one's home institution in order to acquire data, information, or insights that significantly inform one's research."[1] For professional scholars and graduate students, field research can mean spending months at a time in a foreign country; this is a veritable rite of passage for many students of comparative politics. Some field researchers behave much like anthropologists, embedding themselves in the host country and participating in the routines of daily life. Other researchers operate more like traditional political scientists and administer a mass survey or visit foreign archives. As we saw in chapter 4, a growing number of political scientists are conducting field experiments in foreign countries. In all these instances, the evidence collected is absolutely essential to the study.

Doing this type of field research requires considerable skill (often including mastery of a foreign language), as well as sensitivity to a number of ethical issues.[2] At the other end of the spectrum, field research can entail visiting an important archive or conducting a few interviews within one's own country. The time spent is measured in days, not months. This kind of field research usually supplements whatever evidence has been collected from the library and online. Perhaps the available sources seem quite biased, making further triangulation a priority. Or, the author could need to fill an important gap in a causal chain. Many years ago, when conducting research for my dissertation, I had trouble finding much evidence about a few provisions in the US tax code. (Apparently, the *New York Times* and the *Washington Post* didn't care about the Targeted Jobs Tax Credit nearly as deeply as I did.) After traveling to Washington, DC, and interviewing some tax policy experts, several of whom had worked for the government, I had a much better idea of who pushed for these programs and why.[3] Realistically, this limited kind of field research—perhaps involving phone interviews, or travel to a nearby office, city, or state—is what undergraduates are most likely to undertake.

Somewhere between these two extremes are political scientists who conduct sustained field research within their own country. Richard Fenno spent considerable time shadowing more than a dozen members of Congress as they operated in their home districts. He wanted to observe firsthand how legislators interacted with their constituents. Before Fenno, scholars who studied Congress focused almost exclusively on legislators' behavior in Congress or on the campaign trail.[4] Cathy Cohen's analysis of the politics of AIDS did incorporate stories from major media outlets and votes in Congress. However, because she was particularly interested in the connections between race and AIDS—a subject largely ignored by mainstream sources—she included numerous "conversations and oral interviews with activists, community leaders, elected and appointed officials, and people living with AIDS in New York City between the years 1990 and 1993."[5] That evidence provided important insights that were unavailable from existing documents.

NOTES

1. Diana Kapiszewski, Lauren M. MacLean, and Benjamin L. Read, *Field Research in Political Science: Practices and Principles* (New York: Cambridge University Press, 2015), p. 1.

2. See, e.g., ibid.; Edward Schatz, ed., *Political Ethnography: What Immersion Contributes to the Study of Power* (Chicago: University of Chicago Press, 2009).

3. For advice about in-depth interviews, see Joel D. Aberbach and Bert A. Rockman, "Conducting and Coding Elite Interviews," *PS: Political Science and Politics* 35, no. 4 (December 2002): 673–76; Beth L. Leech, "Asking Questions: Techniques for Semistructured Interviews," *PS: Political Science and Politics* 35, no. 4 (December 2002): 665–68; Mosley, *Interview Research in Political Science*; and Brian Rathbun, "Interviewing and Qualitative Field Methods: Pragmatism and Practicalities," in *The Oxford Handbook of Political Methodology*, ed. Janet M. Box-Steffensmeier, Henry E. Brady, and David Collier (New York: Oxford University Press, 2008), pp. 685–701.

4. Richard F. Fenno Jr., *Home Style: House Members in Their Districts* (Boston: Little, Brown, 1978).

5. Cathy J. Cohen, *The Boundaries of Blackness: AIDS and the Breakdown of Black Politics* (Chicago: University of Chicago Press, 1999), pp. 27–28.

CHAPTER SIX

There is another way to work with documents, a much different way. Rather than deliberately selecting a sample of written records, some political scientists prefer to work with a random sample of documents or even the entire population. Doing so reduces the chances of cherry-picking their evidence, or being accused of doing so. Instead of relying on subjective interpretations of those documents, many of these same scholars convert the written text into a set of numbers whose meaning seems more objective. Researchers' bias thus has less room to operate, and the whole process becomes more machinelike. In fact, a number of software programs are available to analyze these documents. The general technique is called **content analysis**, and it blurs the line separating so-called quantitative from qualitative research.*

A highly simplified version of content analysis goes something like this.[34] Scholars begin by identifying a population of documents that is relevant to their research question. These tend to be highly authoritative documents such as party platforms, legislative hearings, judicial opinions, or articles in well-respected newspapers and magazines. The next decision is whether to analyze all these documents[35] or a random subset. For example, when Maurits van der Veen was analyzing foreign aid debates in four European legislatures over a fifty-year span, he picked years ending in 0, 2, 5, and 8. One study mentioned in chapter 5 relied on a computer program to pick one-quarter of the available Supreme Court cases for more detailed content analysis.[36]

Researchers then define the unit of analysis. It could be as small as a word or phrase, as large as the entire document, or something in between such as the paragraph. For each unit, we need to establish certain coding rules that will guide us in analyzing the document. In effect, we need to identify certain variables within the document and denote the potential values for each variable. Some coding rules are simple, such as whether or not a specific subject was mentioned. Other rules require more judgment, such as whether the overall tone was positive, negative, or mixed.

One of my favorite examples of content analysis was performed by Martin Gilens as part of a larger study concerning public attitudes toward welfare.[37] In the first part of his book, Gilens shows that public support for welfare and welfare recipients was much lower than for any other social program or group in the United States. Through careful analysis of opinion polls, he

* Chapter 4 distinguished between variable-oriented and case-oriented research designs. In some ways those who perform content analysis are treating each document as a source of variables to be extracted, rather than as a distinct case that needs to be understood holistically.

found that many whites associated blacks with being lazy and with receiving welfare, which in turn diminished their support for welfare programs. Where did those negative stereotypes come from? One hypothesis—from the media. Gilens selected three major newsmagazines and identified every single article related to poverty or welfare that appeared between 1950 and 1992. For each article he noted the year of publication, the specific groups featured (e.g., the homeless, the elderly poor), the tone, and the race of the individuals in any accompanying photos. His assumption—based on prior research—was that people tend to remember visual images and general tone more than the specific facts of a given story. What Gilens found was striking. These newsmagazines consistently featured more pictures of black people when the tone of the story was negative than when the tone was positive. The proportion of black faces was unrelated to the percentage of blacks in poverty or on welfare at the time. Gilens then performed a similar content analysis on a smaller set of television news broadcasts and found the same pattern. As a result, the media emerged as one source of those negative stereotypes. Had Gilens cited a handful of news stories from across four decades and found racial bias, readers might have wondered if he had chosen a few extreme outliers to make his case. Content analysis of hundreds and hundreds of articles made his results appear less subject to manipulation.

Once we have moved from words to numbers, we can tap into a whole new set of analytic techniques. Simple counts and percentages, which are common in content analysis, could be all that we need. Many times, however, political scientists use more sophisticated techniques such as cross-tabulation and multiple regression in order to determine what happened and why. The next chapter offers a brief introduction to working with numbers, which can be found almost everywhere in the world of politics. Much like this chapter, chapter 7 will emphasize key concepts and general strategies more than specific techniques. I have no illusions that these last two chapters will enable you to detect all forms of bias, master triangulation of evidence, conduct field research, perform content analysis, calculate correlation coefficients, or build good regression models. All those skills require much more training and experience than what I offer here. With that disclaimer in mind, let's start thinking about what quality, variety, and a sense of proportion mean when using numbers as evidence.

PRACTICE: INSPECTING

1. Triangulation of evidence. For each of the following studies, identify the main types of documents (e.g., government documents, newspaper articles,

interviews) used as evidence. For which specific parts of the argum[...] author(s) rely on multiple types of evidence?

Stephen Biddle, Jeffrey A. Friedman, and Jacob N. Shapiro, "Testing the Surge: Why Did Violence Decline in Iraq in 2007?," *International Security* 37, no. 1 (Summer 2012): 7–40;

David E. Broockman, "The 'Problem of Preferences': Medicare and Business Support for the Welfare State," *Studies in American Political Development* 26, no. 2 (October 2012): 83–106;

Omar G. Encarnación, "International Influence, Domestic Activism, and Gay Rights in Argentina," *Political Science Quarterly* 128, no. 4 (Winter 2013/2014): 687–716;

Ellen M. Immergut, "The Rules of the Game: The Logic of Health Policy-Making in France, Switzerland, and Sweden," in *Structuring Politics: Historical Institutionalism in Comparative Analysis*, ed. Sven Steinmo, Kathleen Thelen, and Frank Longstreth (New York: Cambridge University Press, 1992), pp. 57–89;

Amy Oakes, "Diversionary War and Argentina's Invasion of the Falklands Islands," *Security Studies* 15, no. 3 (July–September 2006): 431–63;

Maya Tudor, "Explaining Democracy's Origins: Lessons from South Asia," *Comparative Politics* 45, no. 3 (April 2013): 253–72;

Richard M. Valelly, *The Two Reconstructions: The Struggle for Black Enfranchisement* (Chicago: University of Chicago Press, 2004), chapter 6.

2. Content analysis. For each of the following studies, describe how the author converted words into numbers. Then explain whether you do or do not believe that the resulting evidence was authoritative and unbiased.

Frank R. Baumgartner and Bryan D. Jones, *Agendas and Instability in American Politics* (Chicago: University of Chicago Press, 1993), especially chapter 4;

Martin Gilens, "Race and Poverty in America: Public Misperceptions and the American News Media," *Public Opinion Quarterly* 60, no. 4 (Winter 1996): 515–41; or Martin Gilens, *Why Americans Hate Welfare: Race, Media, and the Politics of Antipoverty Policy* (Chicago: University of Chicago Press, 1999), chapters 5–6;

Deborah Welch Larson, "Problems of Content Analysis in Foreign-Policy Research: Notes from the Study of the Origins of Cold War Belief Systems," *International Studies Quarterly* 32, 2 (June 1988): 241–55;

A. Maurits van der Veen, *Ideas, Interests and Foreign Aid* (New York, NY: Cambridge University Press, 2011), especially chapter 3.

important article challenging the standard measure

Jeffrey Mondak and Mitchell Sanders, "Tolerance and

,998," *American Journal of Political Science* 47, no. 3 (July

that article is now more than a decade old. Has either author

ing about tolerance since then, and had it peer-reviewed before

on? If so, name the article(s) or book(s). Have other authors cited that

article in their subsequent research? If so, name a few examples.

d a newspaper article about politics that seems biased, and describe the
nature of that bias. What additional evidence would you require in order to feel
more confident about the accuracy of this article?

3. None of the following claims would qualify as common knowledge. What kinds
of evidence would you need to gather in order to support each claim? (Hint:
there is more than one right answer to this question.)

"Prime minister Tony Blair sent British troops to Iraq in 2003 in order to
promote democracy in the Middle East."

"Public-sector corruption in Turkmenistan is rampant. As a result, Western
businesses have been very reluctant to invest there."

"Given the state of the economy, president George W. Bush was likely to lose
the 2004 election. Fortunately for Bush, his main challenger, John Kerry,
ran a terrible campaign."

"Botswana has largely avoided the resource curse because the national
government has been accountable to its citizens and has wisely spent the
revenues generated by the country's diamonds."

"For many years the Social Security Administration had a reputation as one of
Washington's most competent bureaucracies."

7

USING NUMBERS AS EVIDENCE

Political scientists have mixed feelings about their profession's dependence on numbers. On the one hand, numerical evidence seems admirably transparent. Scholars frequently make their datasets widely available; indeed, some academic journals require authors to do so when publishing an article. Scholars try to describe their statistical techniques clearly and report their main findings with precision (e.g., "Among the countries in this study, a 10-point increase in the high school graduation rate is associated with a 3.6-point increase in voter turnout"). Those who analyze politics with formal models lay out their mathematical proofs line by line. All these steps are supposed to make it easier for others to inspect the work, challenge it, or build off it. In short, numbers make cumulative knowledge possible. They help put the science in political science. This is one reason why some undergraduate programs and most graduate programs in political science insist that students take at least one course in statistics.

Research based largely on written documents seems less transparent. The notes and bibliographies just indicate where to find the evidence. Readers would still have to spend considerable time tracking down the source material and sifting through it. Authors seldom explain why they incorporated a few bits of evidence from a particular document but excluded the rest. Some of the sources, published in a foreign language or stored in a far-away archive, are practically inaccessible to most people. The conclusions are often less precise, stating that some factor was associated with some outcome, or that factor *A* mattered more than factor *B*. This is not exactly the fast track to intellectual progress. No wonder that most of the articles published in the *American Political Science Review*, the premier journal in the discipline, rely on quantitative analysis of numerical evidence.[1]

On the other hand, political scientists can be very skeptical of numbers and those who analyze them. We often repeat Mark Twain's quip about the three types of lies—lies, damn lies, and statistics.* We refer, only half-jokingly, to beating or torturing the data until they confess.[2] We understand that long before BFF and YOLO entered the lexicon, computer scientists

---

* Or this from Twain: "Facts are stubborn things, but statistics are pliable."

coined the term GIGO—garbage in, garbage out. GIGO means that when our numerical measures are defective, our analysis of those numbers will likely be flawed. Most of the time, our measures are imperfect. Sometimes the numbers we need are simply unavailable.[3] Given these constraints, maybe it would be more honest to conclude that factor *A* is more important than *B*, and not that *A* is 21 percent more important. Political scientists can point to numerous occasions when statistical analysis turned out to be highly misleading. The vignette from chapter 3, concerning the distribution of stimulus funds during the Great Recession, is but one example. And some statistical techniques are so advanced, or esoteric, that few of us can truly inspect the work. So much for transparency.

In their own way, numbers can be just as tricky to work with as words. Handled poorly, both forms of evidence can undermine whatever virtues our project might have with respect to research design or case selection. We should handle all our evidence with care (much like a good trial lawyer). The next section of this chapter discusses what quality, variety, and a sense of proportion mean when working with numbers as evidence. Because we already touched on important concepts such as bias and triangulation in chapter 6, I will not belabor these points. The rest of this chapter will introduce readers to a few techniques for analyzing numerical data. The emphasis will be on commonly used techniques that help us answer the fundamental questions of what happened, why, and who cares. How can we determine whether two variables are directly or inversely related? How do we check for spuriousness? Which of our results are significant and which are not so important? Can we use the same statistical techniques whether our measures are nominal, ordinal, interval, or ratio? Although I recommend taking at least one course in statistics to learn the answers to these kinds of questions, this chapter will provide a basic introduction to general strategies and key concepts.

QUALITY, VARIETY, A SENSE OF PROPORTION

Before we perform any computations, we need to evaluate the quality of our numerical data. Our numbers should be authoritative, coming from either official or well-respected sources. Students of US politics often work with government statistics from the Census Bureau or the Office of Management and Budget. Students of comparative politics and international relations might use statistics from a foreign government or from intergovernmental entities such as the United Nations and World Bank. Oftentimes these are the best numbers available. Still, it pays to check for defects. The government of Argentina, for example, has had a reputation for understating that country's inflation rate. By a lot. The situation got so bad that in 2011 the International Monetary Fund decided to find a more credible source for Argentina's inflation numbers. Shortly thereafter, the *Economist* did likewise, saying that it was "tired of being an unwilling party to what appears to be a deliberate attempt to deceive voters and swindle investors." The same article noted that China's official economic figures "can be dodgy."[4] Some academic studies find that authoritarian regimes tend to report overly optimistic numbers, which then biases the relationship between regime type and economic growth in their favor.[5]

Governments aren't the only place to find authoritative numbers. Some governments, particularly in poor or conflict-ridden countries, lack the wherewithal to collect many statistics. Even if they have the capacity, we probably wouldn't trust any government to measure itself on certain dimensions ("Sound the horns! The President of Vuvuzela is proud to announce that his government is corruption-free"). Those numbers could be biased. We therefore rely on nongovernmental organizations such as Transparency International to measure levels of public-sector corruption by country. We count on Freedom House and several other outfits to tell us how well governments around the world protect political rights and civil liberties. Government-sponsored opinion polls could also be prone to bias ("Welcome to North Korea, where trust in government always tops 99 percent"). Fortunately, we can turn to the World Values Survey, the International Social Survey Programme, the American National Election Studies, major media outlets, and several other organizations to measure public opinion. Many, many scholars have relied on these sources for authoritative survey data. Those who study international conflict can turn to the Correlates of War dataset, which originated at the University of Michigan, or the Armed Conflict Dataset, which is connected to Uppsala University in Sweden. Teams of researchers have developed many other datasets related to politics (e.g., AidData, Policy Agendas).

Although these sources appear credible, and are widely used, they still have limitations. As we learned in chapter 2, scholars disagree about how to measure big concepts like democracy and tolerance, and thus any numerical indicator could be considered deficient. An index could exclude a key dimension, include extraneous measures, or aggregate the components without clear justification. Even if they agreed on the conceptual definition and key dimensions, political scientists might disagree about the appropriate level of measurement, such as ordinal versus interval. Moreover, anyone who works closely with these data sources realizes that some of their numbers are, well, dodgy. For decades, the American National Election Studies has been asking people a simple question about voting. The self-reported turnout figure for presidential elections has hovered between 70 and 80 percent since the 1960s. The true figures, however, are usually 15 to 20 points lower.[6] Why such a big gap? Well, many people feel that good citizens should vote, and they give the socially desirable answer even if they did not vote. If we cited these ANES figures to show that voter turnout in the United States compares favorably with turnout in much of Europe, we'd look stupid.

Because measurement error is such a pervasive threat, political scientists often analyze relationships in multiple ways. Suppose we are interested in the relationship between education and political participation across many countries. From our review of the existing literature, we discover that education has been measured at the ratio or the ordinal levels, depending on the author and the countries studied. The ratio measures include percentage of high school graduates, percentage of college graduates, and percentage of literate people. The ordinal measure could be as simple as one with three categories reflecting the highest level of attainment—less than high school, high school graduate, more than high school. We also have found several measures of political participation in the literature. We might then employ statistical procedures (e.g., correlation, cross-tabulation) to compute the relationships between each measure of each variable. We would now be triangulating our evidence. If all the results were fairly similar, we'd feel more confident about characterizing the relationship between education and participation.[7] If the results varied, then we would note where and how much measurement mattered. Either result could be substantively interesting.

Political scientists take this approach all the time. I will mention two examples that should be familiar by now. When Ellen Immergut was testing the relationship between "doctor power" and government involvement in health care, she measured the former in three different ways: the number of doctors as a share of the total population; the percentage of doctors who belonged to the country's major medical association; and the percentage of members of Parliament who were doctors. All three numerical measures captured different aspects of the abstract concept, doctor power. None of the measures, however, aligned as expected with health policy in her three country cases, enabling Immergut to dismiss this explanation.[8] When Michael Ross was testing different causal mechanisms linking natural resources to democracy across many countries, one possibility was repression. More oil revenues might generate the resources needed for governments to crack down on anyone pushing for democracy. He measured this variable two ways, as military spending/gross national product and as military personnel/labor force. The first measure didn't turn out to be statistically significant, but the second one was. By itself, a large military budget wasn't that important; the money had to be spent on soldiers. More oil, more soldiers, less democracy.[9] As these two examples suggest, this approach to numerical evidence can be used whether the *n* of the study is small or large. In our role as inspectors, we should notice whether authors measure their key variables in more than one way in order to demonstrate the robustness of their findings. Where possible, we should adopt this same approach in our own research. Unless we have high confidence in our numerical measures, triangulation makes good sense.

As mentioned in chapter 4, large-*n* comparisons are usually better equipped than small-*n* case studies to detect and deal with spuriousness. More cases enable us to analyze more combinations of variables. Someone analyzing the survey responses of 1000-plus individuals or even the characteristics of 100-plus countries has enough cases to test for a variety of potentially confounding variables. Of course, we shouldn't include every single numeric variable we could lay our hands on. We need to focus on theoretically relevant variables. For a relationship between education and voter turnout, we might control for income, ideology, and age . . . but not how many times per year one eats at Chipotle. Checking for the influence of other variables could entail building a number of statistical regression models. Ross did just that when analyzing the relationship between natural resources and democracy: he built three different models to control for geography, and each of those models included controls for per capita income and percentage of Muslims in each country. When testing for possible causal mechanisms, he created at least three statistical models for each mechanism.[10]

Triangulation of numerical evidence, then, can involve multiple measures of a single concept, or multiple combinations of different measures. It can also—and you will have to trust me on this one—involve different statistical techniques applied to the same set of data.[11] When comparing the overall performance of linear regression models (performance meaning how well the model fits with the data), some political scientists prefer to compute an adjusted R-squared statistic, while others favor calculating the standard error of the estimate (typically written as SEE). To satisfy these two audiences, we could report both figures.[12] When working with panel data, covering many cases over several years, scholars have to assume random effects or fixed effects for relevant variables that were excluded from their models. They might test both assumptions and report the results. If and when you learn more about statistics, you will encounter many other instances in which there is no one right way to analyze relationships among numeric variables. Statistical analysis often requires judgment calls, making it part

art and part science. The more room for judgment, the greater the need for triangulation.

A sense of proportion, in my experience, works a bit differently for numbers than words. Those who work with numbers are less likely to rely on common knowledge. Most people don't know simple facts such as average voter turnout or military spending levels in any country besides their own (and maybe not even that). Researchers typically have to identify the sources for all their numbers. However, those who work with numbers are more likely to rely heavily on a single authoritative source, compared with their colleagues who work primarily with documents. The statistical analysis of attitudes toward immigrants, mentioned earlier in this book, was based largely on evidence from the 2002–3 edition of the European Social Survey.[13] A project designed to explain differences in voter turnout among the American states might be based almost entirely on numbers from the US Census Bureau. In these kinds of projects, a sense of proportion can mean supporting a claim with multiple pieces of evidence from one source of data, rather than individual pieces of evidence from multiple sources (which is how political scientists usually work with documents). In other respects, though, a sense of proportion leads us to treat numerical and textual evidence alike. We still need more evidence when the facts or their interpretation is in dispute. We still need more evidence to prove that A caused B than to show that A and B covary.

The rest of this chapter presents a very quick introduction to statistics, the equivalent of a one-hour tour of the British Museum. My intent is to expose readers to some simple but potentially powerful ways of analyzing numbers, with the hopes that they will be able to read the literature more effectively and will want to learn more. Statistics can tell us a lot about what happened and why in politics, if they are used properly. Among other things, we need to match our statistical procedures to the level of measurement in our data. We'll start with one variable of data, then two, and finally three or more variables.

ANALYZING A SINGLE VARIABLE

Because political scientists are interested in relationships, most of our statistical techniques involve two or more variables. Nevertheless, there are times when analysis of just one variable can be useful. For one thing, it can inform our case selection: we can identify typical cases and outliers for more intensive study.[14] It can also tell us whether our data are distributed normally or abnormally, which could influence any subsequent statistical analysis we perform. Good descriptive work often requires us to generalize about

CHAPTER SEVEN

a single variable. When John Sides and Jack Citrin were analyzing European attitudes toward immigrants, their first table of numbers revealed what percentage of Europeans felt positively, neutrally, or negatively about possible consequences of immigration.[15] Someone studying the incumbency advantage in Congress might want to calculate the average margin of victory when legislators stand for reelection. Someone else investigating border conflicts in the twentieth century might want to know how many were resolved in less than a year and how many lasted longer than ten years.

The first piece of information we need concerns the precision of our numbers. Some numbers are expressed with pinpoint accuracy, while others are better thought of as good approximations. Often the degree of precision depends on whether our numbers originated from a sample or the entire population. Samples produce numbers plus or minus some margin of error, leaving us very confident that the true number lies somewhere within that margin of error. Presidential approval ratings are often based on a sample of the national population, maybe between 1000 and 1500 people. Although the media might report the approval rating as 44 percent, the true number in the population is probably somewhere between 41 and 47 percent (44 ± a 3-point margin of error); it's quite unlikely that the true number in the population is exactly 44.00 percent. If the approval rating in two months is 42 percent, the media might report a decline, and they might be correct. It's also possible, given the margin of error, that the real story is no change, or even an increase in approval. Numbers drawn from larger samples, such as the US Current Population Survey, have smaller margins of error. Numbers drawn from entire populations are even more precise. When countries report their infant mortality rates or the total number of voters in the last election, those numbers typically reflect every single birth and every single voter. The bottom line is that we should not exaggerate the precision of our numbers, especially when they provide a crucial piece of evidence for our arguments.

If we are working with a group of numbers, the next piece of information we might need is a typical value, or what is known as a **measure of central tendency**. How we calculate it depends on the variable's level of measurement (see chapter 2). For a nominal variable such as region or religion, we use the **mode**, meaning the most common value. According to the *CIA World Factbook*, the main religions in Singapore are Buddhism (34%), Christianity (18%), no religion (16%), Islam (14%), Taoism (11%), and Hinduism (5%). The modal answer is Buddhism; the typical resident of Singapore is Buddhist. In Spain, 94 percent of the population is Roman Catholic, making that the modal religion.[16] Thus, the mode may or may not describe the majority of cases for a given variable. For an ordinal variable, we usually calculate the **median**, which is the middle value. An ordinal variable is one in which the values can be arranged (e.g., from less to more), but the distances between the values are irregular or unknown. Individuals' trust in government is a good example. In 1964, 22 percent of Americans said they trusted the national government to do what was right some of the time, 62 percent said most of the time, and 14 percent said just about always. The middle answer, with half the responses below and half above, would be someone in the group who answered Most of the Time. By 2008, the median had changed: 68 percent replied Some of the Time, compared to only 25 and 5 percent for the other two categories, respectively. The new median answer was Some of the Time, indicating a decline in trust.[17]

When variables are interval or ratio, and the distances between each value are the same, we compute the arithmetic **mean** (what most people call the average). We add all the values and divide the total by the number of cases. At the end of chapter 5, I posted data for twenty-five fictional countries. Three of those variables—per capita income, percentage of high school graduates, and voter turnout—were expressed as ratio measures. In the typical country, voter turnout was 70 percent. On average, 57 percent of the adults in these countries graduated from high school. If you scan that table, you will notice that no country had voter turnout of exactly 70 percent, and none had precisely 57 percent high school graduates. The mean does not have to represent an actual score from our dataset.

Finally, we need some **measure of dispersion**, some indication of how the data are distributed around the typical value. *Distribution* implies clear order, so nominal variables are treated differently from the rest.[18] We are concerned about the dispersion of values for ordinal, interval, and ratio-level measures. The **normal distribution** has a single peak in the middle and is symmetric on both sides—the classic bell curve. The mode, median, and mean are identical. This corresponds to the first image in figure 7.1. When the data take this shape, most of the values cluster near the middle. In the real world of politics, the data don't always behave normally. Political scientists deal with **skewed** (i.e., asymmetric) distributions all the time. Some are **negatively skewed**, which means there is a sizable tail on the left side of the distribution (fig. 7.1, image *b*). That tail typically pulls down the value of the mean so that it is less than the median or the mode. Suppose your quiz grades during a course were 0, 90, 90, 90, and 100. Your mean grade would be a 74, a good bit lower than your median grade of 90. The opposite can also occur. A **positively skewed** distribution has a distinct tail on the right side, which usually pulls the mean above the median (fig. 7.1, image *c*).[19] In-

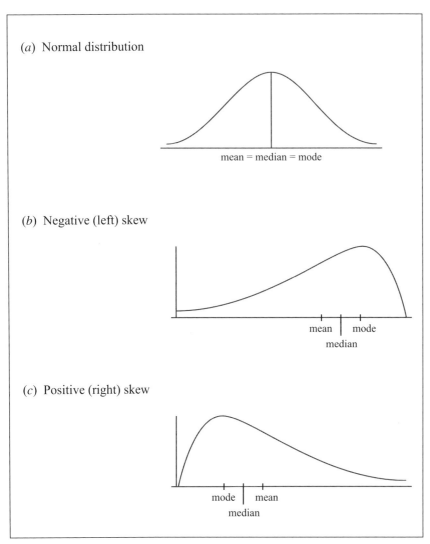

(a) Normal distribution

mean = median = mode

(b) Negative (left) skew

mean   mode
median

(c) Positive (right) skew

mode   mean
median

Figure 7.1. Classic distributions of a single variable. *Note:* The different values for a given variable would appear along the horizontal axis, and their frequency along the vertical axis.

come distribution in countries often takes this shape, as a small number of very wealthy people occupy the right tail of the distribution. Other shapes are also possible. Sometimes we observe a bimodal distribution in which most of the values are clustered around two peaks. Feelings toward a specific political figure could divide people into two distinct camps, with few folks in the middle. The data could be very evenly distributed, with no clear peak. Whenever possible, I advise students to generate pictures of their data so they can see the shape of the distribution. Bar charts, histograms, and box plots can be very useful in this regard (pie charts, not so much).

We have several ways of measuring the distribution of ordinal, interval, and ratio variables. The simplest and probably least helpful is the full **range** of values. Feeling thermometer scales typically allow people to give any number from 0 to 100. If the lowest reported score was a 10 and the highest was a 95, then the range would be 10–95. One downside to the range is that it takes just two observations to define the end points. The vast majority of people might give George W. Bush a rating between a 30 and a 70, but as long as one person said 0 and one person said 100, then they establish the full range. Often a better option is the **interquartile range**, which describes the middle 50 percent of a distribution, between the twenty-fifth and seventy-fifth percentiles. A few extreme outliers will not distort this statistic. Most colleges, for example, report the interquartile range of standardized test scores for their students. Rather than saying only that the average incoming student had an ACT score of, say, 24, they report that the middle half of their students had ACT scores between 20 and 27 (which means that one quarter scored below 20 and one quarter above 27). For household income in the United States, the interquartile range in 2013 was roughly between $25,000 and $90,000. Although Americans making more than $100,000 could feel like they are middle class, they are not, technically speaking, middle income.[20]

Most statistical software packages, such as SPSS and Stata, make it easy to calculate the **standard deviation** and **skewness** of a single variable. Both measures work as long as the variables are interval or ratio. Both measures are based on the distances between every observation and the mean, though the exact mathematical formulas differ. The standard deviation works best when the distribution of values is close to normal. In that case, about two-thirds of the data will be located within one standard deviation above and below the mean, and almost all the data (95%) can be found within two standard deviations of the mean. If the quiz grades for an entire class are normally distributed, with a mean of 83 and a standard deviation of 6.5, then just about everyone earned between a 70 and a 96. When the distribution of a variable is not so normal, the skewness measure works a little better (though truly strange distributions can throw it off). Unlike the standard deviation, whose value is always positive, the skewness measure can be positive or negative. Not surprisingly, a positive number indicates a positive (right) skew, while a negative number indicates a negative (left) skew. A large skewness number, by itself, is not a sign of trouble. Some statisticians advise that when the absolute value of the skewness measure is more than twice the value of its standard error, we should consider the data badly skewed.

Let's return to the fictional dataset from chapter 5. When I analyzed the voter turnout numbers using SPSS, I learned that the mean value was 69.96 percent and the median was 68 percent. The interquartile range extended from 59 to 83.5 percent. The standard deviation was 13.5, meaning that most of the countries fell between 53 and 96 percent turnout. (Joyrida, New Trenton, and Vuvuzela were the only countries to fall outside this range.) The skewness measure was .003, and the standard error of skewness was .464. According to the rule of thumb mentioned above, my voter turnout variable is not skewed, and I should cite the mean as the typical value. In contrast, the five quiz grades mentioned earlier are badly skewed, making the median score of 90 a more typical quiz grade than the mean of 74.

Why should we care if our data are distributed normally or not? Well, a large skew might lead us to rethink our measure of central tendency. In particular, we might want to switch from the mean to the median, or report both. Income in the United States is clearly skewed to the right, thanks to a relatively small number of multimillionaires and billionaires. According to the US Census Bureau, the mean household income in 2013 was $72,641, while the median figure was $51,939.[21] That's a pretty big difference. If we want to talk about the resources available to the typical American household, we should refer to the median income. More people will be clustered around that figure than around the mean. However, if we are comparing incomes across countries, and we want to gauge how much income is available in each country, then the mean might be appropriate. Choosing between the mean and median depends partly on the distribution of the data and partly on the larger questions we are asking. A second reason why the distribution matters is that many statistical techniques for detecting relationships among variables, such as different forms of regression analysis, assume that each variable is normally distributed. When a variable is badly skewed, political scientists usually transform it logarithmically to create a more normal distribution. Ross's statistical models of the resource curse used the natural log of per capita income partly for this reason.[22]

ANALYZING TWO VARIABLES

One requirement for any descriptive or causal relationship is that the values of the measures vary together, either directly or inversely. With case studies, we can pretty much eyeball the data and see if any patterns emerge. That's what Immergut did in dismissing the doctor power hypothesis. Beyond a handful of cases, though, our eyes may deceive us, or our humble brains may not be able to process all the numbers at our fingertips. Thank goodness for computers and statistical software.

When analyzing relationships between variables, we are looking for three pieces of information. The first, and most fundamental, is whether the relationship is **statistically significant**. In lay terms, detecting statistical significance boils down to "hey, I think this relationship really exists." The more precise version is that we have to be 95 percent sure that a relationship exists in the entire population before we call it statistically significant. We have to be very, very confident before making inferences from our data. Put another way, the probability that the null hypothesis is true (i.e., no relationship exists) has to be 5 percent or less. Some political scientists will declare a relationship significant if there is less than a 10 percent chance the null hypothesis is correct, but the bottom line is that we are, by training, a pretty cautious bunch. Being 75 percent sure that a relationship exists is simply not good enough for us. We would rather conclude that a relationship does not exist, even if it really does, than tell the world that a relationship does exist when it really does not.[23]

When the relationship is not statistically significant, we have learned about all we need to know. It makes no sense to say that a relationship between two variables is statistically insignificant, direct, and modest in strength. No relationship means no relationship.* However, when the relationship is statistically significant, we then need to assess its strength. Too often, political scientists say their results are "significant" without clarification. Although many readers will equate significance with substantive importance, it often just means statistically significant; a relationship exists. There's a big difference between statistical and substantive significance. A statistically significant relationship could be weak or strong, trivial or meaningful. If I told you, with utmost confidence, that a 50-point increase in the literacy rate was associated with a 0.5- to 1.0 point increase in voter turnout, you might not be that impressed. A country could make huge improvements to its educational system, and its voter turnout would barely budge. Woo-hoo. Unlike statistical significance, political scientists don't have any

---

*Suppose that a friend asked if you were in a relationship with Taylor, and you said no. If that friend then asked whether your relationship was weak or strong, recent or lengthy, you would likely repeat, with emphasis, that no relationship means no relationship.

common standard for what qualifies as a strong, modest, weak, important, or trivial relationship. Discussing substantive significance is complicated, somewhat subjective, and, in my view, essential. It ties directly to the Who Cares questions that should be central to our work.

Finally, the direction of the relationship is important. We want to know if two variables are directly or inversely related. This is a little tricky with nominal variables, because they have no direction, only distinct categories. It doesn't make sense to state that the more region you have, the more supportive you are of gun control. But we could use statistics to figure out whether, for instance, people who live in the South are less supportive of gun control than people who live in other regions of the United States.

In choosing a specific statistical technique, once again we need to be aware of the level of measurement for our variables. When both variables are **categorical**, meaning nominal or ordinal, we perform a **cross-tabulation** (aka crosstab). This technique is very common in studies of public opinion and voting behavior. Is there a relationship between race (nominal) and support for the death penalty (ordinal)? Are gender and party affiliation related? Is someone's general level of education (ordinal) connected to his support for environmental regulation (ordinal)? Were union members more likely than nonunion members to vote for the left-wing party in the last election?

What we are trying to generate is a table, often called a contingency table, with the values of one variable across the top, creating columns, and the values of the other variable along the side, creating rows. Traditionally, the independent variable creates the columns and the dependent variable the rows. To answer the first question posed above, race would be our column variable and attitudes toward the death penalty would be the row variable. We wouldn't expect attitudes toward the death penalty to change someone from white to black, but we might expect differences in race to affect their attitude on this issue. For this relationship, a very simple table might have two columns (black and white) and four rows (Favor Strongly, Favor Not Strongly, Oppose Not Strongly, Oppose Strongly). Each one of the eight cells would display the total number of respondents, probably from a national survey, who fit in both that column and that row. Because raw numbers can be hard to interpret, we should calculate the column percentages— what percentage of blacks said they strongly favored the death penalty, what percentage said they favored it but not strongly, and so on. We would then compare across the columns, searching for meaningful differences between whites and blacks.

While the differences could be so stark that we know something must be going on, it helps to calculate a few statistics to be sure.* The **Pearson chi-square test** will tell us the statistical significance of the relationship between two categorical variables.[24] The exact value of the chi-square statistic is less important than its p-value, which "tells us the probability that we would see the observed relationship between the two variables in our sample data if there were truly no relationship between them in the unobserved population [i.e., the null hypothesis]."[25] By convention, we want to see if that p-value is less than .05, meaning a probability of less than 5 percent. For the strength of the relationship, we can choose among different **measures of association**. If at least one of the variables is nominal, we can calculate lambda, Cramer's V, or Somers' d.† The possible values of these statistics range from 0 to 1; the closer to zero, the weaker the relationship. If both variables are ordinal, such as education level and support for the environment, we usually compute the strength of the relationship with Kendall's tau, gamma, or Spearman's rho.[26] These statistics range from −1 to +1, which tells us both the strength and the direction of the relationship. A negative value for this statistic indicates an inverse relationship, and the closer the number comes to −1, the stronger that relationship. A positive value means a direct relationship, and bigger means stronger. The closer the number gets to zero, from either direction, the weaker the relationship. Nowhere have I seen an authoritative translation of these numbers into plain-language adjectives. A Cramer's V or Kendall's tau of 0.31 might indicate a modest relationship to some researchers and a fairly strong relationship to others.

A concrete example might help reinforce these general points. Let's go back to the question about race and views toward the death penalty. I happen to have saved a piece of the 2000 American National Election Studies (ANES) on my computer, in part because of the historic presidential election that year. That survey includes questions about race and the death penalty, enabling me to construct a crosstab (see table 7.1). Casual inspection of the columns indicates some difference between blacks and whites. Blacks were more than twice as likely as whites to strongly oppose the death penalty, and whites were more likely than blacks to say they favored it strongly. However, for the middle two responses, blacks and whites were very similar. Thus, it's not clear how to characterize the overall relationship. Now is when the summary statistics become helpful. The p-value (.000) of the chi-square sta-

---

* Most of the crosstabs that appear in the media, by contrast, simply print columns of percentages and let readers decide whether any meaningful differences exist.

† Personally, I favor Cramer's V, but you'll have to take me out to dinner before I tell you why.

Table 7.1. Crosstab of race and attitude toward death penalty

	White	Black
Favor strongly (%)	57.7	33.5
Favor (%)	18.3	18.3
Oppose (%)	10.5	12.6
Oppose strongly (%)	13.6	35.6
N	1320	191

Source: American National Election Studies, 2000.
Note: Pearson chi-square = 67.559; p = .000; Cramer's V = .211. Column percentages may not total exactly to 100.0 due to rounding.

tistic confirms that the relationship was statistically significant.* Cramer's V, a measure of association, equaled .211. Personally, I would call this a moderate relationship, but others might differ. The positive sign of Cramer's V doesn't tell us anything, because race is a nominal variable. We need to look at the table of percentages to interpret the direction. To sum up my findings, I might state that "there was a moderate (Cramer's V = .211) and statistically significant relationship between race and attitudes toward the death penalty in 2000. Blacks tended to be less supportive than whites. Over 35 percent of blacks said they opposed the death penalty strongly, compared with just 14 percent of whites."

When both variables are interval or ratio, we employ a different technique—correlation analysis. The **Pearson correlation coefficient** is one of the most common statistics in all of political science.[27] The usual shorthand for the correlation coefficient is r, which can vary from −1 to +1. The farther r moves away from 0, in either a positive or a negative direction, the stronger the relationship. In the context of correlation, the strength refers to the degree of linear fit between our two variables. Imagine a graph with a country's per capita income on the x axis and voter turnout rate on the y axis. Each country in our study would be represented by a single point (e.g., x = $14,047; y = 56%). If all these points happen to form a single line, sloping up-

---

*Although the p-value was reported as .000, we are never 100 percent confident of rejecting the null hypothesis. If SPSS reported numbers out to more decimal places, the true p-value in this example might have been something like .0003.

ward such that higher incomes were associated with greater turnout, then r would equal +1.[28] In real life, the data rarely line up so neatly. The more that our data points depart from a straight line and appear to be scattered randomly, the lower the value of r. When Robert Putnam analyzed the correlation between economic modernity and institutional performance among regions of Italy, most of the data points were fairly close to a line, but not directly on it ($r = .77$). Pippa Norris found a weaker correlation ($r = .20$) between how often Americans read the newspaper and how often they contacted government officials. In general, more of one behavior was associated with more of the other. Nevertheless, one could find a number of people who read the newspaper every day but never contacted an official, and many others who rarely read the newspaper yet frequently made contacts.[29]

Not all relationships in politics are linear, however. Some might be curved, in a variety of ways, and the correlation coefficient will not detect these relationships. The r will be deceptively low. Here is another reason to generate pictures of our data. Working with two interval or ratio variables, we might generate a scatter plot and visually inspect the data for any nonlinear patterns.

Interval- and ratio-level measures are often referred to as **continuous** variables,[30] and the 2000 ANES included a large number of them. Several were classic feeling thermometer questions, where individuals are asked how they feel about a particular politician, group of people, or part of government. These scores can range from 0 (very cold) to 100 (very warm), with a 50 indicating neutral feelings. Table 7.2 displays a correlation matrix for a few of these feeling thermometer questions.[31] Not surprisingly, feelings toward the two major presidential candidates, Al Gore and George W. Bush, were inversely related ($r = -.414$) and statistically significant.* Generally speaking, the warmer individuals felt toward Bush, the colder they felt about Gore, and vice versa. Feelings toward Gore and toward feminists were directly related ($r = .331$), as were feelings about Bush and the military ($r = .270$); both relationships were statistically significant. No major headlines there. Perhaps the most surprising finding, however, was the lack of correlation between respondents' feelings toward feminists and the military. The p-value for statistical significance indicated a 22 percent chance that the null hypothesis was correct. That's well above our 5 percent threshold. As good political scientists, we would have to conclude that no relationship existed between these

---

*In table 7.3 and in many published studies, you will see asterisks used to denote statistical significance. The usual approach is that * means significant at the .05 level, and ** means significant at the .01 level. Still, it pays to read the fine print to be sure.

Table 7.2. Correlation matrix of feeling thermometer scores

	Gore	Bush	Feminists	Military
Al Gore				
r	1	−.414**	.331**	−.072**
Stat. sig.		.000	.000	.005
N	1774	1747	1410	1494
George W. Bush				
r	−.414**	1	−.203**	.270**
Stat. sig.	.000		.000	.000
N	1747	1761	1403	1487
Feminists				
r	.331**	−.203**	1	.033
Stat. sig.	.000	.000		.219
N	1410	1403	1427	1413
The military				
r	−.072**	.270**	.033	1
Stat. sig.	.005	.000	.219	
N	1494	1487	1413	1517

Source: American National Election Studies, 2000.
*Significant at the .05 level.
**Significant at the .01 level.

two variables. Some Americans probably had cool feelings toward feminists and the military, some had warm feelings toward both, but many had mixed feelings. Before analyzing these numbers, I would have been pretty sure that these two variables were inversely related. So I learned something, and that's OK.

Suppose we looked for correlations among the twenty-five fictional countries mentioned in chapter 5. We could do so for voter turnout, per capita income, and percentage of high school graduates, which are all continuous variables. In light of the analysis we just performed on the feeling thermometer scores, the results are a bit puzzling. The correlation between voter turnout and high school graduates is stronger ($r = .473$) than anything we saw in table 7.2. Nevertheless, the *p*-value is .017, which does qualify as statistically significant, but is a bit larger than many of the comparable figures in table 7.2. How can we be less confident of a relationship that seems stronger? In addition, the correlation between voter turnout and per capita income seems pretty strong ($r = .372$), yet it fails our test of statistical significance because the p-value is .067. How can that be? The answer to both questions is the same—because of sample size. For the feeling thermometer questions, we had somewhere between 1400 and 1800 responses. It was much easier to be confident that some relationship existed than when we had just twenty-five countries. In general, the smaller the number of cases, the larger r will need to be before the relationship counts as statistically significant. The flip side is that someone with a huge sample can proudly declare that a certain relationship is statistically significant, even if it turns out to be a very weak relationship.[32]

Closely related to correlation analysis is **simple linear regression**. Instead of establishing whether two variables are related in any way, simple regression requires us to specify a dependent variable and an independent variable. We are edging away from correlation and heading toward causation (though the distance between them is quite large). For a study of education and voter turnout, the researcher could reasonably assume that the former is the independent variable and the latter is the dependent variable. Among the twenty-five fictional countries we have been analyzing, a simple linear regression tells us that on average, a 10-point increase in the percentage of high school graduates is connected to a 3.6-point increase in voter turnout. It also tells us that variation in the percentage of high school graduates across these countries accounts for about 19 percent of the variation in voter turnout. I will explain where these numbers came from in a minute when we get to multiple regression analysis, which is used much more frequently than simple regression.

Crosstabs, correlations, and simple regressions are the most common forms of bivariate data analysis. Periodically, we want to analyze a bivariate relationship between a categorical variable and a continuous variable, and in that case we'll need a different technique. For instance, suppose we wanted to assess the relationship between gender and the feeling thermometer scores for Hillary Clinton. Or perhaps we had a continuous measure of political tolerance, for individuals in any country, and we wanted to see if it was related to religious affiliation. One option is the **difference-of-means test**, which works best when the independent variable is categorical and the dependent is continuous.[33] The basic idea is to compare the means (and the overall distributions) for each value of the categorical variable. A difference-of-means test would compare, for instance, how men and women felt toward Hillary Clinton, or how Christians, Muslims, and Hindus scored on a tolerance scale.[34] The relevant measure of association is called eta-squared, and its values can range from 0 to 1. Statistical significance can be established with a *t*-test if we are comparing two groups, or with an *F*-test for two or more groups.

What happens if we use the wrong statistical procedure? Well, our answer could range anywhere from almost right to terribly wrong. Suppose we are analyzing two nominal variables with a crosstab, and we measure the strength of their relationship with Kendall's tau, which is appropriate for two ordinal variables, instead of with Cramer's V. Chances are good (but not guaranteed) that we will get close to the correct answer, in part because nominal and ordinal variables are both categorical. Our statistical analysis might look a bit careless, but not deeply flawed. However, if we use a crosstab when we should create a correlation matrix, or vice versa, then the odds of making a big mistake increase substantially. We might "find" a relationship that does not really exist, or dismiss a relationship that really does. Confusing categorical variables with continuous variables could seriously damage our analysis.

ANALYZING THREE OR MORE VARIABLES

For most political scientists, the real payoff of statistical analysis comes when we tackle three or more variables at once. Now we can check for spuriousness and start ruling out certain hypotheses. Now we can determine which of our independent variables are more or less strongly related to our dependent variable. We may even be able to capture interactions between our independent variables. No longer do we have to pretend that politics is shaped by discrete pairs of variables.

At the most general level, political scientists use multivariate data analysis to exert a certain measure of control over complex and often mysterious political phenomena. Control is key. In chapter 4, we learned one way that political scientists establish control over some slice of the political world—through experiments. The experimental research design, in its purest form, allows researchers to manipulate a single independent variable while holding every other possible influence constant. Any observed change in the dependent variable must be linked to change in that one independent variable. The independent variable might even be said to cause the change (though the precise causal mechanism is often obscure). Many features of the political world, however, don't lend themselves to experimentation, for practical and ethical reasons. Political scientists who rely on observational designs, especially those who conduct large-*n* comparisons, use statistical techniques to approximate the kind of control generated by experiments.

Multivariate techniques often build on approaches to analyzing two variables of numeric data. With categorical data, for instance, we can run a crosstab controlling for a third variable. Basically what happens is that original crosstab is divided into separate crosstabs for each value of the control variable.[35] We then compare these new crosstabs to one another and see how much they differ. Perhaps we would like to know if the observed relationship between race and views toward the death penalty held true for men and for women. In other words, we want to control for gender. After running a **crosstab with control**, we discover that gender does not matter much, at least not in 2000. The relationship between race and views toward the death penalty is statistically significant overall, and for men, and for women. The measure of association is a bit stronger for men than women (Cramer's V = .247 versus .190), but nothing dramatic. Our next move is to toss out gender and try controlling for education; our dataset has an ordinal measure that divides adults into three categories based on their highest level of education (less than high school, high school, more than high school). The results are pretty much the same as for gender. All three of the new crosstabs are statistically significant, and the strength measure varies only a little among them. Now we're more confident that race is connected with views toward the death penalty, because we have controlled for a few other plausible factors, and the key statistics changed little. Had the numbers been much different for one of our control variables, we would have been less confident that race was important. Our original findings would have been partly or entirely spurious.

Unfortunately, controlling for a third variable is about all we can accomplish with crosstabs. If we tried to control for two or three variables at the same time, some of our cell entries could have very few or no observations in them. In fact, if we control for just one more variable with several possible values, such as a 7-point scale for political ideology, the same difficulty can arise. Controlling for a continuous variable like per capita income would aggravate this problem by several orders of magnitude. The underlying problem is that our statistical techniques are based on comparisons between the observed distribution of data in each cell of the table and a hypothetical distribution of values that are unrelated (i.e., compared to the null hypothesis). When some cells have few if any data points, the relationships in the other cells will have to be quite strong before qualifying as statistically significant. In extreme cases, our statistical software will be unable to calculate statistical significance or strength of association.

Working with continuous variables, we could move from correlation to **partial correlation**, which enables us to control for a third variable. To explain why some regional governments in Italy have performed better than others, Putnam tested two general hypotheses, one rooted in economics and

CHAPTER SEVEN

the other in culture. He found a strong, positive correlation ($r = .77$) between his index of economic modernity and his index of institutional performance, and an even stronger correlation ($r = .92$) between his index of civic community and institutional performance. Both relationships were statistically significant, and both seemed quite important. Putnam's next step was to calculate two partial correlations. The first was between economic modernity and institutional performance, controlling for civic community. That one was no longer statistically significant. The second was between civic community and institutional performance, controlling for economic modernity. That relationship did remain statistically significant. As a result, Putnam had evidence that culture was more important than economics in affecting government performance.[36]

Both crosstabs and correlations allow us to move from two to three variables, but not much beyond that. **Multiple regression analysis** builds on simple linear regression and is better equipped to deal with control variables. Instead of just one variable, we can test two, three, six, thirteen—any number of variables simultaneously.[37] Suppose we have just two independent variables (A and B) and one dependent variable (Z). A multiple regression model will allow us to estimate the relationship between A and Z, controlling for B, as well as the relationship between B and Z, controlling for A. For both relationships we can identify the statistical significance, substantive size, and direction. The model can also tell us how much of the variation in Z is accounted for statistically by the combination of A and B. That's a lot of useful information. If we had a somewhat more elaborate model with four independent variables (A, B, C, D), then we could determine the relationship between A and Z, controlling for B, C, and D, and so on. Over the years, several types of regression techniques have been developed to handle different kinds of data and different kinds of research questions. For the examples below, I will use ordinary least squares (typically written as OLS) regression, which is the most basic version.

Based on the data from my twenty-five fictional countries, the simple linear regression revealed that the high school graduates variable was directly related to voter turnout, and statistically significant. On average, a 10-point increase in the education variable was connected to a 3.6-point increase in turnout. Where did those numbers come from? When I checked the output from SPSS, I noticed that the p-value of the high school graduate variable (based on a statistical t-test) was .017. As we know, anything lower than .05 counts as statistically significant. The unstandardized coefficient (reported as B or b) was .364, which means that a 1-unit increase in the independent variable is associated with a .364-unit increase in the dependent variable.

(For ease of expression, I then multiplied both numbers by 10.) To determine the overall power of the model, I relied on the adjusted R-squared statistic, which was .190. This is a close relative of r, the correlation coefficient, and is adjusted for the number of independent variables in the model.[38] The values of the adjusted R-squared can range from 0 to 1, and a .190 means that this one variable accounts for 19 percent of the variation in the dependent variable, voter turnout.*

When I added a second independent variable, per capita income, the results were initially puzzling. Neither independent variable was statistically significant, controlling for the other, and the adjusted R-squared barely moved (.192).[†] In some respects this model seemed worse than my simple linear model. The underlying problem, it turned out, was that my two independent variables were intercorrelated ($r = .427$). With so much overlap in the data, I wouldn't get much added benefit from incorporating both variables into the model. I therefore dropped the income variable and added the measure for voter registration requirements, which wasn't correlated with my education variable.[39] When these latter two variables were combined, the adjusted R-squared jumped up to .335, indicating that my new model could account for one-third of the variation in voter turnout. The statistical significance of the education variable just barely missed the traditional .05 cutoff ($p = .055$). The partial regression coefficient of this variable declined to .271. The voter registration variable, however, was statistically significant ($p = .023$), controlling for education, and the direction of the unstandardized coefficient was negative. That makes sense: as voter registration requirements get tougher, voter turnout declines. The exact value of B was −6.493, meaning that as we move up one unit on the independent variable (e.g., from low to medium), voter turnout drops an average of 6.5 percentage points, controlling for education.

* Is 19 percent a substantively important result? That's a judgment call. In some parts of the discipline, scholars would be satisfied if their model accounted for 5 percent of the variation in their dependent variable, as long as some of their independent variables were statistically significant. After all, politics is often complicated, and we may only be able to grasp a sliver of it at a time. Other political scientists would look at these results and conclude that the omitted variables must be more interesting than the featured variables.

[†] Likewise, the standard error of the estimate (SEE) barely changed. Some political scientists are skeptical of R-squared and adjusted R-squared and prefer to use the SEE when evaluating the entire regression model.

You could easily convince me that both independent variables in this model seem important. We are still 94.5 percent sure that the education variable is statistically significant, controlling for registration requirements. It might be helpful to know which of these two variables is more important substantively, but they are expressed in very different units, making them hard to compare. Fortunately, SPSS also generates a standardized regression coefficient (Beta), which basically strips away the specific units of the variables and calculates how much change in the dependent variable is associated with a one-standard-deviation change in each independent variable. The larger the absolute value of the Beta coefficient, the bigger the possible impact. By this measure, my registration variable (−.426) was a bit more powerful than my education variable (.352).[40] When I added the per capita income variable back in, creating a model with three independent variables, the voter registration variable remained statistically significant, and its unstandardized coefficient was basically unchanged. Neither the income nor the education variable was statistically significant (p = .273 and .178, respectively). Within the confines of this little study of voter turnout, it therefore appears that registration requirements were the most important independent variable, statistically and substantively.

Although a simple example like this one can illustrate the general thinking behind multiple regression analysis, it's atypical, considering the small number of cases and independent variables (and the totally bogus data). Table 7.3 presents a somewhat more realistic model, analyzing attitudes toward climate change. The data come from an Internet-based survey of Americans conducted in 2010. Past studies indicated that political ideology was pretty closely aligned with views toward climate change: conservatives were less likely than liberals to perceive a problem or a need for government action. The author of the survey study, Michael Jones, felt that this ideology measure was too broad. He wanted to test whether more specific measures of belief systems would follow similar patterns. Jones ran a series of OLS regressions with a standard 7-point measure of political ideology, along with four continuous measures for different cultural types (individualist, hierarchical, egalitarian, and fatalist) among the independent variables. He also included controls for education, gender,[41] and factual knowledge of climate change. His dependent variables, only some of which are displayed in table 7.3,[42] asked people to express their level of agreement with certain statements related to climate change, ranging from Completely Disagree (0) to Completely Agree (10). These he treated as continuous measures.[43]

As expected, the general ideology variable was statistically significant and

Table 7.3. Multiple regression: Attitudes toward climate change

	Belief in climate change	Human-caused climate change	Need for action	Renewable energy
Ideology	−.483**	−.671**	−.542**	−.305*
Individualism	−.051	−.128**	−.116**	.067
Hierarchy	.103*	.176**	.111**	.095
Egalitarianism	.092*	.171**	.244**	.021
Fatalism	−.032	−.079	−.150**	.009
Education	−.025	.025	.055	−.137
Gender	−.331	−.369	−.355	−.814*
Climate change knowledge	.339**	.239*	.308**	−.009
Adj. R²	.180	.388	.395	.061
N	262	262	263	255

Source: Michael D. Jones, "Leading the Way to Compromise? Cultural Theory and Climate Change Opinion," PS: Political Science and Politics 44, no. 4 (October 2011): 720–25.
Note: Coefficients are unstandardized.
*Significant at the .05 level.
**Significant at the .01 level.

negative. The more conservative individuals were, the less likely they were to believe in climate change, that human activity caused climate change, or that government action was needed. In results not shown here, conservatives were also less likely to feel that climate change posed a personal or societal risk. The more noteworthy results involved the four cultural types. Even controlling for political ideology, several of these types were statistically significant. Moreover, they didn't all point in the same direction. Whereas individualism was inversely related with most of the dependent variables, hierarchy and egalitarianism were often directly related. Individualists were less likely to believe that climate change was due to human activity ($B = -.128$), or that it was important for the United States to reduce greenhouse gas emissions ($B = -.116$). Hierarchicals and egalitarians felt more strongly that humans were a cause of climate change and that action was needed. To the extent that Americans disagree about climate change, Jones's research suggests that the dividing line is not simply liberals versus conservatives.

Interestingly, respondents weren't as divided over possible policy remedies such as renewable energy, nuclear energy, and cap and trade emission policies. Thus, policy makers might want to avoid debates over the extent and causes of climate change and focus more on remedies.[44]

These examples are just the tip of the multivariate iceberg. All these variables behaved pretty normally. In other research, some variables would be skewed and would need to be converted to log scale. Independent variables can be expressed individually or as interaction terms. Not all the dependent variables that political scientists work with are as continuous as voter turnout rates or feeling thermometer scores. Some are dichotomous, with only two possible values: for example, individuals did or did not vote in the last election; legislators voted for or against a specific bill; countries were at peace or at war. These types of questions are often handled with logistic regression models, a statistical cousin of OLS, or with proportional hazards models. My two examples used cross-sectional data, comparing many observations at a single point in time. When researchers work with time-series or panel data, they need to work with more advanced statistical techniques. Ross's analysis of the resource curse was based on pooled data from more than one hundred countries between the years 1971 and 1997. Read his article carefully and you will see that he employed a version of regression known as Feasible Generalized Least Squares.[45] Regression analysis isn't the only option, either; some analysts prefer a statistical technique called maximum likelihood estimation. It's easy to see why more than one semester of statistics is required to become truly proficient.

FINAL THOUGHTS

Throughout this chapter, I have largely avoided the *c*-word—*causation*. In working through some examples of statistical analysis, I have stressed empirical regularities: whether my variables were connected, associated, linked, correlated. A number of political scientists would have looked at my data and reached stronger conclusions. Race had an impact on attitudes toward the death penalty. On average, a 10-point increase in high school graduates led to a 3.6-point increase in voter turnout. By itself, the education variable explained almost 20 percent of the variation in voter turnout. Lots of different ways to indicate cause and effect.

I hesitated to use this kind of language because of the voices in my head.* The first voices insist that only carefully designed experiments can establish

---

* You probably suspected as much once I started talking about home inspectors and the Glasgow Coma Scale.

causation (see chapter 4). However much I try to account for other influences, I know that I can never control for everything with an observational research design. Some unobserved variable could wipe out, or at least seriously weaken, whatever relationship I might have found. It only takes a minute to think of demographic variables (e.g., age, income) and attitudinal variables (e.g., trust in government, orientation toward the future) that might influence someone's views about climate change, yet were omitted from Jones's study. In general, these voices tell me, the best we can do with observational data is to rule out certain relationships when they fail the test of statistical significance, which is useful knowledge, and to highlight relationships that other scholars could test more definitively with experiments.

The other voices belong to really smart people who are adept at statistical analysis and yet depend on multiple kinds of evidence to prove cause and effect. Some of them are distinguished mathematical statisticians.[46] Others were quoted in chapter 4 saying that detailed case studies are better suited for identifying causal paths and mechanisms than are large-*n* statistical comparisons.[47] Henry Brady, a political scientist who knows a thing or two about numbers, has a terrific illustration of the limitations of statistical models. Shortly after the 2000 US presidential election, one well-publicized regression analysis showed that George W. Bush lost at least ten thousand votes in Florida because the media called the election ten minutes before the polls had closed in the panhandle part of the state. Thus, Bush should have won Florida easily, making the 2000 election much less contentious. Through careful process tracing, using a combination of documents and numbers, Brady demonstrated that the vast majority of Floridians had already voted before the networks made their announcement; that most people who had not voted would not have heard the announcement; and that most people who had not voted but did hear the announcement probably decided to vote anyway. The true number of votes lost was closer to fifty, a far cry from the original estimate.[48]

Putnam's analysis of Italian regional governments did not end with partial correlations. After measuring his key variables and computing their relationships, he then shifted gears, devoting the last two chapters to a historically informed case study of Italy. For one thing, he wanted to show that civic community led to institutional performance, and not vice versa. Timing and sequence are among the key hurdles facing causal arguments. In addition, Putnam wanted to explain exactly how civic-ness can improve the performance of governments. He argued that "social capital" was the key element linking these two variables.[49] While some scholars doubt Putnam's argument, my point here is that he realized that his numbers could only reveal so much.

My statistical analysis did not tell me how race affects views toward the death penalty. I could imagine any number of reasons, such as perceived fairness of the criminal justice system, religious beliefs about taking another person's life, perceived threat of violent criminals in one's community, and historical legacies of slavery and segregation. All plausible, none tested. Until someone figures out how race shapes attitudes toward the death penalty, making a strong claim about causality seems premature (maybe even dodgy). In the meantime, I will try not to beat my data until they confess.

This last chapter, then, isn't really a conclusion. The lessons contained in this guide don't culminate in a sophisticated multiple regression model. Nor do they culminate in a richly detailed case study or a clever experiment. In fact, this book isn't supposed to have a conclusion at all. The whole project is an extended introduction to the study and practice of political science. What happens next depends on you, the reader. The world of politics is complicated, often messy, and sometimes absurd. It would be tempting to view it all with bafflement or contempt if the stakes weren't so damn high. My hope is that knowing some basic concepts and general strategies will better equip you to make sense of politics in the future, and perhaps even inspire you to expand and refine your analytic skills. The world isn't exactly clamoring for more full-time political scientists—but it could always use more people who think carefully and systematically about politics.

PRACTICE: INSPECTING

1. Make sure that you can interpret the numerical tables, figures, and graphs in publications such as those listed below. Focus on the statistical significance, strength, and direction of each relationship.

> Heather K. Evans, Victoria Cordova, and Savannah Sipole, "Twitter Style: An Analysis of How House Candidates Used Twitter in Their 2012 Campaigns," *PS: Political Science and Politics* 47, no. 2 (April 2014): 454–62;
>
> M. Steven Fish, "Islam and Authoritarianism," *World Politics* 55, no. 1 (October 2002): 4–37;
>
> Ronald Inglehart and Christian Welzel, "Changing Mass Priorities: The Link between Modernization and Democracy," *Perspectives on Politics* 8, no. 2 (June 2010): 551–67;
>
> Gary C. Jacobson, "It's Nothing Personal: The Decline of the Incumbency Advantage in US House Elections," *Journal of Politics* 77, no. 3 (July 2015): 861–73;

Michael D. Jones, "Leading the Way to Compromise? Cultural Theory and
Climate Change Opinion," *PS: Political Science and Politics* 44, no. 4
(October 2011): 720–25;

Edward D. Mansfield, Diana C. Mutz, and Laura R. Silver, "Men, Women, Trade,
and Free Markets," *International Studies Quarterly* 59, no. 2 (June 2015):
303–15;

Pippa Norris, "Does Television Erode Social Capital? A Reply to Putnam," *PS:
Political Science and Politics* 29, no. 3 (September 1996): 474–80;

Robert D. Putnam, *Making Democracy Work: Civic Traditions in Modern Italy*
(Princeton, NJ: Princeton University Press, 1993), chapter 4;

Craig Volden and Alan E. Wiseman, *Legislative Effectiveness in the United
States Congress: The Lawmakers* (New York: Cambridge University Press,
2014), chapter 3.

PRACTICE: BUILDING

1. For each of the following pairs of variables, indicate whether a cross-tabulation,
   correlation, or difference-of-means test would be the most appropriate
   statistical technique to employ:

   Ethnic group; trust in government (low, medium, high)

   Per capita income of country; percentage of members of Parliament who are
   female

   Region of UK; party affiliation in UK (Conservative, Green, Labour, Liberal
   Democrat, Scottish National, UK Independence, Other)

   Education level (less than high school, high school grad, some college, college
   grad); views toward same-sex marriage (oppose strongly, oppose, support,
   support strongly)

   Age; feeling thermometer score for any political figure

   Ethnic group; feeling thermometer score for any political figure

2. Liesbet Hooghe wanted to figure out whether working for an international
   organization affected a person's support for supranational norms. If so, would
   that relationship hold, controlling for other possible influences? She surveyed
   top officials at the European Commission about their views toward the
   European Union, and the correlation matrix below displays a small slice of her
   results. How would you interpret these bivariate relationships? Think in terms of
   the statistical significance, direction, and strength.

	Suprana-tionalism	Ideology	Size of country	International education	Length of service
Supranationalism	1	−.17*	.01	.22**	.16*
Ideology		1	−.14	−.05	−.03
Size of country			1	−.04	.40**
Int'l education				1	.01
Length of service					1

Source: Liesbet Hooghe, "Several Roads Lead to International Norms, but Few via International Socialization: A Case Study of the European Commission," *International Organization* 59, no. 4 (October 2005): 861–98.

Notes: Supranationalism measures the extent to which respondents believe that the European Union rather than individual countries should take the lead in governing Europe; ideology is self-reported and ranges from left to right; size of country refers to population in millions; international education of the respondent ranges from low to high; and length of service equals the number of years working for the European Commission.

*p < .05.
**p < .01.

3. How would you interpret the following output from a multiple regression model in which the dependent variable is self-reported political ideology, from left (1) to right (10), in Brazil?

Coefficients	Unstandardized (*B*)	Standardized (Beta)	Sig.
Age	.016	.091	.003
Income level	−.035	−.026	.393
Education level	−.128	−.118	.000
Overall model	R square = .032	Adjusted R square = .030	SEE = 2.770

Source: World Values Survey wave 6 (data for Brazil, 2014).

ACKNOWLEDGMENTS

"Writing a book is a horrible, exhausting struggle, like a long bout of some painful illness. One would never undertake such a thing if one were not driven on by some demon whom one can neither resist nor understand." In making this remark, George Orwell probably captured the experience of many writers. Fortunately, I am not one of them—at least, not this time. Although the process of writing this book took many years and included several periods where I felt stuck, it culminated with months of sustained, enjoyable work. If I was driven on by some demon, it was one that I understood pretty well. I had to find a better way of teaching students how to think like political scientists.

Writing this book never felt horrible because I received help from many people. My biggest debt of gratitude goes to the hundreds of William & Mary students who have taken my Research Methods course over the years. They were patient as I experimented with different ways to teach certain skills and concepts, and a number of them offered specific suggestions. Special thanks go to Ellie Manspile and Max Shipman. Authors of academic books usually try out their ideas at professional conferences and departmental workshops. This book was born in the classroom.

I deeply appreciate feedback from Alan Howard and Rick Valelly, who read most of the chapters. They understood what I was trying to accomplish, kept me focused on my audience, and, just as important, offered genuine encouragement. My wife, Dee Holmes, never seemed to tire of listening to my latest thoughts about such fascinating topics as causal hypotheses and case selection. (Trust me, anyone who spends much time thinking about research methods needs emotional support.) I asked my colleague Dan Doherty for help because of his reputation for teaching Research Methods well. He read the entire manuscript carefully, prompting me to clarify my thoughts and saving me from a few embarrassing mistakes.

At the University of Chicago Press, John Tryneski did more than usher this manuscript through peer review and production. John made sure that every chapter had a strong introduction, and he steered me away from examples or analogies that could strike readers as forced, obscure, or dated. He also persuaded me to spend less time critiquing the leading guides to research methods and more time developing my own approach. This project went through two rounds of peer review at Chicago, first when I had a prospectus and a few chapters to share and then when I had finished the manuscript. The reviewers were generous in their praise and pointed out several places where I could make improvements. Thank you. Sandra Hazel polished my prose with a keen eye for grammar and clarity. Several other people working for the University of Chicago Press—Kelly Finefrock-Creed, Rich Hendel, Melinda Kennedy, Rodney Powell, Kevin Quach, Kathleen Raven, and Holly Smith—helped in ways large and small to turn my manuscript into a professional-looking book. I would like to thank them as well.

At the end of the day, though, only one person is listed as the author. If you want to congratulate someone for writing such a wonderful book or discuss ways of turning this into a Broadway musical, then you know who to contact—me, Chris Howard. I'd love to talk. But if all you can offer is backhanded compliments or penetrating criticism, well, you may be right, and I'll try to do better next time.

NOTES

INTRODUCTION

1. For other examples from medicine and business, see Atul Gawande, *The Checklist Manifesto: How to Get Things Right* (New York: Metropolitan Books, 2009).

2. I blame this habit partly on the steady diet of standardized tests that students are fed in high school; all too often, these tests stress factual details at the expense of larger concepts and critical thinking skills.

3. More originality could be expected in a senior seminar paper or undergraduate honors thesis, and certainly in graduate-level work.

4. Tracy Kidder and Richard Todd, *Good Prose: The Art of Nonfiction* (New York: Random House, 2013), p. 70.

5. Daniel N. Posner, "The Political Salience of Cultural Difference: Why Chewas and Tumbukas Are Allies in Zambia and Adversaries in Malawi," *American Political Science Review* 98, no. 4 (November 2004): 529–45. The quote represents my take on Posner's argument.

6. For example, anyone who argues that Truman's decision to drop a nuclear bomb on Japan in 1945 was due to Republicans' historic gains in the 1946 congressional elections probably holds unusual beliefs about time travel.

7. While beliefs, parables, and myths play a vital role in every society, their power doesn't hinge on empirical evidence. I might believe that the fable of the Ant and the Grasshopper teaches some good lessons about working hard and planning ahead, but I would be hard-pressed to find actual talking insects.

CHAPTER ONE

1. James E. Short, *How Much Media? 2013 Report on American Consumers* (Marshall School of Business, University of Southern California, October 2013), available at http://classic.marshall.usc.edu/assets/161/25995.pdf.

2. Farhad Manjoo, "You Won't Finish This Article" (June 6, 2013), available at http://www.slate.com/articles/technology/technology/2013/06/how_people_read_online_why_you_won_t_finish_this_article.html.

3. Gerald Graff and Cathy Birkenstein, *They Say, I Say: The Moves That Matter in Academic Writing*, 2nd ed. (New York: W. W. Norton, 2010).

4. In my experience, the typical lit review is roughly 10%–20% of the length of the entire project. This translates to one chapter (sometimes less) of a university press book and to a few pages at most in a scholarly journal article. In unpublished work, such as an undergraduate honors thesis, the fraction could be larger.

5. However, scholars often connect their research to different literatures in separate publications, each targeted at a somewhat different audience.

6. Of course, it depends on how one defines *democracy* and *war*. Possible exceptions to the democratic peace include the War of 1812 (between the United States and England) and the Indo-Pakistani War of the late 1940s.

7. American National Election Studies, table 5A.1, available at http://www .electionstudies.org/nesguide/toptable/tab5a_1.htm. Accessed February 29, 2016.

8. Sometimes political scientists organize their lit reviews around methodologies—ways of studying politics—rather than prevailing descriptions of or explanations for some part of the political world. Someone interested in voter turnout, for example, might contrast what we have learned from mass surveys to what we have learned from field experiments. Once in a great while, the lit review is organized historically, indicating how our understanding of some political phenomena has changed over time.

9. Pure replication studies are rare in political science. They are more common in fields such as physics and pharmacology.

10. Descriptive hypotheses will be discussed more fully in chapter 2.

11. E.g., Michael Ross, "Does Oil Hinder Democracy?," *World Politics* 53, no. 3 (April 2001): 325–61.

12. E.g., Jonathan Di John, *From Windfall to Curse? Oil and Industrialization in Venezuela, 1920 to the Present* (University Park: Penn State University Press, 2009); Andrew Rosser, "Escaping the Resource Curse: The Case of Indonesia," *Journal of Contemporary Asia* 37, no. 1 (February 2007): 38–58.

13. Causal hypotheses will be discussed more fully in chapter 3.

14. Stephen Biddle, Jeffrey A. Friedman, and Jacob N. Shapiro, "Testing the Surge: Why Did Violence Decline in Iraq in 2007?," *International Security* 37, no. 1 (Summer 2012): 7–40.

15. We might think of the lit review as a kind of home inspection for an entire neighborhood. In this instance the report would say, "You don't want to buy here. These homes are structurally unsound and about to collapse. You should look for a house in a different neighborhood."

16. Pauline Jones Luong and Erika Weinthal, *Oil Is Not a Curse: Ownership Structure and Institutions in Soviet Successor States* (New York: Cambridge University Press, 2010). The authors also examined Azerbaijan, whose degree of government involvement lies in between the two pairs of cases mentioned here.

17. Robert D. Putnam, *Making Democracy Work: Civic Traditions in Modern Italy* (Princeton, NJ: Princeton University Press, 1993).

18. John Sides and Jack Citrin, "European Opinion about Immigration: The Role of Identities, Interest and Information," *British Journal of Political Science* 37, no. 3 (July 2007): 477–504.

19. Not surprisingly, much of this research is coauthored, with at least one scholar from each discipline.

20. Henry Farrell and Martha Finnemore, "The End of Hypocrisy," *Foreign Affairs* 92, no. 6 (November/December 2013): 22.

21. Daniel N. Posner, "The Political Salience of Cultural Difference: Why Chewas

and Timbukas Are Allies in Zambia and Adversaries in Malawi," *American Political Science Review* 98, no. 4 (November 2004): 529–45.

22. Adam Sheingate, "Still a Jungle," *Democracy: A Journal of Ideas* 25 (Summer 2012): 48–59.

23. Alexander Lee, "Who Becomes a Terrorist? Poverty, Education, and the Origins of Political Violence," *World Politics* 63, no. 2 (April 2011): 203–45.

24. Gary Orren, "Fall from Grace: The Public's Loss of Faith in Government," in *Why People Don't Trust Government*, ed. Joseph S. Nye, Philip Zelikow, and David C. King (Cambridge, MA: Harvard University Press, 1997), pp. 78, 79.

25. Sides and Citrin, "European Opinion about Immigration," 502.

26. Notice that the chapter titles tend to be quite broad. The scope isn't public attitudes toward Hispanic immigration or American attitudes toward immigration. It's public attitudes toward immigration.

27. Using this approach, you might also discover chapters about terrorism in the *Annual Review of Sociology* and the *Annual Review of Law and Social Science* that would be worth reading.

28. Disclosure: I was one of three editors for the *Oxford Handbook of U.S. Social Policy*, and I contributed a chapter to the *Oxford Handbook of American Political Development*. Not surprisingly, my opinion of handbooks like these is pretty positive.

29. In addition, the peer review process for edited volumes isn't always as rigorous as it is for academic journal articles and books, making the quality of each volume less predictable.

30. Christopher Blattman, "Children and War: How 'Soft' Research Can Answer the Hard Questions in Political Science," *Perspectives on Politics* 10, no. 2 (June 2010): 403–13. This journal has become a good source of review essays.

31. Marc Hetherington, "Review Article: Putting Polarization in Perspective," *British Journal of Political Science* 39 (2009): 413–48.

CHAPTER TWO

1. Michael P. McDonald and Samuel L. Popkin, "The Myth of the Vanishing Voter," *American Political Science Review* 95, no. 4 (December 2001): 963–74 and sources cited therein.

2. M. Steven Fish, "Islam and Authoritarianism," *World Politics* 55, no. 1 (October 2002): 4–37; Richard N. Haass, "Towards Greater Democracy in the Muslim World," speech delivered to the Council on Foreign Relations, December 4, 2002; available at http://www.cfr.org/religion/towards-greater-democracy-muslim-world/p5283; Sanford Lakoff, "The Reality of Muslim Exceptionalism," *Journal of Democracy* 15, no. 4 (October 2004): 133–39; Alfred Stepan with Graeme B. Robertson, "An 'Arab' More Than 'Muslim' Electoral Gap," *Journal of Democracy* 14, 3 no. (July 2003): 30–44; Alfred Stepan and Graeme B. Robertson, "Arab, Not Muslim Exceptionalism," *Journal of Democracy* 15, no. 4 (October 2004): 140–46. Thanks to Debra Shushan for suggesting this example.

3. Christopher Howard, *The Hidden Welfare State: Tax Expenditures and Social*

Policy in the United States (Princeton, NJ: Princeton University Press, 1997); Christopher Howard, *The Welfare State Nobody Knows: Debunking Myths about U.S. Social Policy* (Princeton, NJ: Princeton University Press, 2007).

4. For a longer and more sophisticated version of this argument, see John Gerring, "Mere Description," *British Journal of Political Science* 42, no. 4 (October 2012): 721–46.

5. Technically, then, both of these examples involve relationships between two variables—democracy and time, in the case of China, and gender and political participation.

6. Keep in mind that those previous studies could include the work of theorists. Anyone working with the concept of democracy might be guided by Aristotle or Robert Dahl, just as someone dealing with war might look to Hobbes or von Clausewitz.

7. Jon R. Lindsay, "Stuxnet and the Limits of Cyber Warfare," *Security Studies* 22, no. 3 (2013): 372.

8. Locke and Thelen point out that the specific meaning of concepts can differ from country to country, which complicates the tasks of measurement and comparison. Labor success, for instance, might entail something different in Germany than the United States given their histories. Richard M. Locke and Kathleen Thelen, "Apples and Oranges Revisited: Contextualized Comparisons and the Study of Comparative Labor Politics," *Politics and Society* 23, no. 3 (September 1995): 337–67.

9. Philip H. Pollock, *The Essentials of Political Analysis*, 4th ed. (Washington, DC: CQ Press, 2012), p. 11.

10. Moving in the other direction, from more aggregate to more differentiated units of analysis, is tricky. This is called an ecological inference, and it could lead to an ecological fallacy. Put simply, what's true of the whole may or may not be true of every part. If we collect information about US voting behavior at the state level, for example, the results won't necessarily hold at the individual or group level. Just because 61% of all voters in Alabama chose Mitt Romney in the 2012 presidential election doesn't mean also that 61% of blacks in Alabama voted for Romney. In fact, only about 4% of blacks in Alabama did. Sometimes, however, we lack evidence at lower levels and need to make an ecological inference. Readers who want to learn more about this problem and possible solutions to it might start by consulting work by Gary King and by David Freedman.

11. "One advantage of using criteria devised by another researcher is that your results cannot be contaminated by the temptation to bend definitions so as to get the results that you expect." Paul Collier, *The Bottom Billion: Why the Poorest Countries Are Failing and What Can Be Done about It* (New York: Oxford University Press, 2007), p. 18.

12. E.g., Michael Coppedge, Angel Alvarez, and Claudia Maldonado, "Two Persistent Dimensions of Democracy: Contestation and Inclusiveness," *Journal of Politics* 70, no. 3 (July 2008): 632–47.

13. The inspiration for this diagram comes from Gerardo Munck and Jay Verkuilen, "Conceptualizing and Measuring Democracy: Alternative Indices," *Comparative Political Studies* 35, no. 1 (February 2002): 5–34, especially figure 1.

14. Seth Mydans, "Recalculating Happiness in a Himalayan Kingdom," *New York Times*, May 6, 2009. The term "gross national happiness" was introduced by King Wangchuck in 1972. A new government under Prime Minister Tobgay is relying less on this index. Gardiner Harris, "Index of Happiness? Bhutan's New Leader Prefers More Concrete Goals," *New York Times*, October 5, 2013.

15. Other sets of answers are certainly possible.

16. When comas are labeled *mild*, *moderate*, or *severe*, that is an ordinal measure. Notice that the mild range includes three points on the Glasgow Coma Scale (from 13 to 15), while moderate includes four points (from 9 to 12) and severe, six (from 3 to 8). The scale isn't divided evenly.

17. It is unclear whether the full Glasgow Coma Scale would be an interval or ratio measure, because a score of 0 is impossible. I suspect this was done for emotional and psychological reasons. Imagine that your father was seriously injured and unresponsive to any external stimuli. His heart was still beating, but otherwise showed no signs of life. The last thing you'd want to hear from a doctor is that your father is a zero. ("Sure, he forgets my birthday sometimes, and he drinks too much on the weekends, but dammit, he's no zero!") Hence, the lowest possible score is a 3, which may offer a sliver of hope. Fortunately for us, we can analyze the numerical scores from this kind of scale with the same statistical techniques, regardless of whether it is interval or ratio.

18. Similarly, some guides rate colleges and universities by giving an exact numerical score (e.g., 75, 93), while others prefer categorical labels such as *most selective*, *more selective*, and *selective*.

19. See, e.g., Michael Fischer et al., "Inter-rater Reliability of the Full Outline of Un-Responsiveness Score and the Glasgow Coma Score in Critically Ill Patients: A Prospective Observational Study," *Critical Care* 14, no. 2 (April 2010): R64; Michelle Gill et al., "Interrater Reliability of 3 Simplified Neurologic Scales Applied to Adults Presenting to the Emergency Department with Altered Levels of Consciousness," *Annals of Emergency Medicine* 49, no. 4 (April 2007): 403–7.

20. Munck and Verkuilen, "Conceptualizing and Measuring Democracy."

21. My own experience indicates that political scientists are less likely to establish the construct validity of their measures than the content validity.

22. Technically, if one or more of our measures are nominal, we can't refer to the relationship as direct or inverse. Nominal measures don't have higher and lower values. Nonetheless, we can still indicate the expected direction of those relationships. For instance, hypothesizing that religion (nominal) and views toward abortion are related is a bit vague. We might clarify by noting that we expect Catholics and Muslims to be more opposed to abortion than are members of other religions.

23. Data from the 2012 American National Election Studies were analyzed via the Survey Documentation and Analysis website at http://sda.berkeley.edu/sdaweb /analysis/?dataset=nes2012. Accessed January 7, 2016.

24. Howard, *The Welfare State Nobody Knows*, chapters 2 and 5.

CHAPTER THREE

1. *Recovery Act: Hearing before the Committee on Transportation and Infrastructure, United States House of Representatives, One Hundred Eleventh Congress, Second Session, March 26, 2010* (Washington, DC: Government Printing Office, 2010). According to de Rugy, Democratic districts received over 2.5 times more aid than Republican districts (p. 52).

2. Nate Silver, "Study Claiming Link between Stimulus Funding and Partisanship Is Manifestly Flawed" (April 1, 2010), available at http://fivethirtyeight.com/features/study -claiming-link-between-stimulus/.

3. Available at newrepublic.com/article/74220/case-study-hackery. Accessed February 29, 2016.

4. Silver also questioned how de Rugy had measured some of her variables, and felt that she had omitted potentially important economic and demographic variables.

5. Note: some of these districts may have been redrawn after the 2010 Census.

6. De Rugy earned her PhD in economics from the Sorbonne (France), which could mean that she was unfamiliar with important details of American politics. "Knowing what you don't know" might be another general lesson to take away here.

7. Political theorists, in contrast, tend to define *theory* more broadly. For them, a theory could be used to describe, explain, or judge some feature of the political world.

8. Some textbooks also mention antecedent variables, which occur before the independent variables. At that point, though, we might consider these antecedent variables to be our independent variables, and our independent variables to be intervening variables. For the purposes of this guide, knowing how to work with independent, intervening, and dependent variables will suffice.

9. E.g., Gary King, Robert O. Keohane, and Sidney Verba, *Designing Social Inquiry: Scientific Inference in Qualitative Research* (Princeton, NJ: Princeton University Press, 1994), pp. 29–31.

10. For a classic discussion of correlation versus causation, see David Dessler, "Beyond Correlations: Toward a Causal Theory of War," *International Studies Quarterly* 35, no. 3 (September 1991): 337–55.

11. E.g., Janet Buttolph Johnson and H. T. Reynolds, *Political Science Research Methods*, 7th ed. (Thousand Oaks, CA: CQ Press, 2012), pp. 167–70.

12. E.g., Paul M. Kellstedt and Guy D. Whitten, *The Fundamentals of Political Science Research*, 2nd ed. (New York: Cambridge University Press, 2013), pp. 54–56 (the quotation appears on p. 55); Robert D. Putnam, "Tuning in, Tuning Out: The Strange Disappearance of Social Capital in America," *PS: Political Science and Politics* 28, no. 4 (December 1995): 664–83.

13. John Gerring, "Causation: A Unified Framework for the Social Sciences," *Journal of Theoretical Politics* 17, no. 2 (April 2005): 167. This article discusses different ways that social scientists think about causation which, while interesting and important, are beyond the scope of this introductory guide.

14. Alan S. Gerber and Donald P. Green, "The Effects of Canvassing, Telephone

Calls, and Direct Mail on Voter Turnout: A Field Experiment," *American Political Science Review* 94, no. 3 (September 2000): 653–63.

15. Ibid., p. 662.

16. Alexander L. George and Andrew Bennett, *Case Studies and Theory Development in the Social Sciences* (Cambridge, MA: MIT Press, 2005); John Gerring, "Causal Mechanisms: Yes, But . . . ," *Comparative Political Studies* 43, no. 11 (November 2010): 499–526.

17. David Grant, "Redskins Rule: How Football Outcomes Predict the Presidential Election," *Christian Science Monitor*, November 4, 2012. The exceptions were in 2004 and 2012.

18. For these and other strange examples, go to tylervigen.com/spurious-corre lations. Accessed February 24, 2016.

19. At one point in the hearings, de Rugy boldly stated, "This is why we do regression analysis rather than just comparing numbers, . . . because it controls for all the variation there could be" (*Recovery Act*, p. 33). This statement is misleading, because de Rugy did not include all the potentially relevant independent variables in her regression model. More generally, we would need an experimental design to control for all possible sources of variation (see chapter 4), and her study was not an experiment.

20. Veronique de Rugy, *Stimulus Facts—Period 2*, Working Paper no. 10–05, Mercatus Center, George Mason University (April 7, 2010), available at http://mercatus.org /publication/stimulus-facts.

21. For a number of years, scholars have noticed that couples with daughters are more likely to divorce than couples with sons. Some then assumed that daughters somehow caused divorce. A recent study, however, suggests that that relationship may be spurious: prior stress in a relationship may lead to having daughters, and to getting divorced. How so? Female embryos appear to be sturdier than male embryos, and thus better able to survive a stressful pregnancy. Couples heading for divorce are therefore more likely to have daughters. Amar Hamoudi and Jenna Nobles, "Do Daughters Really Cause Divorce? Stress, Pregnancy, and Family Composition," *Demography* 51, no. 4 (August 2014): 1423–49.

22. Michael Ross, "Does Oil Hinder Democracy?," *World Politics* 53, no. 3 (April 2001): 325–61.

23. Putnam, "Tuning in, Tuning Out." A shorter version of his argument also appeared as "The Strange Disappearance of Civic America," *American Prospect* 24 (Winter 1996): 34–48.

24. In this example, it's also possible that the two intervening variables, daily interaction with gays and lesbians and general tolerance, could be influencing each other.

25. See, e.g., Joseph Wright and Matthew Winters, "The Politics of Effective Foreign Aid," *Annual Review of Political Science* 13 (2010): 61–80.

26. Gerring, "Causal Mechanisms: Yes, But. . . ."

27. Sarah C. P. Williams, "How Stress Can Clog Your Arteries," *Science*, June 22, 2014, available at http://news.sciencemag.org/biology/2014/06/how-stress-can-clog -your-arteries.

28. Pauline Jones Luong and Erika Weinthal, *Oil Is Not a Curse: Ownership Structure and Institutions in Soviet Successor States* (New York: Cambridge University Press, 2010); Ross, "Does Oil Hinder Democracy?"

29. Jason Reifler and Jeffrey Lazarus, "Partisanship and Policy Priorities in the Distribution of Economic Stimulus Funds" (September 1, 2010), available at http://papers.ssrn.com/abstract=1670161.

30. Many political scientists feel the same way about their parts of the discipline as Robert Keohane does about international politics: "Causal inferences are particularly difficult in international politics, where each major event seems to have multiple contributing causes and to be sufficiently different from other events of the same name that aggregation is problematic. There was only one French Revolution and only one World War I. However important it may have been, the Orange Revolution in the Ukraine was not very similar to the French Revolution, nor can the Iraq War be closely matched with World War I." Robert O. Keohane, "Political Science as a Vocation," *PS: Political Science and Politics* 42, no. 2 (April 2009): 362.

31. Putnam, "Tuning in, Tuning Out," p. 671.

32. Massive amounts of water may cause the plant to die as well, regardless of the amount of sunlight, suggesting a curvilinear relationship between water and plant growth.

33. In statistical analyses, these interactions are usually modeled as the product of two independent variables (e.g., Education × Gender).

34. Ellen M. Immergut, *Health Politics: Interests and Institutions in Western Europe* (New York: Cambridge University Press, 1992).

35. This concept is used in many different disciplines, including biology and psychology. For a general discussion of equifinality in politics, see George and Bennett, *Case Studies and Theory Development in the Social Sciences*.

36. Elizabeth A. Stanley and John P. Sawyer, "The Equifinality of War Termination: Multiple Paths to Ending War," *Journal of Conflict Resolution* 53, no. 5 (October 2009): 651–76; the quotation appears on p. 652.

37. See, e.g., the October 2012 and April 2014 issues of *PS: Political Science and Politics*, which include several articles about forecasting US elections. Many of the authors featured here have also written books, journal articles, and chapters in edited volumes about this topic. For other countries, see the June 2011 issue of *Electoral Studies*, which includes a special symposium on forecasting elections in Britain; Éric Bélanger and Jean-François Godbout, "Forecasting Canadian Federal Elections," *PS: Political Science and Politics* 43, no. 4 (October 2010): 691–99; and Helmut Norpoth and Thomas Gschwend, "Chancellor Model Picks Merkel in 2013 German Election," *PS: Political Science and Politics* 46, no. 3 (July 2013): 481–82.

38. D. W. Miller, "Election Results Leave Political Scientists Defensive over Forecasting Models," *Chronicle of Higher Education* 47, no. 2 (November 17, 2000), A24. Gore's advantage in these models was partly due to the economy, which was quite strong in 1999 and 2000, thus favoring the candidate from the incumbent party.

39. Political scientists aren't the only ones who find the world to be a complicated

place, one that often defies prediction. As US defense secretary Robert Gates admitted in 2011: "When it comes to predicting the location and nature of our next military engagements, since Vietnam, our record has been perfect. We have never once gotten it right, from the Mayaguez to Grenada, Panama, Somalia, the Balkans, Haiti, Kuwait, Iraq, and more—we had no idea a year before any of these missions that we would be so engaged." That same year, when Marine Corps General James Mattis testified before Congress, he admitted that "as we look toward the future, I have been a horrible prophet. I have never fought anywhere I expected to in all my years." Both quotations come from Micah Zenko, "100% Right 0% of the Time: Why the U.S. Military Can't Predict the Next War," *Foreign Policy*, October 16, 2012.

CHAPTER FOUR

1. Fifty years ago, the distinguished political scientist Gabriel Almond argued that "it makes no sense to speak of a comparative politics in political science, since if it is a science, it goes without saying that it is comparative in its approach." Gabriel A. Almond, "Political Theory and Political Science," *American Political Science Review* 60, no. 4 (December 1966): 878.

2. In chapter 2, we discussed the validity of individual measures, using terms such as *face validity* and *construct validity*. *Internal validity* and *external validity* refer to the entire research design, which is quite different.

3. Robert D. Putnam, *Making Democracy Work: Civic Traditions in Modern Italy* (Princeton, NJ: Princeton University Press, 1993).

4. Michael Ross, "Does Oil Hinder Democracy?," *World Politics* 53, no. 3 (April 2001): 325–61 and Pauline Jones Luong and Erika Weinthal, *Oil Is Not a Curse: Ownership Structure and Institutions in Soviet Successor States* (New York: Cambridge University Press, 2010).

5. The distinction between experimental and observational research designs is not ideal, because researchers who run experiments also make observations. But it's better than experimental versus nonexperimental, which is sometimes used. Defining something by what it's not seldom offers much insight. Do you enjoy listening to nonclassical music? Have you ever met an immigrant from non-Latin America?

6. E.g., Donatella della Porta, "Comparative Analysis: Case-Oriented versus Variable-Oriented Research," in *Approaches and Methodologies in the Social Sciences: A Pluralist Perspective*, ed. Donatella della Porta and Michael Keating (Cambridge, UK: Cambridge University Press, 2008), pp. 198–222; Charles Ragin, *The Comparative Method: Moving beyond Qualitative and Quantitative Strategies* (Berkeley: University of California Press, 1987).

7. Alan S. Gerber and Donald P. Green, "The Effects of Canvassing, Telephone Calls, and Direct Mail on Voter Turnout: A Field Experiment," *American Political Science Review* 94, no. 3 (September 2000): 653–63; Ross, "Does Oil Hinder Democracy?"

8. Ellen M. Immergut, *Health Politics: Interests and Institutions in Western Europe* (New York: Cambridge University Press, 1992).

9. Researchers who conduct case studies, in contrast, often work with nominal- or

ordinal-level variables. They may be skeptical that important variables in politics are best expressed as precise numbers. Saying that a country is more or less democratic may be more defensible than labeling it a 1 or a 5.5.

10. That said, Ross picked these causal mechanisms in part because prior case studies had shown their importance.

11. Missing from this chapter is a discussion of interpretive research designs. Although these designs bear an affinity with case studies, interpretive scholars are less interested in describing general patterns or developing causal explanations, which are the bread and butter of mainstream political science (and this guide). Interpretivists are more interested in understanding "the meanings that shape actions and institutions, and the ways in which they do so" (Mark Bevir and R. A. W. Rhodes, "Interpretive Theory," in *Theories and Methods in Political Science*, ed. David Marsh and Gerry Stoker, 2nd ed. [London: Palgrave Macmillan, 2002], p. 131). They often draw inspiration from cultural anthropology, history, and Continental philosophy. Nor will this chapter discuss formal models. Although some of these models (e.g., prisoners' dilemma) can be introduced in nontechnical language, many of them require a specialized knowledge of mathematics beyond what I can offer in this guide.

12. For brief introductions to experimental designs, see James N. Druckman, Donald P. Green, James H. Kuklinski, and Arthur Lupia, "Experiments: An Introduction to Core Concepts," in *Cambridge Handbook of Experimental Political Science*, ed. Druckman, Green, Kuklinski, and Lupia (New York: Cambridge University Press, 2011), pp. 15–26; Susan D. Hyde, "Experiments in International Relations: Lab, Survey, and Field," *Annual Review of Political Science* 18 (2015): 403–24; Rose McDermott, "The Ten Commandments of Experiments," *PS: Political Science and Politics* 46, no. 3 (July 2013): 605–10; and Rebecca B. Morton and Kenneth C. Williams, "Experimentation in Political Science," in *The Oxford Handbook of Political Methodology*, ed. Janet M. Box-Steffensmeier, Henry E. Brady, and David Collier (New York: Oxford University Press, 2008), pp. 339–56.

13. Not every experiment has to recruit individuals to participate. Election observers might be assigned at random to some precincts in a country, and researchers would then measure voter turnout in precincts with and without observers.

14. We probably wouldn't care if the members of one group happened to love broccoli and the other group did not. The only systematic differences between the groups that matter would have to be theoretically relevant to the puzzle we are studying.

15. The control group might be idle while the other group is receiving a treatment, but not necessarily. In an experiment testing the impact of the media on public opinion, the control group might watch the regular evening news while the treatment group watched the regular news plus an extra story about national defense. The regular news for the control group might be considered the equivalent of a placebo in a medical experiment. See Shanto Iyengar, Mark D. Peters, and Donald R. Kinder, "Experimental Demonstrations of the 'Not-So-Minimal' Consequences of Television News Programs," *American Political Science Review* 76, no. 4 (December 1982): 848–58.

16. Researchers would report an average treatment effect, a number that would not

describe exactly the experience of every individual in the treatment group. And many researchers would try several permutations of the treatment to better understand the causal effects. If an experiment about racial attitudes involved showing participants a photo of a young black male, it would be hard to know from just that photo whether respondents were reacting to his race, gender, age, or some combination.

17. Alan S. Gerber and Donald P. Green, *Field Experiments: Design, Analysis, and Interpretation* (New York: W. W. Norton, 2012), p. 5.

18. Not every political scientist recognizes the within-subjects design as a true experiment, because random assignment to two or more groups is missing. They might refer to this design instead as a quasi experiment.

19. If you flip a fair coin ten times, the probability that you will end up with five heads and five tails is only about 25 percent.

20. E.g., John A. Nyman, "Health Plan Switching and Attrition Bias in the RAND Health Insurance Experiment," *Journal of Health Politics, Policy and Law* 33, no. 2 (April 2008): 309–17.

21. As in, "Oh, I get it—you guys are running an experiment about climate change. You probably hope that all this scientific information will make me more concerned about the environment. Sure, I can make that happen."

22. Iyengar, Peters, and Kinder, "Experimental Demonstrations of the 'Not-So-Minimal' Consequences of Television News Programs."

23. Markus Prior and Arthur Lupia, "Money, Time, and Political Knowledge," *American Journal of Political Science* 52, no. 1 (January 2008): 169–83.

24. In addition, some experimenters may exaggerate the importance of their treatment variable. Simply because an effect is found doesn't mean that effect is larger than other treatments the experiment failed to test.

25. Darren Schreiber and Marco Iacoboni, "Huxtables on the Brain: An fMRI Study of Race and Norm Violation," *Political Psychology* 33, no. 3 (June 2012): 313–30.

26. E.g., Paul M. Sniderman and Edward G. Carmines, *Reaching beyond Race* (Cambridge, MA: Harvard University Press, 1997).

27. Jason Barabas and Jennifer Jerit, "Are Survey Experiments Externally Valid?," *American Political Science Review* 104, no. 2 (May 2010): 226–42; Brian J. Gaines, James H. Kuklinski, and Paul J. Quirk, "The Logic of the Survey Experiment Reexamined," *Political Analysis* 15, no. 1 (Winter 2007): 1–20.

28. Gerber and Green, *Field Experiments*, especially pp. 8–13.

29. Gerber and Green, "The Effects of Canvassing, Telephone Calls, and Direct Mail on Voter Turnout"; Andrew Beath, Fotini Christia, and Ruben Enikolopov, "Empowering Women through Development Aid: Evidence from a Field Experiment in Afghanistan," *American Political Science Review* 107, no. 3 (August 2013): 540–57.

30. E.g., Susan D. Hyde, "Experimenting in Democracy Promotion: International Observers and the 2004 Presidential Elections in Indonesia," *Perspectives on Politics* 8, no. 2 (June 2010): 511–27. International observers were assigned at random to different parts of Indonesia during the 2004 presidential election. The expectation was that such observers could help boost turnout, or perhaps discourage corruption. But

some parts of the country were ruled out from the start, because they were too remote or too dangerous. Many of the districts without election observers, that never had a chance to be observed, were different from districts with observers in ways that could have affected voter turnout. Remote or dangerous areas could have had lower turnout or more corruption than the rest of the country.

31. Dylan Scott, "Profs Bumble into Big Legal Trouble after Election Experiment Goes Way Wrong" (October 27, 2014), available at http://talkingpointsmemo.com /dc/montana-election-mailer-state-seal-stanford-dartmouth-professors. Field experiments are tricky in this regard, because researchers don't usually obtain consent from the ultimate subjects of their study. To learn more about these ethical considerations, see Marcatan Humphreys, "Ethical Challenges of Embedded Experimentation," *Comparative Democratization* 9, no. 3 (October 2011): 10+, available at http://www.ned.org /apsa-cd/APSA-CDOctober2011.pdf.

32. Daniel E. Ho and Kosuke Imai, "Estimating Causal Effects of Ballot Order from a Randomized Natural Experiment: The California Alphabet Lottery, 1978–2002," *Public Opinion Quarterly* 72, no. 2 (Summer 2008): 216–40. In one election, candidates with last names beginning with P might be listed first, followed by last names beginning with F, then M, and so on. For an example drawn from Canadian politics, see Peter John Loewen, Royce Koop, Jaime Settle, and James H. Fowler, "A Natural Experiment in Proposal Power and Electoral Success," *American Journal of Political Science* 58, no.1 (January 2014): 189–96.

33. Daniel N. Posner, "The Political Salience of Cultural Difference: Why Chewas and Tumbukas Are Allies in Zambia and Adversaries in Malawi," *American Political Science Review* 98, no. 4 (November 2004): 529–45. For a broadly similar approach, see Diana Dumitru and Carter Johnson, "Constructing Interethnic Conflict and Cooperation: Why Some People Harmed Jews and Others Helped Them during the Holocaust in Romania," *World Politics* 63, no. 1 (January 2011): 1–42. Note that some scholars define natural experiments broadly to include quasi experiments.

34. Daniel Maliniak, Amy Oakes, Susan Peterson, and Michael J. Tierney, "International Relations in the US Academy," *International Studies Quarterly* 55, no. 2 (June 2011): 437–64.

35. "*Any study based on observational (i.e., nonexperimental) data faces the fundamental challenge of eliminating rival explanations* . . . . Experiments eliminate rival explanations by randomly assigning the values of the explanatory variable to the units being analyzed. By contrast, in all observational studies, eliminating rival explanations is a daunting challenge." Henry E. Brady, David Collier, and Jason Seawright, "Refocusing the Discussion of Methodology," in *Rethinking Social Inquiry: Diverse Tools, Shared Standards*, ed. Henry E. Brady and David Collier (Lanham, MD: Rowman and Littlefield, 2004), pp. 10–11 (italics in original).

36. Occasionally you will encounter a panel design, which looks quite similar. The main difference is that the exact same units are included in every year. Usually those units are people. One of the best known is the Panel Study of Income Dynamics, which

began in 1968 and has been tracking the economic ups and downs of thousands of Americans.

37. Ross, "Does Oil Hinder Democracy?"; Cullen S. Hendrix and Wendy H. Wong, "When Is the Pen Truly Mighty? Regime Type and the Efficacy of Naming and Shaming in Curbing Human Rights Abuses," *British Journal of Political Science* 43, no. 3 (July 2013): 651–72; Larry M. Bartels, *Unequal Democracy: The Political Economy of the New Gilded Age* (Princeton, NJ: Princeton University Press, 2008). Returning to the example of guns and crime, we might collect crime-related data for all fifty states, and not just Ohio, between 1970 and 2010.

38. A list of classic case studies would include Graham Allison, *Essence of Decision: Explaining the Cuban Missile Crisis* (Boston: Little, Brown, 1971); Robert Dahl, *Who Governs? Democracy and Power in an American City* (New Haven, CT: Yale University Press, 1961); Martha Derthick, *Policymaking for Social Security* (Washington, DC: Brookings Institution, 1979); Seymour Martin Lipset, Martin Trow, and James Coleman, *Union Democracy: The Internal Politics of the International Typographical Union* (Glencoe, IL: Free Press, 1956); Jeffrey L. Pressman and Aaron Wildavsky, *Implementation* (Berkeley: University of California Press, 1973); Putnam, *Making Democracy Work*; and Theda Skocpol, *States and Social Revolutions: A Comparative Analysis of France, Russia, and China* (New York: Cambridge University Press, 1979). Some traditional methods textbooks don't discuss case studies at all.

39. John Gerring, *Case Study Research: Principles and Practices* (New York: Cambridge University Press, 2007), p. 20.

40. Some book-length treatments could feature up to a half-dozen cases, but much above this number and authors could sacrifice the needed analytic depth.

41. Robert K. Yin, *Case Study Research: Design and Methods*, 5th ed. (Thousand Oaks, CA: Sage, 2014).

42. Put another way, sometimes the path is as important as the destination.

43. Stephen Biddle, Jeffrey A. Friedman, and Jacob N. Shapiro, "Testing the Surge: Why Did Violence Decline in Iraq in 2007?," *International Security* 37, no. 1 (Summer 2012): 7–40.

44. Gerring, *Case Study Research*, p. 173. To learn more about process tracing, read chapter 7 in this book as well as Alexander L. George and Andrew Bennett, *Case Studies and Theory Development in the Social Sciences* (Cambridge, MA: MIT Press, 2005), chapter 10, and Andrew Bennett and Jeffrey T. Checkel, eds., *Process Tracing: From Metaphor to Analytic Tool* (Cambridge, UK: Cambridge University Press, 2015).

45. The importance of using a variety of written sources will be discussed further in chapter 6.

46. To learn more about types of case studies and their uses, see Jack S. Levy, "Case Studies: Types, Designs, and Logics of Inference," *Conflict Management and Peace Science* 25, no. 1 (Spring 2008): 1–18.

47. E.g., Zeev Maoz and Bruce Russett, "Normative and Structural Causes of Democratic Peace, 1946–1986," *American Political Science Review* 87, no. 3 (September 1993):

624–38; John R. Oneal and Bruce M. Russett, "The Classical Liberals Were Right: Democracy, Interdependence, and Conflict, 1950–1985," *International Studies Quarterly* 41, no. 2 (June 1997): 267–69. Note: a number of political scientists who study the democratic peace draw inspiration from Immanuel Kant, a political theorist.

48. Andrew Bennett and Alexander George, "An Alliance of Statistical and Case Study Methods: Research on the Interdemocratic Peace," *APSA-CP Newsletter* 9, no. 1 (Winter 1998): 6 (italics in original).

49. E.g., Miriam Fendius Elman, ed., *Paths to Peace: Is Democracy the Answer?* (Cambridge, MA: MIT Press, 1997); Christopher Layne, "Kant or Cant: The Myth of the Democratic Peace," *International Security* 19, no. 2 (Autumn 1994): 5–49; John M. Owen IV, *Liberal Peace, Liberal War: American Politics and International Security* (Ithaca, NY: Cornell University Press, 1997).

50. Michael R. Tomz and Jessica L. P. Weeks, "Public Opinion and the Democratic Peace," *American Political Science Review* 107, no. 4 (December 2013): 849–65.

51. Originally, triangulation referred to the process by which navigators and surveyors would establish the exact location of some distant point. They would measure the distance from different positions (typically three), and those measures would converge on the true result. Although the ultimate goal of multimethod research in the social sciences is to generate a more coherent and complete answer to a research question, the different methods could produce inconsistent or conflicting results instead. It turns out that the edge of a wooded property is much easier to determine than the edge of a rebellion. Bruce L. Berg and Howard Lune, *Qualitative Research Methods for the Social Sciences*, 8th ed. (Boston: Pearson, 2012), pp. 5–8; Sandra Mathison, "Why Triangulate?," *Educational Researcher* 17, no. 2 (March 1988): 13–17.

52. Edward D. Mansfield and Jack Snyder, *Electing to Fight: Why Emerging Democracies Go to War* (Cambridge, MA: MIT Press, 2007); Katerina Linos, *The Democratic Foundations of Policy Diffusion: How Health, Family, and Employment Laws Spread across Countries* (New York: Oxford University Press, 2013); Nicholas J. G. Winter, *Dangerous Frames: How Ideas about Race and Gender Shape Public Opinion* (Chicago: University of Chicago Press, 2008). For a more skeptical view of this trend, see Amel Ahmed and Rudra Sil, "When Multi-Method Research Subverts Methodological Pluralism—or, Why We Still Need Single-Method Research," *Perspectives on Politics* 10, no. 4 (December 2012): 935–53.

53. Dara Kay Cohen, "Explaining Rape during Civil War: Cross-National Evidence (1980–2009)," *American Political Science Review* 107, no. 3 (August 2013): 461–77; the quotation appears on page 474. Some scholars even manage to employ three or more research designs in a single study. See, e.g., Ben W. Ansell and David J. Samuels, *Inequality and Democratization: An Elite-Competition Approach* (New York: Cambridge University Press, 2014); Lisa L. Martin, *Coercive Cooperation: Explaining Multilateral Economic Sanctions* (Princeton, NJ: Princeton University Press, 1993).

CHAPTER FIVE

1. Why would political scientists try to trick us? This might seem like a rude question, but political scientists are human, which means they have cognitive blind spots

and long-standing commitments. Perhaps they have a professional stake in showing that a favored theory works well (e.g., "In the ongoing debate of institutions versus culture, I shall always come down on the side of institutions"). Or, political scientists may have a personal stake in proving that a certain policy has succeeded or failed. Analysis can turn into advocacy pretty easily. A healthy skepticism is warranted in politics, whether statements are made by public officials or seemingly neutral observers.

2. Jason Seawright and John Gerring, "Case Selection Techniques in Case Study Research: A Menu of Qualitative and Quantitative Options," *Political Research Quarterly* 61, no. 2 (June 2008): 294–308; Stephen Van Evera, *Guide to Methods for Students of Political Science* (Ithaca, NY: Cornell University Press, 1997), chapter 2.

3. Ryan Krog, Paul J. Wahlbeck, and Forrest Maltzman, "Judicial Preferences and Strategic Legal Argument in the U.S. Supreme Court" (PDF of manuscript, 2014).

4. For a more detailed discussion of samples and polls, see Herbert Asher, *Polling and the Public: What Every Citizen Should Know*, 8th ed. (Washington, DC: CQ Press, 2011); Michael W. Traugott and Paul J. Lavrakas, *The Voter's Guide to Election Polls*, 4th ed. (Lanham, MD: Rowman and Littlefield, 2008).

5. Sam Whitt and Rick K. Wilson, "The Dictator Game, Fairness and Ethnicity in Postwar Bosnia," *American Journal of Political Science* 51, no. 3 (July 2007): 655–68.

6. Seawright and Gerring ran a computer simulation involving a single variable with values ranging from 0 to 1. In one iteration, the computer selected 500 random samples of 1000 cases each. In the second iteration, the computer selected 500 random samples of 5 cases each. Although the average value of the variable was very close to 0.5 in both iterations, which is what we would expect, the variation in individual samples was much greater with just 5 cases (Seawright and Gerring, "Case Selection Techniques in Case Study Research").

7. For a similar approach, see Cherie D. Maestas, Sarah Fulton, L. Sandy Maisel, and Walter J. Stone, "When to Risk It? Institutions, Ambitions, and the Decision to Run for the U.S. House," *American Political Science Review* 100, no. 2 (May 2006): 195–208.

8. Kathryn Edin and Laura Lein, *Making Ends Meet: How Single Mothers Survive Welfare and Low-Wage Work* (New York: Russell Sage Foundation, 1997). For a similar approach in a much different context, see Paula M. Pickering, *Peacebuilding in the Balkans: The View from the Ground Floor* (Ithaca, NY: Cornell University Press, 2007).

9. E.g., Earl Babbie, *The Practice of Social Research*, 13th ed. (Belmont, CA: Wadsworth), pp. 187–88.

10. Steven Shepard, "Americans Continue to Drop Their Landline Phones," *National Journal*, December 18, 2013; available at http://www.nationaljournal.com/hotline-on-call/americans-continue-to-drop-their-landline-phones-20131218.

11. Benjamin I. Page, "The Semi-Sovereign Public," in *Navigating Public Opinion: Polls, Policy, and the Future of American Democracy*, ed. Jeff Manza, Fay Lomax Cook, and Benjamin I. Page (New York: Oxford University Press, 2002), pp. 325–44.

12. Andrew Beath, Fotini Christia, and Ruben Enikolopov, "Empowering Women Through Development Aid: Evidence from a Field Experiment in Afghanistan," *American Political Science Review* 107, no. 3 (August 2013): 540–57; Susan D. Hyde, "Exper-

imenting in Democracy Promotion: International Observers and the 2004 Presidential Elections in Indonesia," *Perspectives on Politics* 8, no. 2 (June 2010): 511–27.

13. Dominic Lusinchi, " 'President' Landon and the 1936 *Literary Digest* Poll: Were Automobile and Telephone Owners to Blame?," *Social Science Quarterly* 36, no. 1 (Spring 2012): 23–54; Peverill Squire, "Why the 1936 *Literary Digest* Poll Failed," *Public Opinion Quarterly* 52, no. 1 (Spring 1988): 125–33.

14. Tom W. Smith and Jaesok Son, *Trends in Public Attitudes towards Abortion* (Chicago: National Opinion Research Center, May 2013).

15. For instance, Weaver and Lerman relied on a panel study of children from disadvantaged families in the United States. They noted (p. 821) that those families had been drawn from a sample of cities with at least two hundred thousand people. Readers then know that the sample may not reflect the entire US population. Vesla M. Weaver and Amy E. Lerman, "Political Consequences of the Carceral State," *American Political Science Review* 104, no. 4 (November 2010): 817–33.

16. Ellen M. Immergut, *Health Politics: Interests and Institutions in Western Europe* (New York: Cambridge University Press, 1992).

17. Eric M. Patashnik, *Reforms at Risk: What Happens after Major Policy Changes Are Enacted* (Princeton, NJ: Princeton University Press, 2008); Melissa Nobles, *Shades of Citizenship: Race and the Census in Modern Politics* (Stanford, CA: Stanford University Press, 2000).

18. John Gerring, *Case Study Research: Principles and Practices* (New York: Cambridge University Press, 2007); Van Evera, *Guide to Methods for Students of Political Science*.

19. Daniel W. Drezner, *The System Worked: How the World Stopped Another Great Depression* (New York: Oxford University Press, 2014).

20. Charles Lipson, *How to Write a BA Thesis: A Practical Guide from Your First Ideas to Your Finished Paper* (Chicago: University of Chicago Press, 2005), p. 105.

21. Arend Lijphart, *The Politics of Accommodation: Pluralism and Democracy in the Netherlands* (Berkeley: University of California Press, 1968).

22. Robert D. Putnam, *Making Democracy Work: Civic Traditions in Modern Italy* (Princeton, NJ: Princeton University Press, 1993).

23. Richard M. Valelly, *The Two Reconstructions: The Struggle for Black Enfranchisement* (Chicago: University of Chicago Press, 2004).

24. Barbara Geddes, "How the Cases You Choose Affect the Answers You Get: Selection Bias in Comparative Politics," *Political Analysis* 2, no. 1 (1990): 131–50.

25. Stephen Biddle, Jeffrey A. Friedman, and Jacob N. Shapiro, "Testing the Surge: Why Did Violence Decline in Iraq in 2007?," *International Security* 37, no. 1 (Summer 2012): 7–40.

26. Gerring, *Case Study Research*, chap. 5; Seawright and Gerring, "Case Selection Techniques in Case Study Research." *Deviant* in this context means "highly unusual," not "creepy."

27. David Collier, James Mahoney, and Jason Seawright, "Claiming Too Much? Warnings about Selection Bias," in *Rethinking Social Inquiry: Diverse Tools, Shared Stan-*

dards, ed. Henry E. Brady and David Collier (Lanham, MD: Rowman and Littlefield, 2004), pp. 85–102. Much of this chapter is a direct response to scholars such as Geddes.

28. Collier, Mahoney, and Seawright, "Claiming Too Much?"

29. Van Evera, *Guide to Methods for Students of Political Science*, p. 79.

CHAPTER SIX

1. Asking how many sources are needed can also be a mistake because some topics have more sources available than others. When I allow students to pick a research topic in my social policy class, those who choose Social Security are going to have a lot more to work with than those who choose Workers' Compensation. I suspect the same would be true in an international security class if one student wanted to research the Cold War while another wanted to learn more about Paraguay's foreign policy.

2. On the positive side, I also discovered that most of my students had enough preparation in math to make our little forays into statistics less painful than anticipated.

3. No system is foolproof; some defective products still work their way into building supply stores and people's homes. Yet virtually all producers and consumers recognize the importance of creating and following certain standards.

4. See, e.g., http://libguides.bgsu.edu/c.php?g=227209&p=1506038 (Bowling Green State University); https://www.college.columbia.edu/academics/integrity -sourcecredibility (Columbia College); http://www.lib.lsu.edu/instruction/evaluation /evaluation20.html (Louisiana State University); http://library.ucsc.edu/help/research /evaluate-the-quality-and-credibility-of-your-sources (University of California–Santa Cruz). All accessed January 7, 2016.

5. Because readers might not be familiar with every source mentioned in a study, it can be helpful to establish their credibility in the text. For instance, instead of stating, "According to Andrew Card, President Bush withdrew from the ABM treaty because . . . ," we might write, "According to Andrew Card, the White House Chief of Staff, President Bush withdrew from the ABM treaty because . . ." I offered similar advice in chapter 1 with regard to writing a literature review.

6. Their news coverage is separate from their op-eds, which tend to favor liberal or conservative positions.

7. For instance, one might determine whether authors identified their sources of evidence so explicitly that readers could locate those sources and verify their claims.

8. The acceptance rate at top-tier journals such as the *American Political Science Review*, *Comparative Politics*, and *International Organization* hovers around 10 percent, and some years is lower.

9. In my experience, the rigor of peer review for edited volumes isn't always equal to that for single-authored or coauthored books.

10. Readers should be careful with papers presented at professional conferences, which may have been accepted based on the title and a short abstract, a fairly minimal form of peer review. Based on my twenty-plus years of experience, some conference

papers are terrific, but many have serious flaws, because authors were trying out new ideas or simply ran out of time to do a good job. The quality of dissertations also varies quite a bit. It often makes sense to wait and see which of them generate peer-reviewed articles and books.

11. Fred Barbash, "Co-Author Disavows Highly Publicized Study on Public Opinion and Same-Sex Marriage," *Washington Post*, May 20, 2015; available at http://www .washingtonpost.com/news/morning-mix/wp/2015/05/20/co-author-disavows-highly -publicized-study-on-public-opinion-and-same-sex-marriage/. Political science isn't the only discipline to experience such problems: Fred Barbash, "Major Publisher Retracts 43 Scientific Papers amid Wider Fake Peer-Review Scandal," *Washington Post*, March 27, 2015; Ferric C. Fang, R. Grant Steen, and Arturo Casadevall, "Misconduct Accounts for the Majority of Retracted Scientific Publications," *Proceedings of the National Academies of Science* 109, no. 42 (October 16, 2012): 17028–33.

12. For a sharp critique of the peer review process, see Stephen M. Walt, "On Academic Rigor," *Foreign Policy*, May 24, 2013; available at http://foreignpolicy.com/2013 /05/24/on-academic-rigor/.

13. This way of thinking about bias has roots in statistics, where analysts commonly distinguish between random error and systematic error. Random error (i.e., "noise") is due to chance. With enough observations, random errors should cancel each other out; they won't bias the results. Systematic error isn't due to chance and likely will bias the results.

14. This example isn't so far-fetched: R. Kent Weaver, *Ending Welfare as We Know It* (Washington, DC: Brookings Institution, 2000), chap. 6.

15. https://www.nraila.org/second-amendment/ (accessed March 12, 2016).

16. For a good discussion of bias in documents, see Cameron G. Thies, "A Pragmatic Guide to Qualitative Historical Analysis in the Study of International Relations," *International Studies Perspectives* 3, no. 4 (November 2002): 351–72.

17. This would be sad and surprising news to Frank Baumgartner, Jeffrey Berry, Matt Grossman, Beth Leech, Anthony Nownes, Catherine Paden, Dara Strolovitch, and many other scholars who have been writing about interest groups in recent years.

18. Jonathan Strickland, "How Google Works" and "Why Is the Google Algorithm So Important?," both available at http://computer.howstuffworks.com (accessed March 12, 2016); Michael Liedtke, "Google to Favor 'Mobile-Friendly' Sites In Search," *Huffington Post*, April 17, 2015; available at http://www.huffingtonpost.com/2015/04/17/google -search-update_n_7085642.html.

19. If we want to beat the home-building metaphor into the ground, then these specialized databases would be considered the academic equivalents of Lowe's and Home Depot.

20. Freedom House, "*Freedom in the World 2015* Methodology"; available at https:// freedomhouse.org/sites/default/files/Methodology_FIW_2015.pdf. Accessed February 29, 2016.

21. E.g., Ellen M. Immergut, *Health Politics: Interests and Institutions in Western Europe* (New York: Cambridge University Press, 1992).

22. John Gerring, *Case Study Research: Principles and Practices* (New York: Cambridge University Press, 2007), p. 173.

23. Practically by definition, a multimethod research design requires several types of evidence.

24. Gary King, Robert O. Keohane, and Sidney Verba, "The Importance of Research Design," in *Rethinking Social Inquiry: Diverse Tools, Shared Standards*, ed. Henry E. Brady and David Collier (Lanham, MD: Rowman and Littlefield, 2004), p. 192.

25. Mary Gallagher, "Capturing Meaning and Confronting Measurement," in *Interview Research in Political Science*, ed. Layna Mosley (Ithaca, NY: Cornell University Press, 2013), p. 194. See also B. Guy Peters, *Strategies for Comparative Research in Political Science* (New York: Palgrave Macmillan, 2013), pp. 104–8. By contrast, triangulation in politics means finding a point between and often above two extremes. President Bill Clinton was one of the best-known practitioners of triangulation as he positioned himself between liberal Democrats and conservative Republicans in Congress.

26. Thies, "A Pragmatic Guide to Qualitative Historical Analysis in the Study of International Relations"; see also Ian S. Lustick, "History, Historiography, and Political Science: Multiple Historical Records and the Problem of Selection Bias," *American Political Science Review* 90, no. 3 (September 1996): 605–18.

27. E.g., Filippo Sabetti, "Path Dependency and Civic Culture: Some Lessons from Italy about Interpreting Social Experiments," *Politics and Society* 24, no. 1 (March 1996): 19–44; Sidney Tarrow, "Making Social Science Work across Space and Time: A Critical Reflection on Robert Putnam's *Making Democracy Work*," *American Political Science Review* 90, no. 2 (June 1996): 389–97.

28. The short answer is yes. See Daniel Béland, *Social Security: History and Politics from the New Deal to the Privatization Debate* (Lawrence: University Press of Kansas, 2005).

29. Gary King, Robert O. Keohane, and Sidney Verba, *Designing Social Inquiry: Scientific Inference in Qualitative Research* (Princeton, NJ: Princeton University Press, 1994). As they note on page 8, one hallmark of any scientific discipline is that the procedures are public. For an interesting discussion about transparency in research that relies heavily on documents, see the symposium in *Security Studies* 23, no. 4 (2014): 657–714.

30. Jill Quadagno, *One Nation, Uninsured: Why the U.S. Has No National Health Insurance* (New York: Oxford University Press, 2005); Paul Starr, *The Social Transformation of American Medicine* (New York: Basic Books, 1982). These scholars still might disagree about how and how much the AMA mattered.

31. Lustick, "History, Historiography, and Political Science"; Thies, "A Pragmatic Guide to Qualitative Historical Analysis in the Study of International Relations."

32. The author's personal opinions do not need a citation, either.

33. Another option is to see whether previous studies have treated a certain fact as common knowledge. If several have, then it may be safe to follow suit. For instance, the Online Writing Lab at Purdue University suggests that *several* equals five credible sources (https://owl.english.purdue.edu/owl/resource/589/2/; accessed January 7, 2016).

34. To learn more about content analysis, readers might consult Paul S. Gray, John B. Williamson, David A. Karp, and John R. Dalphin, *The Research Imagination: An Introduction to Qualitative and Quantitative Methods* (New York: Cambridge University Press, 2007), chapter 13; Justin Grimmer and Brandon M. Stewart, "Text as Data: The Promise and Pitfalls of Automatic Content Analysis Methods for Political Texts," *Political Analysis* 21, no. 3 (Summer 2013): 267–97; and Klaus Krippendorff, *Content Analysis: An Introduction to Its Methodology*, 3rd ed. (Thousand Oaks, CA: Sage, 2013).

35. E.g., John Gerring, *Party Ideologies in America, 1828–1996* (New York: Cambridge University Press, 2001); Martin Gilens, "Race and Poverty in America: Public Misperceptions and the American News Media," *Public Opinion Quarterly* 60, no. 4 (Winter 1996): 515–41.

36. Ryan Krog, Paul J. Wahlbeck, and Forrest Maltzman, "Judicial Preferences and Strategic Legal Argument in the U.S. Supreme Court" (PDF of manuscript, 2014); A. Maurits van der Veen, *Ideas, Interests and Foreign Aid* (New York: Cambridge University Press, 2011).

37. Martin Gilens, *Why Americans Hate Welfare: Race, Media, and the Politics of Antipoverty Policy* (Chicago: University of Chicago Press, 1999).

CHAPTER SEVEN

1. John Ishiyama, "Annual Report of the Editors of the *American Political Science Review*, 2013–2014," *PS: Political Science and Politics* 48, no. 2 (April 2015): 396–99. As mentioned before, the length of the standard journal article also favors variable-oriented research designs and quantitative techniques.

2. Bonus grammar lesson: because *data* is the plural of *datum*, it's correct to say "beating the data until they confess."

3. E.g., Matt Ford, "The Missing Statistics of Criminal Justice," *Atlantic*, May 31, 2015; available at http://www.theatlantic.com/politics/archive/2015/05/what-we-dont-know-about-mass-incarceration/394520/.

4. "Don't Lie to Me, Argentina," *Economist*, February 25, 2012; available at http://www.economist.com/node/21548242; see also Juan Forero, "A Quiet Battle over Argentina's Inflation Rate," *Washington Post*, October 31, 2011; available at http://www.washingtonpost.com/world/americas/a-quiet-battle-over-argentinas-inflation-rate/2011/10/29/gIQAEiUjYM_story.html.

5. Christopher S. P. Magee and John A. Doces, "Reconsidering Regime Type and Growth: Lies, Dictatorships, and Statistics," *International Studies Quarterly* 59, no. 2 (June 2015): 223–37.

6. See table 6A.2 at http://www.electionstudies.org/nesguide/toptable/tab6a_2.htm (accessed February 29, 2016). For more accurate turnout figures, see http://www.electproject.org/national-1789-present (accessed February 29, 2016).

7. In this situation, scholars often work with one measure in the text, but indicate in a footnote or endnote that other measures of the same concept produced similar results.

8. Ellen M. Immergut, "The Rules of the Game: The Logic of Health Policy-Making

in France, Switzerland, and Sweden," in *Structuring Politics: Historical Institutionalism in Comparative Analysis*, ed. Sven Steinmo, Kathleen Thelen, and Frank Longstreth (New York: Cambridge University Press, 1992), pp. 57–89.

9. Michael L. Ross, "Does Oil Hinder Democracy?," *World Politics* 53, no. 3 (April 2001): 325–61.

10. Ibid.

11. In fact, those who rely on statistical analysis will often cite more sources to justify their measurement of key variables and their techniques than their sources of data.

12. We might also report the statistical significance of the entire model, which is determined by an *F*-test.

13. John Sides and Jack Citrin, "European Opinion about Immigration: The Role of Identities, Interests and Information," *British Journal of Political Science* 37, no. 3 (July 2007): 477–504.

14. Let's return to the resource curse for a minute. Suppose we are studying the most resource-dependent countries in the world, and we want to know how well they protect political rights. According to the 7-point scale developed by Freedom House, many of these countries will score near the bottom, either a 5 (e.g., Kuwait), 6 (e.g., Brunei, Libya), or 7 (e.g., Saudi Arabia). These are typical cases. A few countries, though, score near the top (e.g., Norway, a 1). These are the outliers.

15. Sides and Citrin, "European Opinion about Immigration."

16. See https://www.cia.gov/library/publications/resources/the-world-factbook/. Accessed March 1, 2016.

17. See http://www.electionstudies.org/nesguide/toptable/tab5a_1.htm. Accessed February 29, 2016.

18. For nominal variables, the distribution is simply the full list of categories and their values, much as I did with religion in Singapore.

19. It's possible for the mean to be greater than the median in a negatively skewed distribution, and for the mean to be less than the median in a positively skewed distribution. This can happen if the distribution has several peaks, or if one tail is short and thick while the other tail is long and skinny.

20. Please note that we report any type of range from point A to point B, and not simply the distance between A and B. If I told you that the interquartile range for household income was $65,000, you wouldn't know if that meant between $10,000 and $75,000, between $50,200 and $115,200, or something else. Instead, I report that range as being from $25,000 to $90,000.

21. Carmen DeNavas-Walt and Bernadette D. Proctor, *Income and Poverty in the United States: 2013*, Current Population Reports, P60-249 (Washington, DC: Government Printing Office, 2014), table A-1.

22. Ross, "Does Oil Hinder Democracy?"

23. Statisticians distinguish between type I errors ("false positives") and type II errors ("false negatives"). Political scientists would much rather commit a type II than type I error.

24. However, if the n is small (e.g., less than 50), some statisticians prefer to use Fisher's exact test instead of chi-square.

25. Paul M. Kellstedt and Guy D. Whitten, *The Fundamentals of Political Science Research*, 2nd ed. (New York: Cambridge University Press, 2013), pp. 147–48.

26. As an added wrinkle, we use Kendall's tau-b if the contingency table is perfectly square, and tau-c if it's not. A square table is one with equal numbers of columns and rows (2×2, 3×3). In my example of race and attitudes toward the death penalty, the table would be 2×4, and thus we would use tau-*c*. In practice, the values for these two versions of tau tend to be very close.

27. As you can see, certain techniques are often named for the statistician who developed them.

28. Nonetheless, if our data form a perfectly horizontal line, then r would not be computed. When every different value on the x axis is associated with the same value on the y axis, we do not have covariation; our y variable would be a constant. The same logic applies to a perfectly vertical line, which would make the x variable constant.

29. Robert D. Putnam, *Making Democracy Work: Civic Traditions in Modern Italy* (Princeton, NJ: Princeton University Press, 1993), p. 85; Pippa Norris, "Does Television Erode Social Capital? A Reply to Putnam," *PS: Political Science and Politics* 29, no. 3 (September 1996): 476.

30. Throughout this chapter, I will distinguish between categorical (nominal, ordinal) and continuous (interval, ratio) variables. This is pretty standard practice among political scientists. Some scholars, however, feel that interval and ratio variables can be continuous or discrete, which is similar to the difference between real numbers and integers; the former can be expressed as a fraction, while the latter cannot. These scholars might therefore contrast categorical to quantitative variables.

31. A correlation matrix is symmetrical on either side of a diagonal running from the top left to bottom right of the matrix. Thus, we only need to pay attention to half these numbers, since the other half are duplicates.

32. This same insight applies to crosstabs as well. A relationship between two ordinal variables could have a Kendall's tau of .08 and be statistically significant, while a different pair of variables from a smaller dataset registered a Kendall's tau of .13 and was not statistically significant.

33. This kind of test is more common in psychology and education, where researchers might want to compare the performance of men and women, boys and girls, blacks and whites, etc., on any number of continuous measures (e.g., a third-grade reading test, an introvert-extrovert scale).

34. According to the 2000 ANES, there was a statistically significant difference between the way men and women felt about Hillary Clinton, but it was a fairly minor difference. On average, women viewed her more positively, but there were considerable differences of opinion among women and among men.

35. Thus, the basic logic is akin to a difference-of-means test.

36. Putnam, *Making Democracy Work*, chapter 4.

37. Political scientists disagree about how many independent variables are appro-

priate in a regression model. Some recommend an upper limit of three, based on theoretical and statistical constraints, whereas many others believe the number can and should be higher. To get a taste of these arguments, see the Winter 2005 issue of *Conflict Management and Peace Science*, particularly the articles by James Lee Ray, John Oneal and Bruce Russett, and Christopher Achen.

38. Throwing in just about any independent variable, no matter how theoretically irrelevant, can boost the R-squared value of a multiple regression model. Just by chance, some of the variation in that variable will match up with some of the variation in the dependent variable.

39. For the purpose of this exercise, I took a leap of faith in considering my voter registration variable to be an interval measure, ranging in value from 1 (very low requirements) to 5 (very high).

40. Some political scientists shy away from the standardized coefficient, in part because they don't like to drop valuable information such as the units of each variable.

41. Gender is the one nominal-level measure in this model. With only two values, it would be considered a dichotomous or "dummy" variable. It appears that women were scored a 0 and men a 1. Because gender has only two values, it's harder for OLS regression to detect a statistically significant relationship. That explains why some of the larger *B* coefficients for gender are not statistically significant in table 7.3.

42. Increasingly, political scientists display their statistical results with graphs, figures, and maps rather than tables of numbers. The visual display of information is an important topic in the social sciences generally, but not one that I have time to address in this guide. As a start, consider Jonathan P. Kastellec and Eduardo L. Leoni, "Using Graphs Instead of Tables in Political Science," *Perspectives on Politics* 5, no. 4 (December 2007): 755–71.

43. Michael D. Jones, "Leading the Way to Compromise? Cultural Theory and Climate Change Opinion," *PS: Political Science and Politics* 44, no. 4 (October 2011): 720–25.

44. Ibid.

45. Ross, "Does Oil Hinder Democracy?"

46. "I see no cases in which regression equations, let alone the more complex methods, have succeeded as engines for discovering causal relationships." David Freedman, "From Association to Causation via Regression," *Advances in Applied Mathematics* 18, no. 1 (January 1997): 60.

Similarly, note how two veteran political scientists, Jan Leighley and Jonathan Nagler, describe their statistical analysis of voter turnout: "In estimating a multivariable model we generally describe the 'dependent' variable as being 'caused' by the . . . explanatory variables. However, the assumption of causality is not based on the data analysis or the model specified but on a model of the real world presumed by the analyst. The data analysis is merely showing the conditional relationships among the observed data and not establishing causality. To be consistent with conventional usage, we will refer to the *marginal effect* of one of our explanatory . . . variables on turnout. However, we are not making the claim that such observational evidence demonstrates causality" (Jan Leighley and Jonathan Nagler, *Who Votes Now? Demographics, Issues,*

Inequality, and Turnout in the United States [Princeton, NJ: Princeton University Press, 2014], p. 57).

47. E.g., Dara Kay Cohen, "Explaining Rape during Civil War: Cross-National Evidence (1980–2009)," *American Political Science Review* 107, no. 3 (August 2013): 461–77.

48. Henry E. Brady, "Data-Set Observations versus Causal-Process Observations: The 2000 U.S. Presidential Election," in *Rethinking Social Inquiry: Diverse Tools, Shared Standards*, ed. Henry E. Brady and David Collier (Lanham, MD: Rowman and Littlefield, 2004), pp. 267–71.

49. Putnam, *Making Democracy Work*.

INDEX

linear, 54, 184; positive, 54n. *See also* spuriousness

reliability, 38, 49–50, 155; inter-coder/inter-rater, 49–50; test-retest, 50

research design, 8–9, 93–94; experimental versus observational, 97–98; formal model, 210n11; interpretive, 210n11; multimethod, 113–14; quantitative versus qualitative, 97; variable-oriented versus case-oriented, 98–99. *See also* case study; experiment; large-*n* statistical comparison

review essay, 32, 34, 203n30

sample, 96n, 102–4, 118–20; convenience, 123–24, 130; margin of error, 120, 175; nonrandom, 123; random, 102, 118, 120–25, 132, 139, 165, 215n6; simple random, 121; snowball, 123–24; stratified random, 122, 126; systematic random, 121. *See also* population

selecting on the dependent variable, 135. *See also* bias

skewness. *See* measure of dispersion

small-*n* case study. *See* case study

spuriousness: controlling for, 57–58, 94, 96, 99, 132, 173; definition, 53, 55–57; examples, 72–75, 106–7, 162, 188, 207n21. *See also* relationship

statistical significance, 10, 180, 182, 184–90,

194, 221n12; Pearson chi-square test, 182–83, 222n24; and substantive importance, 180–81, 190n*, 191

tautology, 3, 51

theory, 66–67, 206n7

transparency, 40, 65, 126, 139, 159, 169–70, 219n29

triangulation, 214n51; of evidence, 156–57, 159–62, 164, 172–74; methodological, 113–14; in politics, 219n25

unit of analysis, 41–44, 59, 165

validity, 49–50, 81, 117, 155–57; construct, 51–52, 205n21; content, 51, 205n21; external, 94–96, 98, 101–5, 108–10, 118–32, 137–38, 209n2; face, 51–52, 72; internal, 94–97, 99, 101–2, 104–6, 108–10, 118, 121, 131–39, 209n2

variables, 48, 94, 131; antecedent, 206n8; categorical, 181–82, 186–87, 205n18, 222n30; continuous, 184–88, 191, 193, 222n30, 222n33; dependent, 67–68; dummy, 48n; endogenous, 78; exogenous, 78; independent, 67–68, 97–98, 223n38; interactions between, 21, 82–83, 111, 187, 208n33; intervening, 20, 68–69, 78–81, 110, 206n8, 207n24

verification, 53, 111, 156, 162